Money, Land and Trade

The Islamic Mediterranean

Programme Chair Robert Ilbert
Series Editor Randi Deguilhem

Published and forthcoming

MONEY, LAND AND TRADE

An Economic History of the Muslim Mediterranean

Edited by

Nelly Hanna

I.B.Tauris *Publishers*
LONDON · NEW YORK

in association with
The European Science Foundation, Strasbourg, France

Published in 2002 by I.B.Tauris & Co Ltd
6 Salem Road, London W2 4BU
175 Fifth Avenue, New York NY 10010
Website: http://www.ibtauris.com
in association with The European Science Foundation, Strasbourg, France

In the United States and Canada distributed by Palgrave Macmillan, a division of
St. Martin's Press, 175 Fifth Avenue, New York NY 10010

ISBN 1 86064 699 9

A full CIP record for this book is available from the British Library
A full CIP record for this book is available from the Library of Congress

Library of Congress catalog card: available

Typeset in Baskerville by Dexter Haven Associates, London
Printed and bound in Great Britain

Contents

List of Tables

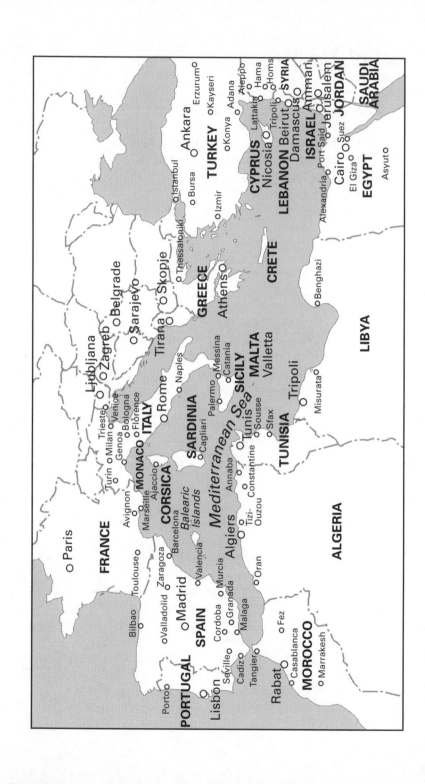

INTRODUCTION

Nelly Hanna

The present volume publishes a number of studies that were presented at seminars held at the Department of Arabic Studies at the American University in Cairo during 1997 and 1998. The studies fall within the overall theme of the research programme, 'Individual and society in the Mediterranean Muslim world', sponsored by the European Science Foundation (ESF). At the same time, the more immediate concern of the seminars, which operated under research group four (modes of production), was to bring together recent studies on the economic history of the region. Much of this research is based on new types of sources and approaches.

The choice of subject can be justified on a number of grounds. Of all the domains in the history of the Middle East, the economic history still lags behind the political, diplomatic and social. This is especially true of the period prior to modern times. A number of reasons explain this situation. First of all, sources for this period are not as abundant as they are for the modern and contemporary periods. There are few or no systematic statistics or figures for revenues and expenditures concerning such matters as imports and exports and incomes. Too often, economic history was written using European sources such as traveller and consular reports, as well as European archival sources. For many periods, Arabic chronicles were too few and far apart to be coherent. Nevertheless, a wealth of material is found in the archives of the Ottoman and Arab world that was unknown and unexplored until a generation ago.

Studies of the Middle Eastern economy have also been slow to take off, due to traditional methodological approaches. Scholars of the previous generation have all too often considered that, prior to the nineteenth century, there was no economic history to be written, because the Middle East had experienced no change in economic conditions since ancient times. They considered that, for about a millennium, economic and material conditions in trade, agriculture and production were generally stationary. In fact, they thought that conditions had not changed until European models and capitalism were introduced into the region. Change, when it did occur, was the result of outside forces, taking place only with the introduction of European-style banking, modern agricultural methods and rapid communications. Consequently, research concentrated on the modern and contemporary periods, on those changes termed 'modernisation' and on the adoption of European models. Scholars assumed that before the nineteenth century, changes in individual fortunes occurred, but that they did not affect the global economy. Proponents of this view considered that Islamic societies could be studied independently of economic and material life because these factors did not play a significant role in such societies until the nineteenth century.[1] Thus, in addition to the problem with sources, assumption about the history of the region further discouraged scholarship in the field for a long time.

More recently, economic history has come to the fore in Middle Eastern studies. This is, to a certain extent, due to the work of a number of scholars who were working within the theory of incorporation into the capitalist economy. This approach, developed by Immanuel Wallerstein and applied by historians to the Ottoman Empire, attempted to overcome some of the weaknesses in traditional approaches. Huri Inan-Islamoglu, for example, published work which showed that change was organic, that economies changed because of internal reasons.[2] In the case of the Ottoman Empire, the centralised economy of the sixteenth century gave way to an economy in which the state had less control, opening the way for the penetration of European capitalism and the eventual incorporation of the empire into the European capitalist economy.

Significant scholarship is now emerging that questions the incorporation approach. For one thing, this approach tends to treat peripheries as undifferentiated masses, following a similar pattern regardless of basic regional differences. Thus, patterns that developed in South America would not differ essentially from those in India or the Middle East. This generalising concept of incorporation theory does not sufficiently take into consideration the dynamism of peripheral regions and the consequent changes that can take place there regardless of those instigated by core areas.[3]

The research contained within this volume deals with a variety of subjects, including works on crafts and production. Hamdani analyses the organisation of artisans into guilds, Rafeq considers the guild system in Damascus, Ghazaleh covers the transition from the guild to the factory system in Cairo and Kredian explores the transition from family textile workshops to textile establishments. A number of the studies, such as those by 'Abbas and Hakim, are concerned with agriculture – specifically with the concept of property – while those by Michel and Elbendary analyse the organisation and management of land in relation to both agriculture and pasturage. From a financial point of view, Alleaume and Pamuk look at monetary factors to study long-term effects over a wide region of the Mediterranean, notably regarding the bankruptcies which occurred at the end of the nineteenth century. 'Ashmawi's contribution explores the role of Greek money-lenders in nineteenth-century rural Egypt in peasants' dispossession of their land. The chapter by Girgis studies the numerous ways in which Coptic priests could earn their living.

The research in this volume uses a diversity of sources and methods: for example, private family papers have been used as a source for studying textile history, popular literature has enlightened the researcher about rural life, and deeds have been studied. Yet despite these diversities, the studies share a number of themes that go beyond the specific concern of economic history. They also investigate certain dimensions of the individual within the economic context.

Taken together, the research contained in this volume provides new perspectives on the debates regarding approach, challenging some of the dominant paradigms on the history of the Muslim Mediterranean world. Furthermore, they provide a perspective on the individual, sometimes as an actor in the economic scene and sometimes as an embodiment of the surrounding social and economic forces. In terms of methodology, the contribution by Kredian shows that individual lives can be the mirror through which one may analyse and understand a particular social group or general phenomena. As Gran suggests, biography is a useful tool to understand society: by studying an individual life, one can come to an understanding of social forces at play. The role of the individual in bringing about long-term change is also a matter of debate, to which Alleaume and Pamuk's research contribute new elements.

This volume also offers studies of peripheries and rural areas in terms of content, approach and sources. Historical research has tended to concentrate on urban areas for obvious reasons: they have written records that rural or peripheral areas often do not. On the methodological level, Gran argues that in order to have an overall understanding of a period, it is of paramount importance to include, on one hand, peripheral groups such as peasants, landless workers and village notables and, on the other hand, people from deprived regions. He therefore argues for studies of peripheral regions such as Upper Egypt, a relatively deprived area which was exploited by the wealthier Delta region.

The problem of sources is acute for such studies. Two contributions in this volume propose the use of non-traditional sources to study the history of peripheral areas. Kredian's work is based on private family papers that go back to the beginning of the twentieth century. These papers belonged to an Armenian family living in a small isolated town of some 3000 households in Gurin, Anatolia. By studying these papers and oral history, the fortune of this family of textile workers can be followed through a period of general crisis in the lands of the Ottoman Empire. 'Ashmawi's study also uses non-traditional sources. Through both popular and learned literary sources, as well as through other forms of expression such as cinema and song, he examines the image of Greek money-lenders in rural Egypt that was formed at the end of the nineteenth century.

Other articles use their sources in new ways. Girgis, who based his article on documents from the Coptic patriarchate in

Cairo, shows new dimensions in which these can be used to shed light on larger society, as well as on priests in the low ranks of the religious hierarchy.

Another dimension of the study of peripheries emerges in a number of articles concerned with rural areas and agricultural land. They show that societies which are often described as simple and static were, in fact, quite complex and had a considerable ability to adapt to changing conditions. Moroccan rural society, for instance, recognised the concept of private property in relation to agricultural land and collective property in relation to pasture land. In order to confront population growth, agricultural land was expanded during the second half of the nineteenth century to meet the new demand for agricultural products, at the expense of collectively owned pastures. Individuals were allowed by the community to appropriate this land, thus bringing about a considerable expansion in agriculture.

Likewise, the weavers of Gurin first produced belts which they sold to the neighbouring Kurdish population, these belts being part of the Kurds' traditional clothing. At a time when severe competition from machine-made European textiles was destroying many artisanal workshops in various regions of the Middle East, these weavers were attempting to maintain their business by mechanising their weaving. In the early years of the twentieth century, the business grew and spread to Kayseri, Adana, Konya and, from 1912, Aleppo.

A further contribution made by this volume is that it proposes models other than the 'impact of the West' model which has dominated social and economic studies for a long time. The methodology proposed by Gran is concerned with both approach and content. For him, the forces of change are less a result of contact with the West than the result of inner dynamics, notably the struggle between different groups in society.

Hamdani adds a new dimension to the debate on the appearance of guilds. A number of scholars have argued for a fairly late appearance of guilds in the Islamic world. Hamdani suggests that their arguments are based on a European definition of the guild as being an autonomous association with a juristic personality distinct from that of the individuals who compose it. He considers that these norms were part of the specifically European experience. If, however, one understands a guild to be an association of workers in a craft who have grouped together, one sees that guild-like groups emerged at an earlier date than is usually thought.

Studies by Alleaume and Pamuk also contribute to this debate. Both offer an new explanation for the bankruptcy that took place at the end of the nineteenth century in several areas of the Ottoman Empire, including Egypt, Anatolia and Tunis. Alleaume and Pamuk consider long-term monetary trends as a major factor in the crisis, which led to the interference of European powers in the finances of the area, rather than mismanagement of the economy by ineffective rulers, overly ambitious plans to modernise their countries along European lines, unwise expenditures on reforms or the rulers' love of luxury.

Another contribution to the debate is more specifically related to the individual in the economic context. The study of the individual, both in general history and in the context of economic history, has received little attention in Middle Eastern studies. The dominant trend in the historiography of Europe has been to consider that the concept of the individual was invented and developed in Europe, that it was part of the European experience and that consequently non-European societies, that is traditional societies, were only introduced to it when they came into close contact with Europeans. One of the problems with this argument is that the definition of the individual was based on European experience. This helped to emphasise the European experience as being the norm by which others were to be measured.[4]

Scholars who studied the history of the Mediterranean Muslim region tended to confirm these views. They considered that the individual there was completely dominated by outer forces such as family, the guild, the state and Islam. The views that Gibb and Bowen expressed reflected a general opinion held by many. For them, the individual was entirely dominated by social, religious and political forces. Individual initiative was stifled and individual action and decision-making was restricted by rules and regulations. Only in the modern period, starting with the nineteenth century, as a result of contact with the West, was the individual able to break away from some of these restrictions. These scholars did not distinguish between one region and another, between rural and urban; neither did they differentiate between types of activity, nor between social classes. They took these statements to be generally applicable.

As European scholarship developed and refined the concepts related to the individual in Islamic society in the course of the last few decades, the views expressed by Gibb and Bowen continued to be standard.[5] Little serious attention was given to the issues that were explored in relation to European history such as the process or mechanisms of individuation or the relation of the individual to the group in terms of legal or property rights. In addition, scholars have also explored the relationship between the individual and certain forms or aspects of Christianity.[6] But the link between Islam and the individual is yet to be explored, especially in relation to Sufism, which emphasises a deeply personal relation with God. Although most scholars will agree that certain particular forms of individual behaviour were peculiar to the European experience, there is still much to investigate in this domain in relation to non-European societies.

Through concrete studies, the research in this volume attempts to outline a Mediterranean experience of the individual, specifically in an economic context. The issues that are analysed move around a number of points. One of these is the question of private property, a matter closely related to the concept of the individual. In both Marxist and liberal thought, the right to own and to dispose freely of one's property are an essential part of the emergence of the individual. Some consider these rights to be part of a European experience which emerged fairly recently. The dominant historiography of the Middle East has supported this view, including the idea that the right to own private property was, for most Arab countries within the Ottoman Empire, established by a law issued by the Ottoman Porte in 1858; that is the Land Law, which gave individuals the right to own and freely dispose of landed property. Prior to this law, so the thinking went, property was either state-owned (agricultural land) or collectively owned (pastoral land).

The studies in this volume address this matter from another angle. Individual private property is shown to have existed before the nineteenth century, before intensive contacts with Europe were established, predating the 1858 Land Law by a long time.

'Abbas demonstrates, in fact, that as far back as pharaonic times, some lands were privately owned, while Michel's research on Morocco indicates that peasants owned agricultural land. That private ownership of land was not the only form of ownership is an important matter brought up by Hakim, who found that several forms and degrees of land ownership co-existed which gave the holder multiple rights – the right to inherit, pawn or give land to a third party. Even when a person did not have full ownership rights over a piece of land, he could plant what he wanted, sell the produce, pass the land on to another person to plant etc. Thus, there existed a wide spectrum of alternatives to the presence or absence of individual private property. Consequently, the insistence on private property (in the absolute sense) as the only moving force does not seem justified in this context. To understand private ownership within a rigid context set up through a European context is to see an incomplete picture of the situation. The general view, supported by research published in this volume, is that private property emerged as a result of certain conditions which prevailed at a particular time rather than the result of a specific legal decision.

Ghazaleh deals with the issue of the individual and collectivity. She questions whether one can establish clear stages of evolution from collective forms in traditional society to individual forms in modern society. The work shows the persistence of traditional forms of labour relations in a modern mechanised factory, namely the Khurunfish textile factory established by Muhammad 'Ali. The documents which Ghazaleh consulted indicate that the factory combined a guild organisation of labour and an individual wage labour organisation, the collective one undertaken through the guild shaykh and the system of recruiting a wage earner. Muhammad 'Ali adapted the model to fit his needs and meet certain conditions. The introduction of modern models borrowed from the West did not eradicate older systems, but co-existed with them.

The confrontation between the individual and society is also analysed in this volume. In much of the historiography of Europe, the emergence of the individual is related to the ability to grow apart from social surroundings. This process brings about a confrontational relation between the individual and society, a confrontation based on the contradictory interests between the two. Confrontation is thus a major theme in the study of the individual's relation to society.

The studies contained in this volume show that under certain geographic or material conditions in the Middle East, it was difficult or impossible for individuals to conceive of their own interests as separate from those of their group or community. They could, in fact, only pursue their interests within the framework of the collectivity. In this context, Rafeq's article shows that guilds attempted to control markets by subsuming smaller guilds under their control. He suggests that at a relatively early stage, capitalist formation was being undertaken in a collective framework by these guilds.

The research by Michel on Moroccan rural communities shows how individual and collective interests co-existed and were a necessary part of people's lives. Thus, the relation between the individual and society did not have to be confrontational but could be complementary, depending on the economic context. Even when private individual ownership did exist, landowners had to have recourse to collective facilities in order to manage their land. Water, for instance, was managed collectively. In the case of cattle owners, pasture land was also collectively used by landowners of the surrounding areas. Because of the very nature of the land, peasants had to share common facilities with each other in order to manage their land. It was sometimes in the interest of individuals to make use of the collectivity in order to further their interests or guarantee their ability to function. The agro-pastoral economy of Morocco moved between individual and collective action and needed both in order to function effectively. Thus, people resorted to collective forms because material conditions such as water shortages pushed them to do so, rather than because of some innate inability to act individually.

Elbendary focuses on a similar issue, in particular the need for the state to manage the Nile waters in order for peasants to be able successfully to plant and harvest their land. Peasants needed some kind of concerted effort in water management in order to survive. It was vital for them to work, at certain levels, within the collectivity. There may have been other levels at which a peasant depended on his individual initiatives, but there are no written records for such matters, because in Egypt, as elsewhere, peasant history was rarely recorded in writing.

Elbendary's research from the peasants' point of view also explores a dimension related to the individual's search for self-interest. It examines a crisis period triggered by an insufficient flooding of the Nile. The main actors during the crisis period were the peasants, who attempted as best as they could to harvest their land, the state, which played a role in water management, and the merchants and bureaucrats, who took advantage of the situation by hoarding grain at a time of severe food shortage. The study shows that the crisis was aggravated by poor management and by merchants and bureaucrats who hoarded cereals and then sold them at a high profit once their price went up. This natural crisis that could have been controlled by careful management turned into a severe famine, partly because of initiatives taken by a few people who acted out of self-interest.

The common subject of two otherwise very different studies dealing with the nineteenth and the beginning of the twentieth century period is the individual in search of material and economic interests. Kredian's ancestors, originally from an Anatolian village confronted with severe economic conditions at the beginning of the twentieth century, tried with some success to adapt their traditional weaving of belts into a moderately large business complete with networks in other important towns. For a while, they met with success. The second study concerns Greek money-lenders who penetrated the Egyptian countryside at the end of the nineteenth century. Their financial success came at the expense of the peasants who were frequently dispossessed of their lands due to unpaid debts. This occurred at a time when imperialism was expanding, when capitalism was spreading to rural areas and when Europeans or their protégés, such as many Greek individuals, enjoyed the legal protection of the mixed courts and, in practical terms, were free of most restrictions incumbent upon Muslims in the area.

Research centred on the study of the individual helps one reach a deeper understanding of the society under study because it enables one to perceive it from an inside angle rather than from the outside. In this, an important dimension is added to the understanding of the ways in which a society and economy function. At the same time, the study of the individual in Islamic societies provides a channel by which to enter a debate that has largely been limited to the European context. The study of experiences in Egypt, Syria, Morocco or Anatolia provides a comparison that can contribute to widen the scope and the perspectives of this topic. It can also help to counterbalance the concept of the 'uniqueness of the West'.

Bibliography

Abercrombie, Nicholas, Stephen Hill and Bryan S. Turner, *Sovereign Individuals of Capitalism*, London, Allen and Unwin, 1986.

Gibb, Hamilton and Harold Bowen, *Islamic Society and the West*, vol. 1, London, Oxford University Press, 1957.

Gurevich, Aaron, *The Origins of European Individualism*, transl. from Russian by Katharine Judelson, Oxford, Blackwell, 1995.

Islamoglu-Inan, Huri (ed.), *The Ottoman Empire and the World Economy*, Cambridge, Cambridge University Press, 1987.

Lapidus, Ira, *A History of Islamic Societies*, Cambridge, Cambridge University Press, 1988.

MacFarlane, Alan, *The Origins of English Individualism, The Family, Property and Social Transition*, Oxford, Blackwell, 1978.

Quataert, Donald, *Ottoman Manufacturing in the Age of the Industrial Revolution*, Cambridge, Cambridge University Press, 1993.

Wallerstein, Immanuel, 'The Ottoman Empire and the Capitalist World-Economy: Some Questions for Research', *Review* 2, Winter 1979, pp. 389–98.

Notes on Introduction

1 Lapidus, 1988, pp. 916–917.
2 Wallerstein, 1979; Islamoglu-Inan, 1987.
3 Quataert, 1993.
4 Gurevich, 1995, pp. 3–13.
5 Gibb and Bowen, 1957, pp. 212–13.
6 MacFarlane, 1978, p. 5; Abercrombie, Hill and Turner, 1986, pp. 57–60, 80–1.

Part One:
LAND

CHAPTER 1

The Individual and the Collectivity in the Agricultural Economy of Pre-colonial Morocco

Nicolas Michel

Is it possible to talk about individualism in traditional societies? To examine this question, this research is based on pre-colonial Morocco before the founding of the Protectorate in 1912. The work covers the entire nineteenth century, but it concentrates on the second half of the century, together with the very first years of the twentieth century.[1] Abundant archival sources exist from this period, with both Moroccan and European travel accounts of ethnographic or anthropological expeditions. The initial changes that came about with the arrival of Europeans – changes limited in content and extent – will not be examined, rather, the focus is turned towards the structures of an agrarian society as they appeared from the remarkably rich collection of sources which were studied.

The answer to the question of the extent of individualism can never be categorical. The point is not to take a stand on whether a society was individualist (although this is often done when talking about the so-called occidental or industrialised society as opposed, polemically, to all other forms of society) but to measure, according to the facts, the relevant respective importance of the individual and the collectivity. Contemporary sources did not describe this individual dimension: no-one wanted to study the lives of specific peasants. It is not until the late twentieth century that this sort of precise documentation can be found.[2] An overall idea can, however, be gleaned from the richness and the diversity of archival sources from the earlier period.

This study will focus on issues relating to Morocco in general, without going into detail about geographical differences. It will present analytical factors which help to distinguish the respective roles of personal and collective initiative within the principal economic activity of rural areas – namely agriculture. This type of study of agricultural life (subsequently relabelled 'traditional') would seem to be the best way to understand the structures of rural society in pre-colonial Morocco.

The Economic and Social Framework

A study of agriculture must be conducted within the double scope of economic and social issues. The economic situation in pre-colonial Morocco was agro-pastoral.[3] With the exception of the semi-desert areas of the Sahara, farming in Morocco was a combination of crop cultivation and cattle-raising. The latter consisted of breeding animals to work and provide manure for the fields, as well as keeping smaller livestock, such as sheep and goats, to sell at markets to provide what was often the main source of income for the farmer. As will be demonstrated below, this combination of crops and livestock was important in both the life of the individual and the collectivity.

Crops usually occupied less *douar* (circle of tents) land than cattle did. They consisted mostly of cereals and some vegetables; some market-gardening took place where the land was well irrigated. Arboriculture (olives, almonds etc) and the limited amount of more commercial cultivation of cotton, sugar cane, hemp and tobacco were never solely undertaken by any group. Each community attempted to produce according to its consumption needs, and thus always gave precedence to cereals. These crops were either run by individuals or families, in what agronomists call 'cultivation workshops'. In general, the size of crop fields corresponded to the area that a plough, pulled by two beasts of burden, the *zuja* (yoke, a word relating both to the harness and to the animals themselves), could manage to work in one season. This was about 10–12 hectares for a pair of oxen, the size obviously varying slightly according to the quality of the soil or of the animals. It is significant that the Moroccan country-side was only measured in *zuja*; no other methods of measurement existed. This emphasises the all-important ownership of a plough and beasts, indispensable to the economic independence of the grower.

Crop-growing was therefore always linked to cattle-raising. Cattle-breeding was considered an individual issue, in that the ownership of animals was personal, but it used the land in a collective way because the pastures were normally owned by the community. As it was extremely difficult to feed livestock in the dry season which, in Mediterranean areas, affected vegetation from approximately May to October, it was crucial that everyone had access to the straw left over in the fields after the spring harvest. Once this was used up, the animals would need other grazing lands that were better protected, to which the whole community would often relocate for the summer months. For the rest of the year, the wasteland surrounding the cultivated fields served as commonage.

The tending of the flocks was usually a family affair, usually done by the women, who looked after milk production, and children, who acted as shepherds for the smaller livestock. Occasionally, there was a herdsman hired by the whole *douar*, or a rota within the families of the community, in which each took their turn in guarding the animals.

As every individual farmer sought to combine crops with livestock,[4] and therefore had to rely on common grasslands, the communal aspects of life were always apparent, as was the collectivity of which every farmer was a member.

The social framework in North Africa, both rural and urban, was tribal or segmentary.[5] Therefore the collectivity referred to in this research was essentially tribal in nature. For the colonial administration, the existence of the tribe was translated by physically dividing the country into confederations, tribes and fractions; in other words, tribal segments were encased geographically. The settlers had a tendency to organise and systemise, designating a specific name for each echelon of the segmentation: the confederation, tribe, sub-tribe etc. In fact, the existing vocabulary was poor: the middle echelons were called *qbila* in Arabic and *taqbilt* in Berber. There were no generic names for the upper echelons, which the French called tribes or confederations. The geographical divisions varied according to the relationship between groups. The limits were the subject of numerous disputes, either carried out by force or by the imposition of legal rights of tribal or allied groups laying claim to the same land. Summer grazing, for reasons already explained, was the main focus of such litigation.

Such segmentation gave a social frame to the individual, within which he could find identification. As individuals lacked given surnames,[6] they were called after their tribal group, at the level appropriate to the person addressing them. They would either be identified by this segmentation of tribes or, if the interlocutor was an outsider, by their geographical origins. Outside Dukkala, for example, one was a Dukkali, even though the different tribes of the region had only regional commonality.

The majority of names of segments were formed from the names of people: for example, Oulade (or Ayt) Brahim, as in 'the sons of...'. This is the simplest genealogical system recognised by all concerned, by which the history of the tribe could be seen as a family tree with all its branches and, sometimes, with its grafts. Certain individuals, usually outsiders cut off from their original roots but integrated into the tribe and its annals, also could bear the name Oulade X, indicating that they were descendants of their line of origin, but were starting a new branch. From these names, although sometimes bastardised (not surprisingly, since they were orally transmitted), it was possible for everyone to demonstrate a connection with the group by using easily defined terms – those of parental links. They were not solely genealogical though, in the sense that they always gave an explanation of landed status, showing for what reasons and under what conditions the founding ancestor (always an outsider) had arrived and had acquired his position and rights for integration into a group.

Ultimately, the group or the segment created a secure framework within which its members could live and work. This came from the *jma'a*, the village assembly, in which adult men met to take collective decisions, or individual leading citizens laid down the laws. Depending on the size of the community, business was carried out at the *jma'a* of the corresponding level. In the territories which came more directly under the control of the Makhzen (the centralised power of the Alids' sultanate) or in *blid el-mahzen*, at the top of the tribal pyramid, an Arab chief would be the one with authority. But at lower levels, it largely fell into the hands of the *jma'as*, and the chiefs only dispensed the most rudimentary administration. The administration of the Makhzen was not incompatible with tribal order.[7] One should not forget that this rural society was armed; every able-bodied man carried a rifle. Disputes often became violent and, when entered into collectively, could break out in war. However, outside the *jma'as*, certain arbitrating systems existed, either through the Makhzen, which imposed its own decisions, or by individuals coming from saintly families – especially in the areas contested by the *blad essiba*, the 'unconquered lands', where links to the Makhzen were weakest.

The tribal framework was coupled with a type of common law (*'urf*), usually oral in nature, under which a wide variety of situations were covered. In certain areas, rulings became recorded in writing, occasionally making reference to neighbouring groups. As a general rule, the countryside did not recognise the *sra'* (Islamic law) with the notable exception of the Sous tribe of Chleuh territories, with its rural *qadis*, its teaching centres for tribal law and its frequent references to the *sra'* in customary law. But even this was not done in the traditional way. Jacques Berque notes that the juridical practice of the Seksoua people from the centre of the High Atlas area, although strongly influenced by Islamic law, had long preferred written proof to oral statements sworn under oath, which went against the *sra'*.[8]

The coherence of the tribal structure constrained the individual in the sense that he could not leave it without risk of marginalisation, as all land was designated to a tribe. 'Any individual's status was based on being a part of a group or being an outsider to a group', noted Julien Couleau. 'To belong to a group was an honour. Shame lay in being on the outside.'[9] Sometimes family quarrels, personal interests or bad luck led members to flee or to be exiled from a group. Stories of pre-colonial Morocco are full of these episodes – always heaping praise on the special qualities possessed by the hero which had enabled him to escape from an impossible situation (and to go on to found a new group). But in reality, most of the outsiders (*mlaqtin, barraniyin*) living in tribal territories lived inglorious lives. Apart from Jews and certain Muslim artisans, potters or smiths who belonged to their own, albeit inferior, groups, outsiders occasionally managed to integrate through adoption or marriage where custom would admit them, according to varying conditions. They could try their luck in the service of great *caïds*, either aiming for direct patronage or being content with fairly menial positions which carried no status, such as with the Sanagita (from Sengiti or Sengit, in what is now Mauritania) who worked as serfs for the great *caïd* Mohu u Hammu of the Zaïan, at the beginning of the 1900s.[10] All that remained was to emigrate into towns; this only happened from certain areas – notably the mountains and oases. But this phenomenon, starting in the nineteenth century, did not really take off until after the beginning of the Protectorate.[11] For the most part, the most sensible way to exist as an individual was to find a way of expressing one's individualism within the tribal structure into which one had been born.[12]

The individual and collective lifestyles were each strictly structured. Both can be seen with particular clarity in the principal economic activity of the region – agriculture.

Property

Property (*milk*) was divided individually[13] when it concerned cultivated fields, water, trees and the tools which worked them. To this was added the collective rights of commonage and the right of pasture that included land lying fallow and stubble fields, which were always considered common grazing land.[14] Land enclosure was usually forbidden or limited. However, a key exception to this was the Haha tribe in the Eastern High Atlas area – an arboricultural region where fields were enclosed by hedges or stones, which made it appear as if it was divided into individual dependencies.

It is important to recognise the absence of the concept of collective land property. That which the Protectorate authorities later called the *blad jma'a*, which they ranked as communal lands, were not lands owned by the community, but were mostly fallow lands surrounding the *douar*'s cultivated fields, on which each member of the *douar* or group had rights. This same land performed different functions during different times of the year, being individual plots for cultivation, joint pasturage or protected plantations.

The most interesting case in which individual and collective rights can be seen to be working in synchronisation was when, due to the needs of a growing population, the land which had until then been used only as commonage was put to cultivation. Two things happened here: if the land proved fruitful, the first occupant, with the tacit agreement of the *jma'a*, cleared it, reclaimed it and became the owner. This practice of agricultural expansion continued until the community considered that the common grazing land left, which was needed in the autumn and winter between the ploughing and the harvest, had shrunk to a critical threshold. This happened, at different times, on the middle Atlantic plains (Chaouïa, Dukkala, Àbda) in the second half of the nineteenth century and the first half of the twentieth.[15] According to more recent studies, this zone became a veritable pioneer area – especially the coastal region of the Sahel,[16] where the earth was poor, but to which corn production in the nineteenth century added value, constantly attracting small groups of impoverished outsiders.[17] Clearly, it held appeal for a great number of individuals in search of something better.

When the available land was less, it was divided up according to members' rights, either by household (where it was divided evenly between those having rights) or by *zuja*, taking account of social inequalities, aiming for greater economic efficiency. These divisions tended to be cyclical, more often than not taking place in areas of greater political instability.[18]

The concept of banning cultivation of land also existed and was recorded from time to time; such land was called *hrum*. For example, under the Protectorate, the *douar* of Oulade Buziri decided that cultivation could not take place without the agreement of the *jma'a*. This regime followed one that had allowed free access to uncultivated land which had until then been plentiful. At the beginning of the Protectorate, demographic pressure forced two successive divisions of the *gaba* (the forest, technically encompassing the entire uncultivated lands comprising forest, maquis and grazing lands). Divisions were carried out between members of the *douar* according to household configuration, but those lands which were previously held by a deceased individual who did not have any heirs now reverted to the *hrum*.[19] Another eighteenth-century example is found under the rule of Mulay Sliman (1792–1822) in the *harim*, the common grazing lands of the Bni Bufrah, situated on the slopes of the Mediterranean. Despite interdiction, these lands began to be taken over by hopeful small landholders. Rather than expel them, the *jma'a* of the tribe took the decision to share the land equally among the households.[20] Such a system seemed to parallel that of official protected grazing rights.

In irrigated areas, water rights were shared (an irrigation turning machine was used, called *nuba* in Arabic and *tiremt* in Berber). Without going into detail about the extraordinary variety of water division,[21] it generally depended upon the respective overall availability of land and water; division was averaged out on that basis.

Ownership of property and rights was carefully protected by local custom, which either forbade or strictly limited outside proprietorship: women could not inherit land, a custom which contradicted Islamic law. Thus, when they married, women could not take land out of the paternal family. In some tribes, under the possible influence of the *sra'*, daughters' rights to land was theoretically allowed: in practice this was circumvented in some way or other. Observing the Gel'aya in the Eastern Rif, Raymond Jamous said: 'It was explained to us that a sister would not claim her share of the family inheritance so as not to cut ties with her original family'.[22] Potential inheritors no longer living in an area were cut off from territorial inheritances.[23] The commune exercised its right of pre-emption (*sfaà*) to the benefit of close relatives, of lineage or of neighbouring groups. Certain customs forbade land to be sold to outsiders[24] or given as gifts whilst the owners were still living,[25] just as they forbade or were strict about access of outsiders to the group by marriage or adoption.

Each tribe adapted customs to its own ends in order to preserve family properties and tribal rights against the threat of outsider infiltration. One example of this can be seen in the Seksoua tribe of the High Atlas mountains, studied by Berque. In this settled region, irrigated land was rare and was defended vigorously by various family lineages who, more often than not, owned it jointly. The major concern was to prevent too much fragmentation, which seemed inevitable in the case of shared succession. Therefore, custom dictated that a part of the land would be retained as the *dimna* or patrimonial reserve and the rest could be inherited. Moreover, the written titles to the property would only be validated on the basis of a proven peaceful tenure (*tasarruf*). These provisions preserved the land within family lineages for centuries.[26] In the slightly different context of the Middle Atlas region, in the semi-nomadic Tamazigt-speaking tribes, the all-important summer pastures were divided and defended by more basic means – the group's strength. Thus, to assure supremacy, outsiders were readily accepted into the group; adult men began to be progressively admitted by the *jma'a* up to the point of actually being allowed inheritance rights.[27]

Agricultural Farming

Within the framework of each cultivation workshop, the personal knowledge and experience of each individual was crucially important. A host of proverbs reminded growers of things to do or to avoid doing, for example, 'Every orphan knows when it is May (harvest-time)', a well-known Prérif proverb.[28] At such important moments, individuals certainly took the initiative. Agricultural farming was an individual or, more exactly, a family affair. It is therefore useful to pause a moment to define the contemporary family.

The census of the Habt tribes, who originated from the hills near Larache, was carried out on 4053 households in 1902 for a new tax, the *tertib*.[29] In 110 households, widowed women were registered as the head of the household. In most traditions, daughters did not inherit land. It was by the more indirect route of the remarriage of widows that land might pass into another family or even to an outsider: 1216 fiscal households were made up of a father and his child or children. In addition, there were 27 cases in which children occupied different houses to their fathers; 127 cases showed brothers living in their deceased father's house; in 203 cases, sons of deceased fathers lived in separate households.

It was very rare for children to leave the parental household before their fathers' death, but a father's death heralded a likely dissolution of the household. The dominating structure was not, therefore, that of the extended family. Mortality, which threatened all age groups, drastically limited the number of children reaching adulthood in their fathers' houses: the majority of households were composed of only one male adult. The above example of the Habt describes a situation common to most of Morocco, apart from the non-nomadic areas in the mountains, where it seems that the extended family structure had been adopted.[30] Thus it was with the Guedmioua, from the Eastern High Atlas region:

> In each family in its strictest sense, sons rarely leave their fathers, even after marriage. Each house frequently shelters three or four households. When their father dies, tradition has it that the brothers continue to live together as long as possible.[31]

In family farms, the collective aspects were very significant. They took several forms. The *twiza* (from the Berber *tiwisi* which passed into Moroccan Arabic), either voluntary or remunerated,[32] was a co-operative cultivation of land, practised at wheat harvest times, and to beat olive trees etc. It was also practised in the Prérif to clear the *matorral* (the shrub and tree vegetation of Northern Morocco). There, the *twiza* was common to different *douars*, where the clearing of the land was shared by a number of active men from each *douar*.[33] In the end, this gave rise to other collective service areas, such as in education, in which the land of the *douar* along with that of the *fqi*, the schoolmaster, was cultivated by *twiza* in rotation by the peasants or, in the case of the *douar* of the Prérif, to the mill and olive presses which were built and used in a collective way.[34] It is interesting to note how this type of behaviour adapted to new techniques. Maize, for example, was introduced into the Atlantic region of Morocco at the beginning of the nineteenth century where, in the Dukkala, the threshing of corn was carried out collectively, each grower in the *douar* taking his turn.[35]

Ritual or folkloric aspects[36] existed in co-operative relationships, for example, over when to start ploughing. Many tribes considered Sunday to be the most favourable day. In certain tribes, only the chief of the village, a sharif or an individual considered to be lucky (called *amzwar* or *aneflus* in Berber) was permitted to plough on this first day. In the Seksoua tribe, no-one would have dared violate the chosen date for ploughing, 17 October of each year, according to the Julian calendar.[37] Other accounts relate that in other areas harvesting would begin earlier if the rains had been favourable.

In addition to anthropological aspects linked to preserving the *baraka* of the fields – the grain, plants etc – certain rites manifested the constraints imposed by the available agricultural space. Recent examples may be used to demonstrate the remarkable richness and diversity of this concept.

The collectivity would intervene when it came to the agricultural calendar: as seen above, it would choose the date when cultivation should start. This was a wise decision, since it served to limit potential damage caused by birds and vermin on a field whose crops ripened more quickly than neighbouring ones. In the same way, the opening and closing dates of common pasturage were also imposed by the collectivity to avoid too great a risk of over-grazing.

In certain semi-nomadic regions, the entire *douar* moved according to crop needs. In the Rommani area (Zaër), for example, the tents would be surrounded by a spiky hedge. They would be erected in the stubble fields of some grower or other, following a sort of auction of manure, since the collectivity's flocks left manure on the fields which would be used as their grazing area. The money collected was deposited with the *jma'a*, which used it as it liked.[38]

The collectivity also intervened in the choice of crop. In the *douar* of the Àbda in the 1980s, the spring crop and its sowing dates were decided each year on the basis of anticipated profitability, after discussion within the *douar*. One of the farmers, aged about 70, who had travelled much and who had an excellent memory, was clearly dominant in these decisions.[39]

These collective intercessions could take more complex forms, notably in the case of crop rotation or in the division of the land into portions, which were then each allocated to the rotation of different crops. The Hayaïna, in the Prérif, only had one biennial rotation:[40] firstly, corn and barley in equal parts (fast-growing *bekri* [broad bean] crops sown in autumn or January) and then millet (a *mazuzi* or late crop), *bekri* and *orobus* (a fodder crop). Fields could also be left fallow.

The explanation behind this rotation lies with the peasants themselves, who decided to regroup the millet fields in the administrative area of the collectivity in order to stop damage from livestock pasturing affecting the stubble fields during the summer growth of the millet. This systematic combination of crops, stretching right throughout the year, also slightly compensated for the lack of much fallow land in this region, which was already densely populated in the pre-colonial era. This sort of rotation was elsewhere combined with a collective herding of flocks (*dula*) or, more precisely, of livestock owned by individuals, which was herded up and driven by a herdsman paid for by the *jma'a*.

Did these collective constraints and interpositions allow room for individual initiative, or did it simply dictate general agricultural routine? As far as agriculture is concerned, it should be said that the constraints of nature are themselves so important in all economic decisions that any innovation could only be relatively minor. However, there was room for some flexibility – the decision to embark on a new crop, for instance. Speculative cultivation was very successful in the Chaouïa and Dukkala areas, which were near exporting ports – particularly with flax, which was introduced by Europeans in 1899,[41] and subsistence crops like maize, which was introduced at the beginning of the nineteenth century and grew everywhere after a few decades, offering completely new resources.[42] There are other examples which demonstrate particular shrewdness and perspicacity. In the village of Ifri on the high Ziz, on the road between Fès and Tafilalt, there was a certain Moha u-lhusayn, the first Aït Izdeg occupant of the village who, whilst selling his dates in Fès around 1920, noticed that almonds were getting a better price, and so planted an almond tree on his return.[43]

The power of example and the search for quick and strong profitability existed here as elsewhere. By the twentieth century, colonisation and the availability of mechanised work were also influences. In the 1980s, in the *douar* of Àbda, the growers would only sow their *hsida* crop (planted in autumn/early winter) when they learned that it had already been sowed in the larger neighbouring farms. It is clear that mechanisation, initiated in larger domains, was taking over everywhere in the countryside by the 1960s.[44] It heralded total change. Pre-colonial Morocco did not have any large farms which were owned individually; there were some large *caïd* domains cultivated by forced labour (and thus probably badly). Most of the landholdings were confined to small sharecroppers and none of them were examples of a model way of farming.

Agricultural Associations

Since custom forbade the sale of lands – or at least made it extremely difficult – it is justifiable to wonder how a peasant coped with his share of an inheritance if it was larger than he could manage on his own. This is where the agricultural associations came in. There were associations of crop cultivation, tree planting and stock raising. The former is particularly interesting for its originality and use of logic.[45] They aimed on the one hand to increase the returns on farms which were generally too low, and on the other hand to increase land utilisation of properties too large for their owners to cultivate themselves. On many of the *zuja*-owning properties, crop associations achieved remarkable results by opening up the hitherto seldom-used practice of hiring help on a daily basis or taking on more regular salaried workers.

Any association is defined by what it brings to its members and how it is remunerated. In Morocco, the crop associations followed local custom, in which the main methods of payment were not up for free negotiation, but were and had always been concluded orally, usually before witnesses. Despite its customary aspects, however, the collectivity did not intervene – this was entirely an individual initiative. It was generally understood that any farm should be the result of five factors:[46] the land, the *zuja*, the seed, human effort (especially that of the ploughman) and other expenses such as the tax on grain. (In the case of *bernisa* crops – crops which required fields to be reworked after harvest, for example broad beans, millet and maize – the cost of the seed was relatively low compared to what the harvest yielded, so the sowing factor was eliminated and only the other four factors counted.)

Interestingly, these factors were considered to have equal value and were thus remunerated with an equal part of the harvest – in other words, one-fifth of the harvest (or a quarter in the case of the *bernisa* crops). This was the 'principle of five-fifths', which determined the returns for all sorts of associations and which could be found almost all over Morocco. They can be classified into two categories: an association between partners in which each side had roughly equal status and an unequal partnership between the owner of the land (*mul l-lerd* or *mul s-si*) and its cultivator. This could be unequal in one of two ways: the *b-el-homs*, in which the sharecropper, or *hammas*, contributed only his work and received one-fifth of the harvest, and the *b-el-hobza*, in which the worker, or *habbaz*, took charge of the entire cultivation and costs incurred, and thus kept four-fifths of the harvest, leaving the owner with the last fifth.

It seems shocking to think that the sharecropper only received one-fifth of the harvest. It is, however, also striking that in the principle of five-fifths, the same value was given to the ownership of the land as was given to human toil. It demonstrated the egalitarian ideal in which peasants believed – an ideal shared all over the country because it was to be found everywhere. 'In my opinion,' comments Couleau, 'the idea of simply dividing equally is because the debate (about the respective values of land and work) applied to the free citizens of the tribe'.[47] This egalitarianism extended out of the tribal framework, since it was possible to hire outsiders as *hammas*. It even provided a type of preferential status for those working on large domains – albeit a servile status, awarded to individuals outside the tribe who were hired by those with influence. The sharecropping status was certainly attractive to these people, for the customs relating to the agricultural associations had to be respected whatever the personal status of the member.

The equality between the *hammas* and his employer was, in other ways, largely theoretical. The sharecropper was often treated as a lowly farmhand. He only had the right to one-fifth of the grain, the straw staying entirely in the master's possession – a fact which made it very hard for him to buy or feed any large livestock, which were indispensable when it came to setting up a smallholding (although this was possible if he could acquire a donkey, the quintessential rustic animal). As he always received his year's food allocation a year in advance, the share which was due him from the harvest only served to reimburse this. And in bad years, a part of his debt was transferred to the following year, leaving him a permanent debtor to the landowner. And so, in reality, in one part of the country, the sharecropper received less than one-fifth of the harvest, his shareholding tending to diminish even whilst the quality of the earth and the yield increased. But for some unknown reason this was not the case everywhere in the rest of Morocco – which has some excellent-quality land – where the *hammas* continued to receive his full fifth share.[48]

Thus, the issue of associations brings the lot of the individual into close focus. A great many adult men never managed to rise to the level of owning a *zuja*.[49] This was for two principal reasons. In the first place, if one man was sufficient in order to drive a yoke of oxen, the crops on the area of ploughed land had to be rapidly tended in the spring. This then required more work: in this sense, it was not technically possible for all peasants to be ploughmen. Secondly, the land area that was actually cultivated was usually less than the capacity of one *zuja* (about 10 hectares for an average yoke of oxen). This micro-farming came about because of the complexities of inheritance shares, in addition to the fact that it was necessary to have acquired a yoke before acquiring land.

This raises the issue of help from the family, for example from younger brothers. In fact, the *b-el-homs* contract often included the employment of a family member (*tba'*) who was not paid, such as the wife or brother of a *hammas*.

The agricultural associations were a means for a great many landless people to partake in farming; for these people, it was a route to a better status in society. A good example of this, showing how the practice continues into modern times, is of a farmer in the Dukkala,[50] born in 1918 in a *nouala* (a reed hut) to a *habbaz* father. Between the age of 8 and 14, he tended flocks for a fixed amount of corn and barley that was given to his father. At 14, he started helping his father on the farm. Then, after his father's death, between the ages of 19 and 21, he was employed as a *hammas* by one of the sharifs. There, when he was 21, he had accumulated enough grain to marry his maternal cousin. His uncle and his father-in-law were then able to buy a bit of land which he rented in *b-el-hobza*. In 1945, the famine which marked the end of the war meant that he lost his job as a *hammas*. His father-in-law died and he inherited a house and a donkey.[51] Becoming a *hammas* once more with a remuneration of thirteen-hundredths of the harvest,[52] thanks to a successful harvest in 1951, he was able to buy a swing-plough, thus becoming a *habbaz* and earning half of the harvest. At the age of 33, with two children, his change in status meant a significant upgrade in his quality of life. Twenty-one years later, aged 54, now with eight children, he was still a *habbaz*, working on four 13-hectare strips of land, with two oxen; he also worked three other plots of land in association. His wife helped him with the winnowing of the maize and the harvesting of the corn and barley, which is relatively unusual for that area.

Such precise documentation of the individual does not exist for times before the beginning of the twentieth century, but there were probably many such examples. Such an image is commonly held of life in the pre-colonial past. This is backed up by some inhabitants from a Habt *douar*, descendants of a group from Rhamna, set up in a forest by Sultan Sidi Mohammed b. 'Abd er-Rahman (1859–73) to be woodcutters and guardians of the main road. According to them, at that time he who owned a *zuja* would work as much land as he could, and he who owned a *ferd* (a beast of burden) would team up with another, while he who had nothing would hire himself out as a *hammas* for one-fifth of the harvest.[53]

Since then, the possibilities for an individual to advance himself have diversified, more or less compensating for the problems – especially since the 1960s – of overcrowding in the countryside. The itinerary from child to goatherd to young *hammas* and adult *habbaz* has lost its classical character. Middle-sized farms cannot grow any larger, but young people try to seize opportunities in small businesses, construction work or mines – or they move to the cities, the only phenomenon to have its roots in tradition: people from certain areas, notably from the mountains and oases, used to seasonally or definitively migrate to the cities.

Conclusion

There is a tendency to describe non-Western societies as having rigid structures which are based not on economic logic but rather, for example, on religious logic. These beliefs frequently come from anthropological observations, concentrating almost completely on internal issues of such societies. In fact, in recently colonised Morocco, despite the fact that much was written from the second half of the nineteenth century, anthropological sources, so rich elsewhere, were relatively rare. By examining how the society worked practically, rather than only focusing on its internal values, one can see clearly that the way in which an individual lived was not solely dictated by social pressures from each segment of society. Compared with other types of society,[54] the economic elements – production and exchange of material goods – were only partly influenced by social customs and obligations. The latter were most evident in the fear of individuals making excess profits within the tribal group, where more important egalitarian ideals existed; this says a great deal about life in the countryside.

The balance between the initiative of the individual and that of the group came about as a flexible response to the economic needs of an agro-pastoral society. The general impression is one of a world of small farmers striving for individual success, but since their economic basis was weak, they needed the protection and strength of their group. In the end, therefore, it was economic need or even the simple fear of poverty that formed the basis of the essential relationship between the individual and the collectivity.

Bibliography

Aspinion, R., *Contribution à l'étude du droit couturier berbère marocain (Étude sur les coutumes des tribus Zaïans)*, Casablanca, Editions A. Moynier, 1946.

Berque, J., *Structures sociales du Haut-Atlas*, Paris, Presses Universitaires de France (PUF), Bibliothèque de sociologie contemporaine, 1955.

– *Le Mahgreb entre deux guerres*, Paris, Editions du Seuil, third ed., 1979.

Chiche, J., 'Déscription de l'hydaulique traditionelle' in *La question hydraulique, t. 1: Petite et moyenne hydraulique au Maroc*, Rabat, 1984, pp. 204–21.

Couleau, J., *La paysannerie marocaine*, Paris, Éditions du CNRS, 1968.

Deliège, R., *Le système des castes*, Paris, PUF ('Que sais-je?' no 2788), 1993.

Gellner, E., *Saints of the Atlas*, London, Wiedenfeld and Nicolson, 1969.

Guillaume, A., *L'Évolution économique de la société rurale marocaine*, Paris, Librairie générale de droit et de jurisprudence, Institut des Haute-Etudes marocaines, Collection des centres d'études juridiques, n.d.

Hart, D.W., 'An ethnographic survey of the Riffian Tribe of Aith Wuryaghil', *Tamuda* 2 (1), 1954.

Hoffman, B.G., *The Structure of Traditional Moroccan Rural Society, Studies in Social Anthropology 2*, The Hague and Paris, Mouton, 1967.

Jamous, R., *Honneur et baraka, les structures sociales traditionelles dans le Rif*, Paris, Maison des Sciences de l'Homme/Cambridge University Press, 1981.

Laoust, E., *Mots et choses berbères*, Paris, Challamel, 1920.

Lazarev, G., 'Répartition de la propriété et organisation villageoise dans le Prérif. L'exemple des Hayaïna', *Revue de géographie du Maroc* 8, 1965, pp. 61–74.

Michaux-Bellaire, E. and G. Salmon, 'Les tribus arabes de la vallée du Lekkoûs', *Archives marocaines* 4, 1905–6, (2), t. 6.

Michel, N., *Une économie de subsistances: Le Maroc précolonial*, 2 vols, Cairo, IFAO, 1997.

Montagne, R., *Les Berbères et le Makhzen dans le Sud du Maroc. Essai sur la transformation politique des Bebères sédentaires (groupe chleuh)*, Paris, Librairie Félix Alcan, 1930.

Noin, D., *La population rurale du Maroc*, Paris, PUF/Publications de l'Université de Rouen, 1970.

Pascon, P., *Études rurales. Idées et enquêtes sur la campagne marocaine*, Rabat, Société marocaine des éditeurs réunis, 1980.

Pascon, P. and H. van den Wusten, *Les Beni Boufrah. Essai d'écologie sociale d'une vallée rifaine (Maroc)*, Raba, Réproductions industrielles, 1983.

Remaury, H., 'Le khammessat et le salariat en milieu agricole marocain', *Revue de géographie du Maroc* 20 (72), 1956, pp. 521–64.

Rosenberger, B., 'Cultures complémentaires et nourritures de substitution au Maroc (XV–XVIII siècle)', *Annals E.S.C.* 35 (3–4), 1980, pp. 485–8.

Westermarck, *Ritual and Belief in Morocco*, London, 1926.

Notes on Chapter 1

1   Michel, 1997.

2   The most important work on this subject comes from the records of the farming training courses of the Agronomic and Veterinary Institute Hasan 11 in Rabat (now I.A.V.S.E.). Each one of these documents gives a chronological account of the farmer, his family and, via oral tradition, the history of his group.

3   Michel, 1997, vol. 1, pp. 121–84.

4   This is also seen in the individual accounts of the I.A.V.S.E. records which clearly show that the acquisition of beasts of burden and small livestock was the essential first step towards becoming a farmer.

5   For anthropological accounts on the North African tribes: Gellner, 1969, pp. 35–69; Jamous, 1981, pp. 29–61, 109–19, 181–8.

6 Only town dwellers had family names, many of which were related to their geographic or ethnic origins. For example, the name 'ed-Dukkali' meant that the person was from the Dukkala region. These urban names were passed down through patrilineage only.

7 Some of the more powerful chiefs completely destroyed the cohesion of certain groups, replacing their *jma'as* by direct administration, which was often described as oppressive. These types of situations, albeit rare, could be called the destruction of one tribal group by another, either by absorption or by complete annihilation.

8 Berque, 1955, pp. 327–30.

9 Couleau, 1968, p. 51.

10 Berque, 1979, p. 119 and note 4.

11 One example is the Ammelne people from the Tafraoute region (Eastern Anti-Atlas area), who are studied by Noin, 1970, vol. 2, pp. 202, 207–8. Oral tradition confirms the migration of this tribe towards the Moroccan towns during the time of Sidi Mohammed b. 'Abd er-Rahman (1859–73); by the beginning of the First World War, this influx had become much more significant in certain villages.

12 In fact, in recent generations it is the very possibility of being able, at last, to make one's fortune elsewhere, that has weakened the whole tribal structure.

13 Family shareholdings must be considered as being a simple variation on individual property, as opposed to being part of the collectivity or having collective rights.

14 It was the right of each member of the collectivity to graze his flock on stubble which had been left in other members' fields.

15 Michel, 1997, vol. 2, pp. 464–7. On individual migrations: Noin, 1970, vol. 1, pp. 270–1.

16 Pascon, 1980.

17 Sometimes, they came from very far: in a *douar* of the Oulade Buziri in Chaouïa, a shaykh installed a family from the Zagora Oasis. This family had suffered the pillaging of their village by the Aït Ourir and the Aït Àtta in the Siba era (early twentieth century): I.A.V.S.E., *Chaouïa*, 1977–1978, binomial 1 (*douar* Oulade Slimane. C.R. Sidi Rahal), p. 6.

18 Michel, 1997, vol. 1, pp. 254–8.

19 I.A.V.S.E., *Chaouïa*, 1977–8, binomial 1 (*douar* Oulade Slimane. C.R. Sidi Rahal), pp. 4–5, 8.

20 Pascon and van den Wusten, 1983, pp. 91–5. Collective grazing was also called '*harim*' by the neighbouring tribe of Bni Ouriagel: Hart, 1954, pp. 65–6.

21 Chiche, 1984.

22 Jamous, 1981, pp. 125–6.

23 For an example of this in the Habt, see Michaux-Bellaire and Salmon, 1905–6, pp. 245–6; they summarise the position of the Habt thus: 'How can it count as your property if you do not use it and you are not there to protect it?'

24 There was an interesting example of this regarding the Beni Meskine in the Krakra *douar* in the 1970s. They had been there for at least one hundred years and had bought commonage from a neighbouring *douar* of the Oulade Àbid. By the 1970s, although it was forbidden for outsiders to own land, 15 hectares appeared to belong to the Oulade Àbid. It is assumed that this aberration came about due to latter day 'exchanges' of wives between the two *douars*. Generally, giving women to outsiders was not done and, in any case, they would become disinherited in this situation which is why the idea that an exchange seemed the most logical and honourable explanation to the *douar* farmer who was interviewed about this subject. I.A.V.S.E., *Chaouïa*, 1977–1978, binomial 5, 3, 8.

25 This was the case for the Zaïan: Aspinion, 1946, p. 169.

26 Berque, 1955, pp. 356–8, 362.

27 Michel, 1997, vol. 1, p. 264, note 85 and Bibliography.

28 I.A.V.S.R. (rural courses), *Taounate*, 1985, trinomial 121 (Arïaïna *douar*, C.R. Aïn Aïcha), *F-mayu kell yitim ta-ihkem b-rayu*. Peasants followed the Julian calendar which was 13 days behind the Gregorian one: Berque, 1979, p. 36 cites the observations of a French settler in Algeria (Marcel Florenchie, *Eux et Nous*, p. 130) on the coming of the harvest and the treading out of the corn: 'The Arab, docile and uncommunicative all winter long changes completely in springtime. One could say that the very thought of the upcoming work on the harvest intoxicates him and puts him into a very special state.'

29 Bibliothèque Royale (*al-hizana al-hasaniyya*), Rabat, register no 450: Michel, 1997, vol. 1, pp. 240–3.

30 Michel, 1997, vol. 1, pp. 244–5. See also Hoffman's synthesis on family structures: Hoffman, 1967, pp. 45–50 and Bibliography.

31 Montagne, 1930, p. 218.

32 The *twiza* also covered obligatory labour due to the grand masters of domaines, especially the *caïds*.

33 I.A.V.S.E., *Taounate*, 1982–83, binomial 1–2 (*douar* Lbabra, C.R. Zrizer), p. 4.

34 On the *twiza* of labour: I.A.V.S.E., *Taounate*, 1982–83, binomial B2–1 (*douar* Ibazine), pp. 44, 50.

35 I.A.V.S.E., *Doukkala*, 1972–73, binomial T2 (*douar* Dhahja, C.R. Tnine Gharbiya), t. 2, p. 229.

36 These are well documented by Westermarck, 1926, vol. 2, pp. 208–52 and Laoust, 1920, particularly pp. 308–21, 330–50, 365–407

37 Berque, 1955, p. 132.

38 I.A.V.S.E., *Rommani*, 1988–89, binomial 3 (*douar* Aït Ben Ghmouch, C.R. Zhiliga), p. 6.

39 I.A.V.S.E., *Àbda*, 1983–84, binomial 32 (*douar* Oulade Houman, C.R. Jmaât Shaïm), p. 75.

40 This rotation was noted and studied by Lazarev, 1965; Michel, 1997, vol. 1, pp. 163, 194–96.

41 Michel, 1997, vol. 2, pp. 452–3.

42 Rosenberger, 1980; Michel, 1997, vol. 1, pp. 149–50, 152–4.

43 I.A.V.S.E., *Errachidia*, 1984–5, binomial 1, pp. 9–10. Another mention (p. 18), indicates that the dating of Moha u-lhusayn, a distant ancestor of the interviewee, is less than precise. His story may have even been confused with others (he was also said to have been a hero in the French Resistance).

44 See examples developed by Guillaume, n.d., pp. 73–6, where, in some cases, modernisation spread from the colonial farms to the traditional smallholdings as early as the 1930s: market-gardening and pesticides around Casablanca, soft wheat from Chaouïa and the Gharb etc.

45 This has been dealt with at greater length in Michel, 1997, vol. 1, pp. 304–14, 317–28.

46 The five-fifths system is presented by Couleau, 1968, pp. 211–21.

47 Couleau, 1968, p. 218.

48 Michel, 1997, vol. 1, pp. 310–12; the detailed research study of Remaury, 1956.

49 See the study on the *tertib* (1901–2) in Michel, 1997, vol. 1, pp. 278–92 and the summary, pp. 301–4.

50 I.A.V.S.E., *Doukkala*, 1972–3, binomial T3 (*douar* Azib El Beghli, C.R. Tnine Gharbiya) (without pagination). The memoirs of these farming courses in the I.A.V. recount the entire personal and family history of each student. This allows us to see how frequent this sort of example was. Naturally, it did not happen to everyone, though some people lived as family helpers all their lives.

51 His wife did not inherit land owned by her father, as girls were excluded from land inheritance.

52 The landowner paid him fourteen-hundredths, of which one-hundredth had to be turned over to the authorities as part of the land tax (*tertib*). Since 1953, according to this interviewee, the

hammas' share was no more than eleven-hundredths, but at that time, it was the employer who paid the *tertib*.

53 I.A.V.S.E., El-Qsar el-kebir (*Larache*) no 85, binomial C2, *douar* of the Rhamna, C.R. Laouamra (without pagination).

54 Compare the much documented Indian caste system, the *jajmani* system summarised by Deliège, 1993, pp. 72–81 and Bibliographies.

CHAPTER 2

Why Study Ownership?
An Approach to the Study of
the Social History of Egypt[1]

Ra'uf 'Abbas Hamid

The study of individual ownership is especially important to social historians because of debates among the various materialist approaches to history. For Marxists, ownership is a historically conditioned form of the appropriation of material wealth expressing the relationships between people in the processes of social production. For them, forms of ownership are a manifestation of the relationships of classes and groups to the means of production. The development of forms of ownership is determined by the development of productive forces. Therefore, changes in modes of production lead towards changes in forms of ownership. Different forms of ownership thus represent different stages in the development of the division of labour.

Even though Marxists and non-Marxists disagree over the five stages of societal development based upon ownership, they generally agree that there is a strong relationship between private ownership and capitalist social formation, and that the development of private ownership is linked to economic classes and liberalism with all its socio-political patterns.

Hence, the study of individual ownership is important for Marxists as well as for liberal historians. Yet, most of the debate among those two groups centred around the European experience. The experiences of the rest of the world, including those of Asia, Africa and Latin America were studied in reference to the European one. Most of these non-European experiences were placed within the frameworks of the 'Asiatic mode of production' by Marxists and 'traditional societies' by liberals. Since the Middle East and the Arab world fall within these two categories, it is therefore important to shed light on their historical experiences and clarify their position vis-à-vis the Marxist and liberal theoretical models. Both are equally Eurocentric, and take the European model as a measure of development by which to judge the experiences of non-European societies.

However, before plunging into the debate about the nature of development of the Middle East and the Arab world and how to deal with Eurocentrism in this context, it is important to discuss ownership in Egypt within its historical context.

Since Egypt was one of the earliest agricultural societies, it was able to produce one of the most sophisticated civilisations of ancient times. Egyptian agriculture depended upon the Nile as its main source of irrigation; its civilisation was thereby almost entirely related to making optimum use of that river which occupied a sacred position in ancient Egyptian culture. This need led to the establishment of a sophisticated irrigation system and the accompanying advancement of sciences related to controlling the river, such as mathematics, engineering and astronomy. The Nile allowed Egypt to establish an important sedentary society that functioned as a catalyst to help establish the earliest centralised government in the world. This government was largely developed according to the need for an authority to control the river and manage agriculture, the basis of the Egyptian economy. The regulation of Nile water and establishment of various irrigation projects necessitated that the government exercise control over agricultural lands and peasants to ensure the financial resources needed to maintain and develop the irrigation system.

Therefore, agricultural lands have theoretically been the property of the state since ancient times. Ancient Egyptian literature is full of clear references to the belief that the lands of Egypt were bestowed on the Pharaoh by the gods. Throughout history, the rulers of Egypt continued to consider this as a right of state, one that they exercised when they needed to reorganise society and its social forces or when grave economic or social crises occurred.

This is not to say that the state busied itself with direct agrarian management. It considered that farmers were its agents in working the land according to a system of land tenure that regulated farmers' rights and duties according to their land-holdings. In return, farmers paid taxes in lieu of rent. These taxes were the financial returns for the right of usufruct.

Importantly, there is clear evidence that land tenures had been inherited since pharaonic times. A farmer could also pawn his tenure or sell his usufruct to others. In pharaonic Egypt, the ruler also bestowed large areas of land on his senior employees. These became their tax-exempt private farms, whose usufruct was held for life. This usufruct was sellable and inheritable.

In ancient times, the ruler usually kept large areas of agricultural land for himself and his family. In the Roman world, these private plantations were known as *gé ousiake*. Most of them were originally uncultivated lands that were granted to senior state officials, who would reclaim and farm them out. During these times, the religious establishment controlled large areas of tax-exempt lands, whose revenues financed temples and the clergy.[2]

After the Arabs conquered Egypt in 641AD, they maintained the system of land tenure that was already in place under the Byzantines. The land itself theoretically became the property of the treasury (*bayt al-mal*), to which farmers paid the land taxes (*kharaj*). But some individuals were granted large estates by the caliphs. These estates became their full property (*milk*), which they could sell and inherit, and upon which they paid tithe (*'ushr*) taxes. This type of land tenure increased with time.

According to the position of three of the Sunni schools of jurisprudence – the Shafi'ites, the Malikis and the Hanbalis – and the Shi'ite schools, farmers who possessed the usufruct of lands owned by the treasury had to pay *kharaj* taxes. However scholars of the Hanafi school considered that land was the property of its farmer and that *kharaj* represented taxes paid to the state in return for its maintenance of public works.[3]

Three ancient systems of land tenure continued to exist throughout the Islamic period: land belonging to the ruler; *kharaji* lands and private property. In the Ayyubid and Mamluk periods the innovative system of military and civil *iqta*'s (tax farms) was introduced. This was a system of tax concessions for agricultural lands granted in return for military and civil services. But even under this system, farmers still retained their usufruct.

There was also an increase in pious endowment (*waqf*) lands founded to support charitable and religious causes.[4]

During the Ottoman period, the system of *iqta'* progressively ceased to exist, and was replaced by *iltizam*, another system of tax farming. However, the three other types of land tenure – *kharaji*, *miri* (state-owned) and *milk* (privately owned) – which included *rizaq* (sing. *rizqa*) lands, continued to exist.[5] In the nineteenth century, two important developments occurred. First, the *lawa'ih al-atyan* (land codes) were promulgated, thus confirming the hitherto customary rights of holders of *kharaji* lands. Secondly, the right of private ownership of *rizaq* agricultural land was granted by the ruler to certain individuals, the *ab'adiyat* and *shafalik* (or *jafalik*). *Ab'adiyat* were uncultivated lands granted by the viceroy to certain persons as a tax-exempt *rizqa*. *Shafalik* were numerous villages granted by Muhammad 'Ali to himself and members of his family as tax-exempt *rizqas*.

Another important legal step came under Khedive Isma'il (1863–79), who was in debt and in desperate need of funds, prompting the state to pass the *muqabala* law in 1871. This law offered the option of converting *miri* and *kharaji* land into private property, in return for paying the equivalent of six years' tax on the land. The option involved an absolute title deed to the land and a subsequent 50 per cent tax reduction. However, after the bankruptcy of the Egyptian treasury, coupled with increased European financial intervention, the government annulled this tax break in 1880, while confirming the absolute title of all those who had paid the muqabala on their land.[6] Finally, in April 1891, a decision was taken whereby this right was extended to all *kharaji* lands – even those where the *muqabala* had not been paid.[7]

The Egyptian model of ownership has tempted some scholars to argue that Egypt fits into the model of the 'Asiatic mode of production'. To explore this idea, Ahmad Sadiq Sa'd wrote a two-volume work in which he attempted to prove that the Egyptian experience fits the Asiatic model.[8] He argued that since land in Egypt was considered to be the property of the state entrusted to the ruler, it was a kind of communal property. Thus, the relationships of production can be described as a type of 'general enslavement', meaning that the individual producers working on the communal holdings were in reality 'slaves' to the state, embodied in the ruler. But a social formation usually includes several modes of production other than the dominant one: it usually comprises transitory characteristics, reflecting internal contradictions within that structure. These contradictions could be the factors behind change, given the appropriate conditions. When these conditions are not available, the status quo is maintained and society remains stagnant. Ahmad Sadiq Sa'd considered that in the case of Egypt, change occurred only under external pressure. He thus viewed the British occupation as having played the major role in driving Egypt towards capitalism. In his eyes, the model of the Asiatic mode of production, as detailed by Marxists, can clearly be identified in Egypt.

First of all, Sa'd argues, there was an absence of individual property in Egypt and a prevalence of communal land tenure; the other systems of land tenure which co-existed were weak and without influence. Secondly, this formation was primitive insofar as it was tied to natural powers but became more developed as it integrated social classes. Thirdly, Egypt was characterised by a strong central government involved in the economy and society: it was not simply a centralised state but a state that had specific roles to play. If these roles were not fulfilled, the whole structure would have collapsed and been subjected to chaos and disorder. In this formation, the ruling class monopolised the surplus and the work of farmers.

Sa'd goes on to assert his theory by referring to what he calls the concept of 'the class/state'. He argues that the property-owning class in Egypt was the ruling class, and that the conformity of state and state institutions with ownership was clear in the Egyptian experience, making it difficult for individuals exterior to the ruling institutions to control the means of production. He stated that this formation, established in Egypt on the basis of a centralised state, inevitably led to stagnation and under-development. This argument is clear even though the evidence that the author himself provides proves that any given incident of breakdown in the central authority was accompanied by a comprehensive breakdown in all social functions. Society regained its vitality only when the central state regained its unity and power. In the Egyptian experience, the central state led to progress and development, maintained the welfare of society and unleashed its potentials.

Samir Amin, also a Marxist scholar, puts forward another perspective on the model of ownership associated with the centralised state. He attempts to provide another interpretation for the Asiatic mode of production, in what he terms the 'tributary mode of production'. The basis of this mode is the presence of a ruling 'tributary' class that centralises surplus through the state. Its superstructure is represented in a strong unifying ideology. This is a powerful system that nevertheless perpetuates itself. It is different from the Western feudal system which, in his view, was characterised by an ability to exceed that of mature tributary formations. Amin agrees with the proponents of the Asiatic mode of production in that the Eastern tributary mode of production, of which he takes Egypt as an example, is linked to underdevelopment, while the European model is the ideal model for progress.[9]

As for the liberal view of the model of ownership within the framework of a centralised state, the proponents of modernisation theory consider the Eastern type of agricultural society to be traditional society within which structures are identical. Such a society is regarded as lacking in institutions which perform their functions in a rational way. Such a society is considered to be self-sufficient and based on kinship relations and a familial system, which provides the political authorities with a large degree of stability. The only way for this type of society to experience modernity is through a capitalist transition, brought about by laying the foundations for individual property ownership and industrialisation. These conditions would lead to the rise in individual property and consequently to the rise of independent social structures and autonomous institutions.[10] Thus, agricultural society in which a centralised state controls the means of production is defined as traditional, backward and stagnant, a society that does not move towards progress except by adopting the Western model for development.

The conclusions of the liberal school do not differ from those reached by Marxists. Both schools of thought consider the European model to be the ideal one for development and progress, and do not see any other alternatives. The only way to realise this model is through achieving an 'industrial revolution' that would be the apogee of a capitalist transformation, with full ownership of the means of production. The only difference between the two schools is that the Asiatic mode of production stresses the alienation of producers from the means of production as a precondition.

Is the Western European model then the ideal measure for development that non-European societies ought to follow if they are not to be doomed to underdevelopment and decline? In other words, are there rigid prototypes on which societies must be modelled, is there one law governing the development of all societies?

To answer this question, one must realise that both Marxism and liberalism used Western Europe as the model for their theories. This particular region of Europe had experienced industrial revolution, which differed from one country to another in shape and content economically, socially, politically and culturally. The circumstances in Eastern Europe, however, were remarkably different to those in Western and Central Europe which experienced capitalism. In fact, the transformation to capitalism in itself caused wide debates over its nature. Different pre-capitalist modes of production co-existed in Eastern Europe alongside the capitalist one. This led to social structures in these countries that differed from those in Western Europe, and which differed from one country to another within Eastern Europe itself.

Marxist and liberal frames of analysis do not provide theoretical ideas that are suitable to explain the development of all types of human society. The theories do not even provide comprehensible explanations for their model, Europe, because of the differences in the circumstances of development from one society to another within Europe itself. Thus, the Eurocentric idea that Europe is the appropriate measure for the development of all societies is questionable. This is especially an issue in dealing with non-European societies, the circumstances of which are markedly different from those of European societies.

The concept of the Asiatic mode of production in the writings of Marx and Engels, subsequently developed by Marxists, is the weakest aspect in Marxist thought. When Marx introduced the idea, he was not well informed about developments outside Europe: his knowledge of the rest of the world was general and superficial. He was confused by ancient Eastern societies which were the centres of ancient civilisation, because their models did not conform to his conceptualisation of the five stages of development of society. He therefore lumped the development of all these societies together in one basket and called it 'the Asiatic mode of production'. To this, other Marxist theorists added the idea of 'oriental despotism', linking it to the idea of the centralised state in hydraulic societies such as China, India and Egypt, despite the fact that the differences between these societies outweighed the similarities. Thus, Marxist thinkers described and categorised these societies as ones in which a stagnant and backward mode of production prevailed. Such an idea is hardly free of racism.

The same applies to the idea of the 'traditional societies' introduced by liberals of the modernisation school. These theorists also study non-European societies as though they were all the same; the differences in the degree of development among these societies are not taken into consideration. Some theories take regions which have provided humanity with important civilisational achievements to be primitive societies taking their first footsteps on the road to development. They consider all that is agrarian to be underdeveloped and stagnant as long as it lacks private ownership and individualism, and as long as its social and political institutions are not similar to their Western counterparts. Thus, it becomes the 'duty' of the West to help those underdeveloped peoples catch up with the train of progress through 'modernisation'. Here, racism is clear in all its connotations. The idea of 'modernisation' is a reproduction of the idea of 'the white man's burden' that was used to legitimise colonial expansion in Asia, Africa and the New World in the nineteenth century.

Society cannot be shaped according to a defined model. It is a changing organic manifestation, the development of which is controlled by material conditions which are not the same in every society. Nor are they necessarily equal in their influence. The role of the material situation in promoting change differs fundamentally from one society to another. A specific theoretical framework cannot explain the development of all societies. Theories are abstractions based on conditions of specific societies: a theory might explain a particular society or it could explain specific stages of development, but it would be a mistake to generalise a theory and turn it into a model that 'must' be applied to 'all' societies. In such a case, societies that do not stand up to the measures of the defined theory would be excluded from the model and be considered anomalies that must be moulded in order to fit the theoretical model.

This is not to say that one should ignore theories. That would be absurd. One may make use of a certain theory in explaining some stages in the development of society – theory can be used as a tool of analysis. The historian must then explain the specificity of the development of other stages which do not fit the theoretical framework. A good example is the criticism of basic Marxist doctrines by neo-Marxists, since empirical studies have indicated that the five-stage theory of traditional Marxist thought, its historical determinism and the role of class struggle in the transition from one stage to another are not accurate.

The ideas of modernisation are also problematic in that change resulting from external influences does not elicit the same result as inner changes unless it touches the basic structures. This logic is difficult to achieve within the framework of modernisation.

Russia, China and Japan are good examples of development that do not fit the theoretical model of stages. It was Russia, not Britain, that had experienced the move to socialism even before its capitalist experience had matured according to Marxist specifications. The same applies to China. Japan experienced its industrial revolution at the hands of a feudal aristocracy according to a framework which employed the cultural heritage of what has been termed a 'traditional society'.

But then where does the Egyptian experience lie in the context of this discussion? What is the role of ownership in determining the framework of that experience? The natural environment and Egypt's strategic geographical position have played an important role in defining its experience. Environmental conditions drove people to collect around the valley of the Nile and to respond to the challenge of that great river in a way that integrated human beings and the environment. As this study has argued, this necessitated a centralised state that strictly regulated the economy, and that provided protection against both natural conditions and external aggression. This needed a detailed division of duties that gave the central administration the power to oversee production in order to ensure the optimum use of all agricultural land so that none would lie fallow.

Thus, the state's role in distributing land tenure among producers became essential to the process. It led to the development of a special form of ownership feebly tied to the state's theoretical right to the land. The state usually did not use this right except when lands were at risk of being lost to desertification or when establishing large public works. The producer (farmer) assumed the burden for this through obligatory *corvée* labour in public works known as *sukhra*. The farmer was also limited in his rights to move or emigrate, which formed a tie between himself and the land. These conditions put aside, the individual producer was totally free to plant what he liked, and could use his landholdings whichever way he chose, including pawning or selling his usufruct. The individual was therefore not a 'slave' but rather someone who could benefit from the fruits of his labour.

A system of pawning, the *gharuqa*, prevailed in Egypt during the Ottoman period until the stabilisation of private ownership in 1891. The *gharuqa*, like many other legal customary practices, seems to have been a continuation of pre-Ottoman customary usages, in that the Ottomans generally kept earlier legal and customary practices in place after their conquest of Egypt. This particular type of pawning was, in reality, a veiled sale of land. It gave the creditor the right to farm the land and to use its produce throughout the terms of the pawn, which were usually in perpetuity.[11] Since the producing farmer's landholdings were already inheritable, one can consider that these landholdings were *de facto* property. The only limitation was that it could not be entrusted to a *waqf*. This was a right reserved only to private ownership which had existed, albeit in a limited fashion, since at least pre-Ottoman times.

Agricultural production in Ottoman Egypt covered the needs of the local and foreign markets. The Egyptian economy was a market economy, not a subsistence one. This applied to both agricultural and craft industries, a fact which explains the flexibility of the economy during the first decade of the nineteenth century, when Muhammad 'Ali steered Egyptian agriculture towards foreign markets. It also explains the success of Egypt's industrialisation, even though it did not follow the European model. There were many similarities in this experience with the Japanese one which came four decades later.

During Muhammad 'Ali's rule, mercantile capital played an important role in commercialising agriculture in Egypt, and in leading it to provide for both local and foreign markets. Commercial houses achieved a remarkable degree of capital accumulation. Central authorities played a regulatory role over the local market and a sometimes protective role when dealing with foreign markets.

The external factor, in this case aggression, played an important role in aborting Muhammad 'Ali's experience. It curtailed the attempt at development and made the Egyptian economy dependent on the European economy. It is within this context that, in the late nineteenth century, laws were promulgated legalising private property. These laws simply legalised hitherto customary practices for the benefit of foreign investors in agricultural credit.

The status of ownership in the Egyptian experience allowed for the rise of a class structure based upon property which was a means to attain power; correspondingly, power was a tool to expand property. There were also opportunities to expand small land tenures, as there existed a rural proletariat.

The role of central power in the Egyptian experience has been fundamental in regulating, monitoring and providing internal and external security. The best example is the correlation between economic and social crises combined with a weak central authority incapable of playing its regulatory and monetary functions. Conversely, society prospered when central power was strong. This is in clear opposition to both Marxist and liberal theories. In fact, the state played a remarkable role in developing social structures under both Muhammad 'Ali and, much later, during the regime of the July 1952 revolution.

Conclusion

Through the study of ownership, it becomes clear that the Egyptian experience has its specificities which must be taken into account when analysing and explaining its historical development. This experience emphasises that there are multiple routes to development, also making clear that scholars are in need of new methodological tools in dealing with societies whose histories go back to ancient times and which have their own specificities. Eurocentric theoretical frameworks are not suitable as methodological tools in dealing with such societies.

Bibliography

'Abbas Hamid, Ra'uf, *al-Nizam al-Ijtima' i fi Misr fi Zill al-Milkiyat al-Zira'iya al-Kabira*, Cairo, Dar al-Fikr al-Hadith, 1973.

Amin, Samir, *Azmat al-mujtama' al-'arabi*, Cairo, Dar al-Mustaqbal al-'Arabi, 1985.

Barakat, 'Ali, *Tatawwur al-milkiyya al-zira'iyya fi Misr 1813–1914 wa Atharuha 'ala al-haraka al-siyasiyya*, Cairo, Dar al-Thaqafa al-Jadida, 1977.

Black, C.E., *The Dynamics of Modernization: A Study in Comparative History*, New York, Harper and Row, 1966.

Cuno, Kenneth M., *The Pasha's Peasants: Land, Society, and Economy in Lower Egypt, 1740–1858*, Cairo, American University in Cairo Press, 1992.

Dusuki, 'Asim al-, *Kibar al-mulak al-zira'iyin wa-dawrahum fi 'l-mujtama' al-misri*, Cairo, Dar al-Thaqafa al-Jadida, 1978.

Eisenstadt, S.N., *Modernization, Protest and Change*, Englewood Cliffs, NJ, Prentice-Hall, 1963.

Grohmann, A., *Arabic Papyri in the Egyptian Library*, 5 vols, Cairo, Dar al-Kutub, 1934.

Lutfi, Suhayr (ed.), *Namat al-intaj al-asyawi wa-waqi' 'l-Mujtama'at al-'arabiyya*, Beirut, Dar al-Kalima, 1984.

Nasr Allah and Muhammad 'Ali, *Tatawwur nizam milkiyat al-aradi fi 'l-islam*, Beirut, Dar al-Thaqafa, 1984.

Pirenne, J., *Histoire d'institutions et du Droit Privé de l'Ancienne Égypte*, Brussels, Fondation Egyptologique de la Reine Elisabeth1936.

Rostovtzeff, M., *The Social and Economic History of the Hellenistic World*, Oxford, Oxford University Press, 1964.

Sa'd, Ahmad Sadik, *Tarikh Misr fi daw' mafhum al-namat al-asyawi*, 2 vols, Cairo, Dar al-Thaqafa al-Jadid, 1983.

Yusuf, Mahmud Fahmi, *Kitab al-rahn*, Cairo, Matba'at al-Akhbar, 1913.

Notes on Chapter 2

1   This paper has been translated from Arabic by Amina Elbendary.
2   For details see Pirenne, 1936, vol. 2, pp. 48–52, 358; Rostovtzeff, 1964, pp. 268, 276, 411.

3   Nasr Allah, 1984, pp. 14–17.
4   For related documents, see Grohmann, 1934, vol. 2, pp. 57–69, vol. 3, pp. 67–93, 102–6 and vol. 4, p. 70.
5   *Rizaq* lands were lands designated for the support of local pious and public works. They were subject only to the basic land tax and were usually administered by a family of religious notables in each village: Cuno, 1992, p. 36.
6   *Ibid.*, pp. 203–4.
7   For more details on the development of property rights in the nineteenth century: 'Abbas Hamid, 1973; Dusuki, 1978; Barakat, 1978.
8   Sa'd, 1983. In 1984, Dar al-Kalima arranged a symposium in Beirut to discuss the book. The symposium was supervised by Suhair Lutfi and included Abu Sayf Yusuf, Ahmad Sadiq Sa'd, Galal Amin, Salah Qunsuh, 'Adil Husayn, 'Ali Mukhtar and Fu'ad Mursi. These papers were published by Suhair Lutfi (see Bibliography).
9   Amin, 1985, pp. 78–80.
10 For details: Eisenstadt, 1963; Black, 1966.
11 For more details: Yusuf, 1913, pp. 62–76.

CHAPTER 3

A Multiplicity of Rights: Rural–Urban Contradictions in Early Nineteenth-century Egyptian Land Ownership[1]

Muhammad Hakim

The relationship between city and village in nineteenth-century Egypt has been discussed by most historians in an incidental or peripheral manner. Such studies have focused on three main issues: firstly, the creation of individual 'private property' towards the end of the 1830s; secondly, the phenomenon of 'absentee land ownership', a phenomenon which many scholars consider to date from an earlier period (somewhat paradoxically since, if private property did not exist, landowners, whether absent or present, could hardly have existed either); thirdly, tax relations between the peasantry and the state.

Whether proprietors were 'present' or 'absent' in this sense and whether or not private property was first instituted in the late 1830s, the emphasis in such research is placed on the owner of the property. This explains the exaggerated preoccupation with the names of landowners, the date on which they became owners, their respective shares of property and their classification into groups on the basis of the size of their property. This approach tends to define a large undifferentiated mass which is designated by the general term, *fallah* (peasantry). This homogeneous mass is always an object, exploited or oppressed, reaffirming the principal active role of the property owner, whatever the nature of the property.

Within this perspective, the mid-1840s[2] witnessed the sudden, sharp, unjustified differentiation of the mass of peasants, on the basis of the concept of *hiyaza* (landholding), which such studies introduce with no further comment, as if it were self-explanatory.[3]

The focus on the 'birth' of private property has resulted in a neglect of other forms of agricultural land relations and the reduction of these forms to a mere question of property. Once property is created in these terms and established as the main issue, the question is dealt with in terms of a series of inter-changeable dichotomies: property is thus seen as private or public, legal or customary (based on *'urf*), *de jure* or *de facto*, taking as its object the land itself or the product of the land.

Similarly, the overwhelming focus on 'absentee landowners' has masked the contradictory nature of relations between urban and rural areas. This approach has reduced rural–urban relations to a question of the production cycle, in which absentee landowners failed to invest in projects capable of improving agriculture, as well as to a question of ethics, notably the exploitation of the peasants. If private property is generally perceived as an indicator of economic progress, absentee landowners have been classified as one of the factors responsible for a lack of investment in the agricultural sector and, therefore, as a cause of economic stagnation.

This trend has dominated the historiography of both Egyptian and Western researchers. The only exception to this general trend is Cuno's work, which attempted to move away from it through a shift in focus from private property to the examination of the forms of differentiation among the *fallahs* themselves. However, Cuno focused exclusively on one area of Egypt (Daqahliyya) and repeated the usual clichés concerning Upper Egypt. Yet he did focus on differentiation within the village itself instead of dealing with it as a homogeneous and monolithic entity. This focus gave a preponderant place to the village *a'yan* (notables) to the detriment of the poorer *fallahs*, although these were by far the majority of the villagers. Nor did Cuno make any effort to theorise the specificity of local administrative terminology – with which he was, nonetheless, familiar – that determined the forms of agricultural land relations. He simply referred to these diverse forms as 'landholding'.[4]

Although Cuno's effort to break with the dominant historiographical trend was not completely successful, it remains important as an attempt to tackle land relations, in all their complexity, at the village level.

The historiography of land relations has been dominated by the legal status of the land. This made the question of full legal private property, in the Western tradition, the focus of academic concern with Egypt's economic development. This bias, given the absence of constitutive legal texts before 1858, has given rise to two levels of contradiction concerning agricultural land relations: some scholars believe that the sultan owned the land, while others attribute ownership to the *multazim* or the *fallah*. These same claims are also often made at different points within the same study.

Thus, according to one view, either the sultan, the *multazim* or the *fallah* was the sole owner of agricultural land. According to the second view, diametrically opposed to the first, the sultan, the *multazim* and the *fallah* all owned the land simultaneously. In other words, some scholars postulate a single owner of all land while others posit a multiplicity of owners.

It is important to note that these two pictures change during the period following 1813 and are replaced by the dichotomy between public property (the state as owner) and *de facto* individual property (the *fallah* as owner). This view of the post-1813 period is based on the belief that Muhammad 'Ali abolished the *iltizam* system and, therefore, the space within which the *multazim* had previously mediated agricultural land relations.

These contradictions are essentially the result of the belief that archival sources may be dealt with as 'raw material', a reservoir of facts and positive data. Yet, one also needs to take into account the role of these documents as bearers of state ideology, as tools of control, themselves the outcome of conflicts and a changing balance of power.

Perhaps the best indication of the fact that the archival material itself is at stake is the text of the 1858 decree issued by the Khedive Sa'id. This is the first document to have stated the terms of land ownership so clearly. It stated that the *fallahs* had never inherited land before 1858. This is, however, in complete contradiction with another type of document, the Dafatir Tahqiq al-Uthurat, which records in detail the history of the various forms of agricultural land transactions (inheritance, cession, pawning and rental) from 1814 onward. The dominant historiographical trend, therefore, has not dealt with archives as historical documents and has presumed them to be sources of hard facts and information rather than the expression of a certain set of interests.

Academic discourse has inherited these contradictions by viewing state discourse as a statement of true facts. It has depended on official documents, especially decrees and laws, while disregarding documents related to transactions. It has also been influenced by orientalist discourse, which has clearly been based on information provided in high-level administrative statements. This is the case, for instance, in the turn of the nineteenth-century *Déscription de l'Égypte* and in the writings of Ya'qub Artin, both of which played a groundbreaking role in the formulation of academic discourse on agricultural land relations.

While the *Déscription* was based upon the replies made to the occupation's savants by Husayn Afandi, the *ruznamji* (head of the financial administration), and the Coptic scribes,[5] Artin's writings were based on the compilation of agricultural 'laws' prepared by the Egyptian government during the 1860s at the request of the mixed tribunals. In both cases, the direct goal of this process of codification and compilation was to serve the occupation – first the French and then the British. Both works were also essentially intended for foreign readers, who were accustomed to classifying the world in categories set down by European positive law.

During the past two centuries, the efforts within academic discourse to resolve these contradictions only resulted in their reproduction within a wider and more consistent theoretical framework based on the authority acquired by the scientific production of knowledge – not only in academia, but through-out society. This framework, similar to theories based on the Asiatic/feudal/*kharaj*[6] mode of production or that of the modernisation or oriental despotism paradigm, is only able to perceive that the East is the opposite of the West. In the best of cases, these theories perceive the East as the medieval past of the West, in diametrical contradiction to its capitalist modern present.

The present study attempts to reconsider the issue of agricultural land relations in the nineteenth century without reducing them to a single one of their many forms (that of property) and without creating an artificial contradiction – or assimilation – between custom (*'urf*) and law or between *de facto* or *de jure* relations. It also attempts to rethink the contradictory nature of rural–urban relations instead of dissimulating them behind a limited phenomenon such as absentee land ownership. It tries to avoid narrow modes of classification which force interpretation through the prism of European law or even of political economy that developed within the limitations marked by an administrative law elaborated to control human choice. This study instead undertakes the conceptualisation of the administrative terminology of the period on the supposition that this terminology was a reference understood by contemporaries involved in agricultural land relations, and that it was the administrative reference that regulated the behaviour of these actors. This study also constitutes an endeavour to provide alternative analyses for problems which previous research has addressed by changing the frame of analysis itself.

The Conflict over the Possession of Agricultural Land

In this context, the present study suggests three concepts which may help in determining the basic forms of agricultural land relations and the distribution of these forms between city and village.

The first is possession (*istihwaz*), a term with a wide meaning. It differs from the concept of private property because, in its restricted meaning, it implies any party's right of disposal of a given object (agricultural land) while, in a more general sense, it can also imply complete legal ownership or property rights and, therefore, an individual's absolute freedom to dispose of the land. Between the two extremes are many degrees of possession and many ways of dealing with the property, involving many parties. This concept differs from property, as understood in the West, since it is not determined exclusively in terms of rights to agricultural land, but in terms of each party's rights to returns from exploitation of the land within the production process.

The second is composite rights: this concept refers to a multiplicity of possessors and of the rights of disposal, different in degree, which each party enjoys with reference to the possession of agricultural land or to its product.

The third is comparative rights, a concept that indicates the determination and differentiation of rights among the parties to composite rights pertaining to the land or its product. It also implies the attribution of a relative weight to each party's right to the land or its product.

In light of these three concepts, it is possible to determine the principal forms that land relations took and the way in which they were distributed between city and village. *Hiyaza athariyya*[7] was the rural producer's right to agricultural land, represented in a definite legal form to which the administration applied the term *athar fulan* (literally, 'so-and-so's trace or mark'). This form differs from that which historians have termed as 'holding' or tenure, since these two latter terms imply that the land is in the possession of a person other than the agricultural producer who rents it, whatever the form of the rent. On the other hand, that which the administration referred to as *athar* rights entail the right of cession, association, pawning, rent, inheritance etc. *Iltizam* was also a legal right which granted the *multazim* the same rights as the *athar* possessor (cession/*isqat*, association/*musharaka*, mortgage/*gharuqa*, endowment/*iqaf*) and which gave the *multazim*'s heirs priority in purchasing this right upon the death of its possessor. The rights of the *multazim*, in this case, applied to the same plot of land over which the *athar* possessor enjoyed *athar* rights. Property (*milkiyya*) referred to public (state) property; *athar* or *iltizam* rights were only tributaries or derivatives of property rights. The owner of public property determined the nature and form of *athar* and *iltizam* rights and the relation between them.

It is now possible to explain the legal distribution of the elements in the production process between village and city: the village enjoyed the right of *hiyaza athariyya*, while the city held the right of *iltizam* and public property. However, there was a conflict inherent in the appropriation of the rural means of production, a conflict which not only pitted village against city but also ran through each of the two. The *hiyaza athariyya* represented a locus of conflict between city and village, since the village considered this form of ownership to be a right (from which other rights such as cession, mortgage, association and inheritance flowed), and dealt with it as a legal institution, guaranteed by the judicial system at the village level. The city (that is the *multazim* or the state), however, dealt with it as a responsibility, a task to be discharged by the village. For this reason, the state always enforced the peasants' ties to the land (the object of *athar* rights) and forbade them from abandoning an allocated plot in favour of another plot in a different village.

The best evidence of the conflictual nature of these relations is the promulgation, in the space of only 31 years, of five decrees attempting to regulate the relations of the various parties to the land, specifically in 1827, 1837–8, 1847, 1854 and 1858. If land relations had not been so problematic, there would not have been any need for so many decrees seeking to regulate their various aspects. Further proof lies in the implementation in 1859 of a judicial inspection process in every village, aimed at determining the relation between *athar* possessors and their *athar*, and again in the confiscation of the *athar* from *athar* possessors and its transformation into private property. The land subjected to this transformation was then granted to members of the ruling family who did not live in rural areas, as in the case of the *jafalik* and *'uhad* of Muhammad 'Ali's sons, or to urban members of the high-ranking bureaucratic elite, as in the case of the *ab'adiyat*. *'Uhad* (sing. *'uhda*) was agricultural land granted to high-ranking government officials by villagers who could not afford to pay land tax; they were obliged to pay the tax arrears in advance, pay the land tax, and could enjoy the usufruct. The confiscation of the right to the *athar* and the assignment of the land to other individuals without its transformation into private property, as in the case of the *'uhad*, provides even more proof of this conflict.

The right to the *hiyaza*, however, was also an arena of struggle within the village itself: even at the village level within the judicial system, the legal recognition of such transactions as purchase and sale, inheritance, mortgage or rental was an important source of social differentiation. The *hiyaza* was accumulated by those who had the ability to pay the purchase or mortgage price of land, or by those who owned land to bequeath or rent. This led to the creation and reproduction of a group of *athar* possessors, those who owned a *hiyaza* of 20 *feddans* (1.038 of an acre) and above, larger than the labour-power available within their household. It would appear that this social group was not new, nor was its presence limited to middle and lower

Egypt, contrary to the claims made by previous studies.[8] In fact, such surplus *athar* possessors were also present in upper Egypt. The registers drawn up during the first cadastre or land survey carried out under Muhammad 'Ali mention the existence of this group, which made up a large proportion of the rural population – approximately 3 and 4.1 per cent of all *athar* possessors held approximately 24.7 and 31.4 per cent of total agricultural land in the villages of Kamshish and Akhtab (lower Egypt) respectively. In al-Balayza and al-Hammam (upper Egypt), on the other hand, where it has been stated that the land was held in common (*musha'a*) and redistributed among the cultivators every year, the percentage of surplus *athar* possessors was remarkably even higher than it was in lower Egypt: in these two villages, 5.5 and 12 per cent of all *athar* possessors held 33.9 and 87.5 per cent respectively of total agricultural land.

Although the figures yielded by the second cadastre, of 1820–7, indicate that some reforms had influenced land distribution patterns and thus had affected this social group to a certain extent, the tax registers of 1843–5 demonstrate that this group rapidly regained its position. Indeed, the partial redistribution was not intended to create equality or justice among the *fallahs*, but rather to guarantee the cultivation of all arable land.

With the burden of accumulated financial arrears falling upon the poorest *fallahs*, the sale and mortgage of land increased, as did the phenomenon of desertion, whereupon the land of indebted peasants was transferred to the surplus *athar* possessors.

Here, it is important to emphasise that this phenomenon was not limited to the 1840s (the period on which previous studies have focused), since its causes and the way in which it unfolded were not merely aspects of an economic process, void of political content. Nor was this process – contrary to many scholars' assertions – essentially linked with a conversion to cash crops or with integration into the global economy; as indicated above, it predated these two processes.

In terms of degree, causes, development and effects, this type of differentiation is incompatible with the dominant perception of the homogeneity of rural society. In both scientific and state discourse alike, this homogeneity is assumed to prevail as based on unproven theoretical statements such as family-based production or the Asiatic mode of production. The best-known rumour in Egyptian history, first spread by Artin, also reinforces the idea that rural society was homogeneous since it holds that Muhammad 'Ali distributed plots of between three and five *feddans* to the peasants on the basis of the labour power available within each household.[9]

The struggle between property and *iltizam* rights was characteristic of the nature of agricultural land ownership. This struggle took place within the city itself. Public authority based its appropriation of agricultural land on the right of conquest. The state granted *multazim* the right to hold an *iltizam*, on condition that when they died this right would be terminated in exchange for the *hulwan* or the *musalaha*, a payment equivalent to three times the legal *fa'iz*,[10] as determined by the state, as well as another payment known as the *damima*, which predominates in the financial registers of the late eighteenth and early nineteenth centuries. The payment of the *hulwan* or the *musalaha*, as well as the *damima*, was not only an additional source of income for the state, but also a reconfirmation of its rights as proprietor of the land. Therefore, deaths due to natural causes, in addition to the epidemics, murders at the instigation of the ruler/owner and massacres linked to the military clashes (either among the Mamluks or between the Mamluks and Ottomans) that repeatedly occurred during the second half of the eighteenth century and the first decade of the nineteenth were all opportunities for the (re)confirmation of the state's property rights as against the right to *iltizam*, which had become clearer and more defined at the end of the eighteenth century, if one takes into account the portion of the surplus agricultural product that each received.

For this reason, the campaign to occupy Egypt, led by Hasan Pasha Qabudan in 1786, represented only the most serious attempt to confirm possession as against property rights through the 'second (Ottoman) occupation' of Egypt. The French expedition of 1798–1801 succeeded where Hasan Pasha had failed, confiscating the Mamluks' right to *iltizam*, which amounted to approximately 78 per cent of all land – not two-thirds, as previous studies, following the *Déscription*,[11] have stated. Continual attempts were made by the Ottoman state between 1801 and 1815 to confirm this confiscation; this should perhaps serve as the focal point of this period's historiography. These efforts, again, were based on the right of conquest, exercised by an occupier renewing the occupation and attempting to 'delink' the land from the Mamluks, who had transcended their role as representatives of the Ottomans to become occupiers in their own right, while preserving the external form of the relation between original occupiers and occupiers 'by appointment'.

Simultaneously, a process of replacement was taking place within the ruling class in Egypt. High-ranking Ottoman corps, notably Albanians, began to establish control over most agricultural *iltizams*. In so doing, they replaced the Mamluks either through political oppression, through the confiscation of *iltizams* which were then granted to high-ranking military men, or through economic oppression by way of 'exceptional' and very large financial levies carried out annually or monthly, which led to the impoverishment of many tax farmers. This process forced the Mamluks to renounce their *iltizam* lands which were also distributed to high-ranking military men. The same process also occurred through judicial oppression when the registration of *iltizam* shares was renewed: those who had no written proof of their right to an *iltizam* saw their land confiscated while *iltizams* which had expired upon their holder's death were auctioned off preferentially to military men. Finally, this process was confirmed through the appropriation of Mamluk women, who sought to defend themselves against the confiscation of their own *iltizams* and other possessions.

This process of replacement provides the key to understanding the outcome of the conflict between public property and *iltizam* rights. In this struggle, the *multazims* lost their role as collectors of *kharaj*, the tribute to the central government treasurers (*sayarifa*). They were also stripped of their direct relation to the land and thus to the immediate producers. However, in exchange for the *hulwan*, at the time of the so-called abolition of the tax farms (1813–15) the *multazims* obtained the lifelong right to the total surplus product from *usya* land – a *multazim*'s private land – as well as the total *fa'iz* and *barrani* (informal tax on dairy products) received every year from the *iltizam*. The *multazims* did not receive this directly from the peasants themselves, but from the central treasury. In addition, they received shares in other villages when the right to *iltizam* and the *hiyaza athariyya* was confiscated and the land transformed into private property (the *jafalik* and *'uhad* belonging to Muhammad 'Ali's sons) in 1837.

This process also allows one to understand that the new *multazims* enjoyed the same rights of disposal as the *athar* possessors: the right to cede, endow, vacate, grant or bequeath the object of the *iltizam* – that is the same land over which the *athar* possessor had exercised the same rights. This process is logical in the sense that the new Ottoman tax farmers were high-ranking officials within the state apparatus. The main attempt to oppose the abolition of *iltizam*, following the Citadel massacre of 1811, came from the concubines and wives of these new tax farmers, not from Mamluk women. The military defeat of the Mamluks meant that the confiscation of *iltizam* rights in upper Egypt met with no opposition, because the Ottoman officials did not receive tax farms there. Therefore, after 1811, there was no-one to oppose the state's attempts at confiscation.

In lower Egypt, the Albanians who controlled the state apparatus prevented the state from confiscating tax farms as it had done in the south; here, ironically, instead of the *multazim* collecting money for the state, the state collected money for the *multazim*. This confirms once again the hypothesis that agricultural land relations were not based on sacred legal rights (the *shari'a*, Islamic jurisprudence), but rather on the outcome of a conflict determined by the shifting balance of power, an outcome ultimately codified and enshrined as law.

At any rate, in the conflict between public property and the right to *iltizam*, public property emerged victorious. By 1817, the *multazim* collected only 6.9 per cent of the total *fa'iz* collected from agricultural land.[12] These *iltizams*, moreover, were mainly concentrated in lower Egypt.

The Conflict over Surplus Product

Possession of the rural means of production was not the only object of social struggle over survival opportunities between and within city and village. Possession of surplus product, the result of the agricultural production process, was a complementary aspect of this conflict. Just as the analysis of the 'possession process' should not reduce agricultural land relations to only one of their multiple forms (property), so must the analysis of the creation of surplus product avoid reducing the forms of this product to tax, *kharaj* or rent, forms considered mutually exclusive by many scholars. In this perspective, one may suggest that the forms of land relations determine the various forms of surplus product, which were *kharaj*, profit, rent and *athar* returns.

Rent and tax were united as *kharaj*, since administration and property were incorporated, with the state as owner. *Kharaj* was represented in that portion of the surplus product which, following the administrative terminology, consisted of *miri*, *kushufiyya* and *mudaf.*

Since the *multazim* was considered a lessee, profit was defined as the result of his or her investment in the purchase of the *iltizam* through the *hulwan*, the *musalaha* and the *damima*. This profit, according to the administration's terminology, was made up of *fa'iz*, *barrani* and the net product of the *usya*. This definition also holds true for the possessor of the *'uhda*, who bought the right to the *'uhda* by paying the arrears due from the village. His or her profit resulted from the subsequent collection of these arrears from the peasants (who continued to enjoy *athar* rights) as well as the net product of the land which *athar* holders had deserted.

Owners received rent from their tenants on those lands which had been transformed into private property (*jafalik*, *ab'adiyat*). These lands were in fact exempted from taxation, but even in 1854, when the payment of a tax equivalent to a tenth (*'ushr*) of the net product of the *feddan* was imposed, this did not change the nature of the rent collected from the tenant.

Athar returns were the portion of the net product of the *feddan* which remained for the *athar* possessor in exchange for the *athar* right, after the payment of *kharaj* to the state.

Although wages were not part of the surplus product, they were part of the struggle which determined the volume of this product. Wages were represented in that part of the total product of the *feddan* which the cultivator (not the possessor) received in exchange for the use of his labour power in the agricultural production process.

The distribution of the forms of the agricultural product between the village (*athar* returns and wages) and the city (*kharaj*, profit and rent) must not dissimulate the conflictual nature of possession of the surplus product. This conflict existed both between the village and the city and within each of these entities.

In the *athar* lands, the village's share of the average surplus per *feddan* in 1798 was approximately 77.5 per cent, due to its right to the *hiyaza athariyya*. The city's share, on the other hand, was 22.5 per cent of the average surplus product per *feddan*: the return on urban property and *iltizam* rights.[13] Of course, the village progressively lost these rights throughout the first half of the nineteenth century, to the direct benefit of the city. The urban share rose more than 10 times between 1798 and 1845. This process occurred as the *feddan* itself was shrinking by 16.7 per cent according to preliminary estimates,[14] while the average productivity of the *feddan* declined by half.[15] At the same time, the portion of surplus product being paid in kind increased: approximately 85 per cent of the total surplus product was paid in kind in upper Egypt (Qina, Isna, Jirja, Asiyut, Manfalut, Minia, one-third of Bani Suwayf and one-quarter of Atfih) in 1798. By 1815, taxes in kind were no longer just paid in the south, they were being paid on the essential crops throughout all of Egypt. The collection of taxes paid in kind was generalised through the implementation of the 'monopolies' imposed by Muhammad 'Ali. The change in the nature of the taxes being collected allowed the state to increase its profits indirectly, thanks to the state's imposition of set prices on crops. The obligatory payment of taxes in kind, combined with a state-determined price on crops, eliminated the role of the market in setting prices and allowed the urban-centred state to realise its profits in a different market altogether – outside Egypt.

In the lands which were transformed into private property (*jafalik, ab'adiyat* and *'uhad* – although the latter was not technically private property), rent was an arena of conflict between the village – which received wages, whether in cash or in kind – and the city – which received the surplus product in the form of rent. The stake in this conflict was the definition of the share which each of these secured of the gross product. The share of the rural labourforce was determined at about one-sixth of the net product (allowing for this labourforce's survival); this figure could read one-third in the case of summer crops, as long as the productivity of the *feddan* reached 3.5 or 4 *qintars* of cotton. These portions were obtained as long as the landowner paid the costs of the production process. If the labourforce paid the costs of this process, it could secure up to half of the gross product, including the cost of the labour itself.[16] This means that the urban share did not fall below half the gross product per *feddan* at any time. In 1849, the land transformed into private property covered a total surface of about one million *feddans*. It is therefore possible to estimate the volume of surplus product appropriated from the village by the state in the form of rent by evaluating the average product per *feddan* in cash, multiplying it by one million, then dividing that amount by two. The actual distribution was, of course, very different.

So the conflict between rural and urban areas in terms of possession of surplus product was between rent and *kharaj* and *athar* returns, as well as between rent and the return on the labourforce, whether the wages were in cash or in kind. The conflict within the city itself over possession of the surplus product was manifested in a division between *kharaj* (return of surplus to the state or the public authority which appropriated it due to its dual role as owner and ruler) and profit (proceeding from the right to *iltizam*). The portion of profit in 1798 was approximately 80 per cent of the total surplus product channelled to the city, as opposed to the 20 per cent proceeding from the *kharaj*. In 1818, profit made up only around 7 per cent, while 93 per cent was due to the *kharaj*.[17] This indicates a total inversion of the situation as compared to the base year. Yet, one should take into consideration the fact that some compensation was obtained by those groups which had enjoyed profits in the past: they received high salaries in their posts in the army and within the high echelons of the bureaucracy, as well as for their role in supervising the industrial and commercial projects affiliated to the state. In addition, they received *ab'adiyat*, gifts in cash or in kind (property, furnishings etc).

The second form of conflict within the city itself – between *kharaj* and rent – was unexpected. Most rent returned to members of the ruling family, who benefited from *jafalik* and *'uhad*, while the remaining portion was the result of the *wali*'s donations of *ab'adiyat* to high-ranking employees of the state apparatus. Yet this conflict did occur. It took the form of a disagreement which spread even to the members of the ruling family over the distribution of Muhammad 'Ali's *jafalik* after his death. This disagreement led to the murder of 'Abbas I (the third member of Muhammad 'Ali's family to rule Egypt) at the instigation of his paternal aunt, Zaynab. It also led to the imposition of the *'ushr*[18] in 1854–5, which diminished rent to the benefit of *kharaj*.

As for the conflict within the village itself, it pitted athar returns (*athar* possessors) against the returns on labour (wages – in whatever form) within the framework of the *hiyaza athariyya* lands. Since these were too large for *athar* possessors and their families to exploit them alone, a labourforce was brought in from outside the family, either from among unemployed *fallahs* who had no *athar*, or from among other *athar* possessors whose family labour-power surpassed the surface of their own plots. It is likely that the aim of the conflict between these two rural groups was to determine the share of each in the gross product per *feddan*. It is also probable that the labourforce was able to obtain a share equivalent to one-sixth of the crop, as was the case in the *jafalik* and *'uhad* lands and the *ab'adiyat*.

Conclusion

By concentrating only on the concept of property, it would have been impossible to see either the complexity of these relations to agricultural land or the social conflicts resulting therefrom. The analysis suggested in this work has revealed that economic relations were a highly complex web of conflicts. A similar analysis, applied to relations of power and meaning, could reveal new kinds of conflicts both within and between village and city. Economic, political and conceptual conflicts together may help us better understand social conflict as a whole.

Bibliography

Primary Sources

Dar al-Mahfuzat al-'Umumiyya (DMU), Cairo: Daftar Hisab al-Aqalim al-Bahariyya 'an Wajib Sanat 1233; Daftar Usul Fawayid Multazimin bi-l-Wajh al-Bahari, 1233/1817.

Dar al-Watha'iq al-Qawmiya (DWQ), Daftar Hisab al-Aqalim al-Wusta 'an Wajib Sanat 1233; Daftar Hisab al-Aqalim al-Qibliyya 'an Wajib Sanat 1233; Diwan Ma'iyya Saniyya.

Published Sources

'Abbas Hamid, Ra'uf, *al-Milkiyyat al-zira'iyya al-kabira wa-dawruha fi 'l-mujtama' al-misri 1837–1914*, 2nd ed., Cairo, Dar al-Fikr al-Hadith, 1983.

Amin, Samir, *al-Tabaddul Ghayr al-Mutakafi'*, Beirut, Bulaq, 1974.

Artin, Ya'qub, *al-Ahkam al-Mar'iyya fi Sha'n al-Aradi al-Misriyya*, Bulaq, 1306/1889.

Barakat, 'Ali, *Tatawwur al-milkiyya al-zira'iyya fi Misr 1813–1914 wa Atharuha 'ala al-haraka al-siyasiyya*, Cairo, Dar al-Thaqafa al-Jadida, 1977.

Cuno, Kenneth, *The Pasha's Peasants*, Cairo, American University in Cairo Press, 1992.

Ghurbal, Shafiq, 'Misr 'inda muftaraq al-turuq', *Majallat Kulliyat al-Adab*, Cairo, Cairo University, 1936, vol. 4, part 1, pp. 1–53.

Wasf Misr *(Description de l'Egypte)*, transl. Zuhayr al-Shayib, Cairo, Maktabat al-Khanji, n.d., vols 4 and 5.

Notes on Chapter 3

1 This work has been translated from Arabic by Pascale Ghazaleh.
2 In the mid-1940s, registers (*Mukallafat al-Atyan*) were drawn up of peasants' landholdings (*athar*). These registers are particularly important for researchers, since they recorded each peasant's total holdings. Contrary to the suggestions of some historians, however, neither the differentiation between peasants on the basis of holding size nor the process of registration itself were new phenomena. What was new was the fact that these registers were easier for scholars to read and analyse than others such as the Dafatir al-Tawari' – compiled in 1813 – or even the registers drawn up by the new Ottoman administration at the beginning of the sixteenth century. I am currently preparing a study of these Ottoman registers.
3 See, for example, 'Ali Barakat, 1978. The study published by Ra'uf 'Abbas is characterised by greater conceptual precision and by a relative focus on property as a relation of production, not merely a legal concept.
4 Cuno, 1992, pp. 66–74.
5 Wasf Misr, n.d., vol. 5, pp. 14–20, 22, 25, 26, 30, 38, 45, 58–60, 95–8. Shafiq Ghurbal published Husayn Afandi's manuscript, 1936, pp. 50–1 and 53.
6 For the *kharaj* (the tribute based mode of production): Amin, 1974.
7 Literally, '*athar*' refers to a trace or mark. This expression could thus be rendered 'possession by trace'.

8   Cuno, 1992, pp. 6–74.

9   Artin, 1889, p. 47.

10 Part of the total amount obtained by the *multazim* by virtue of his right to the *iltizam.*

11 Wasf Misr, n.d., vol. 4, p. 156.

12 Daftar Hisab al-Aqalim al-Bahariyya 'an Wajib Sanat 1233, Dar al-Mahfuzat al-'Umumiyya (DMU), Cairo; Daftar Usul Fawayid Multazimin bi-l-Wajh al-Bahari, 1233/1817, Dar al-Watha'iq al-Qawmiya (DWQ); Daftar Hisab al-Aqalim al-Wusta 'an Wajib Sanat 1233, DWQ; Daftar Hisab al-Aqalim al-Qibliyya 'an Wajib Sanat 1233, DWQ. All the figures pertaining to money are calculated on the basis of current value, not constant value, since previous attempts to establish such a value were based on European currency equivalents and not the calculation of local inflation rates in the prices of basic goods. We therefore consider them inaccurate.

13 These percentages are calculated on the basis of data on the productivity per *feddan* estimated by Girard in 1800 for Egypt as a whole. After the elimination of extreme values, the distribution of this wealth between city and village was realised by calculating all the taxes collected by the city (from the Dafatir Tarabi' al-Wilayat, 804, 1601, 1603 and 1612, DMU). The remainder was the share of wealth for the rural areas.

14 Dafatir Iradat wa-Masrufat, 1232/1816, register 1622, DMU. In the land cadastre of 1813, Muhammad 'Ali decreed that one *feddan* measured 333.3 square *qasaba* instead of the 400 square *qasaba* which had officially made up one *feddan* before that date.

15 Calculated on the basis of the following sources: Wasf Misr, n.d., vol. 4, pp. 125–49, 365–87; Diwan al-Jafalik, registers 5673 and 5674, DWQ.

16 Diwan Ma'iyya Saniyya, 'Mulakhasat al-Awamir al-'Aliyya', mahfaza 4, kurras 38, 1251/1833–34, DWQ.

17 I calculated the rates for 1798–1800 on the basis of the Dafatir al-Tarabi', compiled especially for the French expedition (DWQ), and on the basis of Wasf Misr, n.d., vol. 4; for 1818, they are calculated on the basis of the Dafatir Tamwil al-Atyan and the accounts of the *multazims* for the same year (DMU).

18 Literally, the tithe, a tax consisting of the tenth of the net product per *feddan* on land transformed into private property.

CHAPTER 4

The Worst of Times: Crisis Management and *Al-Shidda Al-'Uzma*

Amina A. Elbendary

A number of studies in this volume have explored the relationship between agricultural land and the peasant and the state, in terms of ownership and management. The present contribution explores another dimension of these questions by analysing Nile floods during years of crisis. During years of bad flooding, effective agrarian management by the state was essential for the interests of peasants and agriculture. Yet, during one of the worst floods, management by the state was severely impeded by its inability to control factional fighting in the army and by acts of officials and bureaucrats who, in pursuing their individual interests, helped to create a severe crisis.

Almost every historical survey of Egypt mentions the maxim attributed to Herodotus that 'Egypt...is the gift of the river'.[1] Indeed, for many centuries, the Nile has supported one of the largest populations in the Middle East and, at times, the largest of these populations. One of the continuous themes in Egyptian historiography is the attempt to link Egypt's economic and political fate to that of the Nile. The fluctuations of the Nile affected agricultural production, and excessively low or high floods produced crises that Egypt has often had to face. It is commonly believed, however, that low Nile flooding inevitably caused famine and economic catastrophes: 'It was the economic crises and famines (which Egypt has always suffered periodically when the Nile rises insufficiently) which in the Fatimid period caused most disorders'.[2]

This impression needs to be examined more carefully through study of, for example, some of the famines which occurred under Fatimid rule during the eleventh century. In an attempt to understand the relation of the river to the people, the economy, the state and society, this study concentrates on the most famous and indeed the worst of these famines, *al-shidda al-'uzma*, which occurred during the years 1062–73. This will be compared to Nile management under average flood conditions and two series of crises that were effectively managed by the Fatimid administration.

The Fatimid state, like earlier Egyptian governments, was heavily involved in the management of the Nile and in agriculture in general. Efficient agricultural management was necessary in order to make best use of the Nile water and the fertile soil which depended on the river, so as to ensure abundant harvests and support the large population. This included investment in large-scale projects such as irrigation works and their maintenance, and the administration and co-ordination of those works. Agricultural revenue and taxes were the main sources of state revenue. Good harvests were needed to ensure that large population groupings, especially those located in the cities, were well fed. This was crucial for maintaining order and stability. The state thus needed to be closely involved in agrarian administration. Egypt's agriculture was the main source of its wealth and the basis of its civilisation.

The agricultural year was regulated by the flood of the Nile. The Nile started to 'breathe' in mid-June.[3] In an average flood, the Nile reached the level needed to ensure a good harvest in September. This was 16 cubits, measured at the 'Nilometer' at al-Rawda Island. When it reached this level, the *wafa' al-Nil* was celebrated. The Nile then continued to rise until it reached its maximum level around mid-October.[4] The flood maintained this level for about 12 days, after which the water started to decrease gradually.[5] The water levels of the Nile thus fluctuated during the year, and the height of the flood varied from year to year.

From the time when the flood arrived in summer, government authorities organised the opening of dams and dykes on consecutive dates according to a complex system. This allowed the water into the areas to be cultivated. Ibn Mammati, writing during the early Ayyubid period, lists the usual dates – mostly during the months of September, October and November – for the opening of these irrigation works.[6] The major ones, the *jusur* (dykes) and the *khuljan* (canals), were maintained by the government; individual landholders and farmers paid special taxes for this maintenance.[7] The irrigation of Egypt's different regions had to be co-ordinated carefully in order to ensure that the largest possible area was irrigated sufficiently.

Once the water had flooded the lands, government officials went out to survey and classify it for tax purposes. A given plot of land was classified according to the amount of water that flooded it and in relation to the crop that was last sown on it.[8] The system of crop rotation that was followed meant that a given plot of land was classified differently from year to year. It is this classification which determined both the sown crop and the tax rate; this step was, therefore, an important stage in agrarian administration.[9] *Kharaj* or land tax was the principal source of government revenue. To support agrarian production under normal conditions, the state ensured an adequate supply of good quality seed corn and other seeds to farmers. This 'reinforcement' of farmers is referred to as *taqwiya*, and hence the seeds themselves are called *taqawi*, a word still in use today.

Thus, according to the classification carried out by government officials, the main crops to be grown – grains, cereals, flax, legumes and sugar cane – were planted on the most fertile and well-irrigated lands.[10] After the flood had receded, other lands were planted with vegetables in winter and early spring. By the end of May, the main cash crops were harvested. The grain and other commodities paid as tax were shipped to government depots in Cairo. These were calculated in relation to the harvest and paid in instalments throughout the year until the following season. Thus, the government was involved in various stages of agricultural production during the year. This was necessary to ensure revenues for the state as well as food supplies for the people.

A Nile crisis occurred if the flood level had not reached the minimum level of 16 cubits by September, or if the flood receded quickly.[11] This meant that the area of cultivated land was reduced, irrigated lands received insufficient water and, consequently, the harvest of such a year would be lower than usual.

As water levels were regularly announced by the state during the flood,[12] officials and the public would probably be aware of an impending crisis during the summer and certainly by September. Wealthy individuals among the bureaucratic and merchant classes would start buying and hoarding extra foodstuffs and grain as a precaution against famine.[13] It was individuals from these classes who normally had enough liquid funds to purchase at least a year's consumption of grain in advance. In fact, these classes stored grain even in years of good Nile floods. Nasir-i Khusrau, who visited Egypt in the mid-eleventh century, relates that in a year of a low Nile, the caliph sent for a Coptic merchant in order to buy stored grain from him. The merchant answered that he had enough grain stored to feed bread to all Egyptians for six years.[14] This obviously exaggerated anecdote reveals that merchants and other wealthy individuals could have extensive private granaries which they would naturally fill in times of impending crisis. Such a situation would immediately provoke an increase in prices, even if there were adequate supplies of stored grain.[15] This proto-crisis would occur even before the crops of the low Nile were planted, much less harvested. Thus the individual interests of a few were in direct conflict with those of the rest of the population and, indirectly, with the state.

The population would live off the grain of the previous good harvest until May when the diminished harvest would be collected. However, its precise total volume would only be known to professionals, especially grain merchants and fiscal authorities, thus opening the way for further speculation. The harvest supply would be even further reduced since one-fifth of it would be used as seed in November. All this would increase prices even more.

Once the Nile started rising again in June, calculations and speculations for the coming flood would start. If a good flood came in August and September and the waters remained at a high level long enough, prices still would not decrease much because, during this season, the granaries would continue to be depleted due to the previous low harvest. During this crucial period of a low Nile crisis, the shortage would have to be managed and supplies stretched to last until the following summer.[16] The crisis would last between 15 and 20 months, from the beginning of a low Nile until the grain produced by a subsequent high Nile was harvested.

During the Fatimid era, Egypt was plagued with several *shiddas*, or crises of high prices and famine, generally induced by low Niles. The *shiddas* which occurred during the reigns of the caliphs al-Hakim and al-Zahir were contained by the administrations of the time. Studying the means by which the crises were contained helps understand the disastrous *al-shidda al-'uzma* which followed later. In 395/1004, during the reign of al-Hakim, it was reported that the Nile had reached only 15.7 cubits at the beginning of the irrigation season in September. Prices increased in Cairo and bread was scarce.[17] In 397/1006, the irrigation season began with the Nile at only 14 cubits; subsequently, it only rose to 15.16 cubits, after which it started decreasing. The Mamluk historian Maqrizi explains that this led to price increases as people started buying and hoarding grain.[18] In 398/1007, the Nile was only at 15 cubits in mid-September.[19] Maqrizi reports that it had reached its maximum in July/August, and actually started declining in the last week of September. Bread became so expensive that it was sold damp by bakers to increase its weight.[20] The government also rounded up bakers and beat them, because bread was sold out by nightfall.[21] Several granaries belonging to private individuals were seized and the grain in them was sold to millers at a fixed price.[22] Al-Hakim was obliged to suspend customs and taxes on grain and rice arriving at Cairo ports in order to reduce prices.[23] In 399/1008, the Nile started declining in the last week of September, before reaching 16 cubits.[24] Epidemics spread and many people died.[25] That year, the usual festivals and banquets held during the Feast of the Sacrifice had to be suspended as well as the unofficial Shi'ite Feast of al-Ghadir.[26] According to the Mamluk historian, Ibn Iyas, on the authority of the Fatimid bureaucrat, al-Musabbihi, al-Hakim was informed that the flood was low that year because the Ethiopians had changed the course of the river. The account states that he sent the patriarch to Ethiopia to meet with their king, who ordered that a dam be opened. Consequently, the Nile rose in Egypt.[27] Even if the anecdote is not 'true', it does reflect a politicised and sophisticated understanding of the hydraulics of the Nile, the echoes of which are still clear today.

The reign of al-Hakim's son and successor, al-Zahir, also witnessed serious low Niles and famines which lasted from 414/1023 to 415/1024. In 414/1023, the Nile only reached

14.01 cubits.[28] As would be expected, prices increased rapidly and food was scarce. One of the reasons that prices increased in 415/1024 was because boats loaded with wheat were commandeered by the caliph and taken directly from the ports to the palace.[29] The state confiscated 150 granaries where private individuals hoarded grains;[30] the granaries of several state officials were opened and their grain put on the market.[31] The state then sold grain from the granaries to the millers at a fixed price and millers were instructed not to sell their products above a certain fixed price.[32] Grain brokers, millers and bakers were also rounded up and beaten because the price of bread had increased and flour was adulterated.[33] Just as al-Hakim's administration had done earlier, al-Zahir suspended duties on grain at ports in Cairo.[34]

Low Niles were relatively frequent in medieval Egypt and the state apparatus had certain tried mechanisms to deal with them. Famines that occurred during the reigns of al-Hakim and al-Zahir are instructive in the development of such crises and the ways in which they were typically handled by the government. The interests of certain individuals came into conflict with the state: a crisis was a chance for some individuals to make money. Numerous individuals accentuated the crisis by speculation in grain and hoarding, two of the main causes behind price increases that accompanied low Niles.[35] It is easy to understand that everyone involved in the grain market – government officials, merchants, millers and bakers – would wish to make maximum profit out of a Nile crisis. However, it was the millers and bakers who were often singled out as targets of popular condemnation and government demonstrations of power. The government often held them responsible for shortages in grain and increases in prices.[36]

Yet, the palace itself was also involved in grain deals. For example, al-Zahir monopolised grain coming in at the ports. In fact, according to Maqrizi, the policy of the palace before the mid-eleventh century was to buy large quantities of grain each year in order to trade in it for profit.[37] In other words, state granaries were run for profit as a source of state revenue, not merely to provide the public with food supplies. But once a crisis accelerated, the state interfered with the intention of lowering and controlling prices through various means such as suspending customs duties, fixing market prices and selling grain directly to millers to prevent price increases caused by middlemen.[38] This was necessary for public welfare and to prevent riots if possible. Another measure sometimes taken by the state was to cut palace expenses by cancelling some of the elaborate rituals of the Fatimid court. Not only did these rituals cost the treasury huge amounts of money, but the ostentatious consumption of food and luxuries was provocative in times of crisis.

One measure of control that is unexpectedly missing in the sources which were consulted concerns the importation of grain during these years of shortage.[39] Most of the sources that survive from this period are chronicles and histories rather than archives and state documents. Thus, the nature of the sources themselves limit the type of information that they contain. Maqrizi mentioned only once that grain was being imported from Syria, in 420/1029–30 when the Nile was late in rising.[40] Grain imports from Byzantium do not appear to have been regular especially as Byzantine–Fatimid relations fluctuated.[41] Goitein's study of the Geniza documents that refer to the Jewish community in Cairo in the eleventh century did not find references to significant overseas trade in grains and cereals.[42] This does not totally negate the presence of such trade, especially as the commercial networks of the Geniza community were only one among many which functioned in Egypt. However, different combined strands of evidence suggest that during the Fatimid period Egypt relied more heavily on local production of grain than on imports.[43] This meant that agrarian management and grain stores were crucial, especially in times of crisis.

The measures taken during the reigns of al-Hakim and al-Zahir demonstrate the importance of a strong, efficient and centralised administrative structure in preventing a Nile crisis from becoming an utter catastrophe for the whole population.[44] Such a state institution should have not only been able to extend its authority from the capital to the provinces but also to manage the lower levels of administration. Centralised authority was necessary to co-ordinate the complex and interlinked functions required by the hydraulics of the Nile.

It is, however, important to realise that though the state did manage these difficult situations, serious crises were nevertheless recurrent. They affected people of various classes and social groups differently: in 415/1024, while people were dying of famine in Cairo, the palace could still afford to hold lavish banquets – palace slave troops raided one of these banquets out of hunger.[45] On his way back from the celebrations of the feast of *ghitas* (Epiphany) that year, al-Zahir saw corpses on the streets. He ordered that they be buried at the expense of the state.[46] The state's efforts at effective management could not ensure that the poorest of its subjects did not die of famine.[47] Yet, it did sometimes manage to control and contain the crisis.

'The Greatest Calamity'

The most serious crisis that occurred in the Fatimid period was called *al-shidda al-'uzma*, which literally means 'the greatest calamity'.[48] This is the name commonly given to the series of interlinked crises that lasted from 454/1062 to 466/1073, during the reign of the Fatimid caliph al-Mustansir. Comparing this crisis with earlier ones demonstrates the extent of the disasters which occurred when the forces of nature were left unchecked.

This *shidda* was the greatest Fatimid crisis, in that it was associated with the complete breakdown of government. It was a period of extreme unrest, famine and deprivation during which a large proportion of the population died, while those who could afford to, emigrated to Syria and Iraq. However, in comparing this crisis to other crises that were mainly caused by low Niles, such as those that occurred during the reigns of al-Hakim and al-Zahir, it becomes clear that the Nile level was not the only variable involved in *al-shidda al-'uzma*.

Mustansir's reign had started out with a reasonably competent administration. His *wazir*, al-Yazuri, had quite efficiently managed to handle a Nile crisis in 446/1054 when he took steps to ensure some measure of state control over the grain market which were reminiscent of those taken by preceding regimes. For instance, he forbade merchants from buying grain in advance from peasants – a common procedure that enabled merchants to speculate on the grain and which required the peasants to pay their tax in instalments. Al-Yazuri bought the grain for the state, shipped it to Cairo and fixed its price. He thus managed the crisis for 20 months until the new crop was harvested and prices diminished.[49] But, this able administrator eventually lost both his job and his life, due to palace intrigues.

The period that started with al-Yazuri's assassination is often taken as a period of transition between two eras of Fatimid rule. The first period is characterised by strong caliphs and efficient bureaucrats, while the second is characterised by weaker caliphs and stronger military *wazirs*.[50] During the 16 years following al-Yazuri's assassination, there were 54 *wazir* appointments.[51] This high turnover rate is a sign of the disarray in the administration which began to stabilise only in 466/1073 with the arrival of *amir al-juyush* (commander-in-chief of the army) Badr al-Gamali, who pacified Egypt and reorganised its administration on al-Mustansir's behalf.

Because *shiddas* did not occur in a vacuum, it is relevant briefly to survey the general political situation of the time. The Fatimid state was facing both various external and internal threats during this period. For example, the rise of the Seljuks in the east threatened and finally put an end to the Egyptian presence in most of Syria and Palestine. In an attempt to prevent the rise of the Sunni Seljuks to power in Iraq, the Fatimids expended large sums to support pro-Shi'ite elements there.[52] These efforts failed as did their efforts to maintain a Fatimid presence in Syria. Both were a drain on the financial and human resources of the state. The loss of control over Syria also entailed a decline in revenues. These expenses left the treasury depleted and unable to deal with other internal crises.

Furthermore, the rise of the Seljuks also interrupted Byzantine–Fatimid relations, which had been friendly for several years. Al-Zahir had consciously worked to improve relations with the Byzantines, mainly to neutralise them in the Fatimid confrontation with the Abbasids and then the Seljuks in the east.[53] However, these relations deteriorated when the Seljuks came to power, an event which affected Byzantine–Fatimid trade agreements. This coincided with the *shidda*. Thus, a grain trade route that could have been activated in a time of emergency or crisis was inaccessible to merchants due to the political situation.

While Mustansir's administration had to fight on external fronts, it also had to fight internally. According to Maqrizi, the real *shidda* began with the interfactional power struggle between Ottoman troops and the black troops of the Fatimid army.[54] This

Table 4.1: Nile Levels During *Al-Shidda Al-'Uzma*

Year AH/AD	Nile level in cubits
446/1054	17.40
447/1055	16.40
448/1056	17.13
449/1057	17.30
450/1058	16.12
451/1059	15.23
452/1060	16.90
453/1061	16.18
454/1062	17.16
455/1063	17.12
456/1064	16.30
457/1065	16.10
458–9/1066	16.17
459–60/1067	15.60
460–1/1068	17.18
461–2/1069	16.00
462–3/1070	17.30
463–4/1071	16.10
464–5/1072	16.70
465–6/1073	16.30
466–7/1074	17.70
467–8/1075	16.14

factional fighting gradually developed into all-out war. The post-Yazuri ministers had no real power, and failed to control these disputes within the army.[55] This internal war proved catastrophic to the state, draining the economy in various ways. Having overcome rival factions, the Ottoman troops were in a position to extort large sums of money from the treasury, to the extent that it became bankrupt.[56] This was at a time when the treasury was already drained by the Fatimid's external war effort. Moreover, fighting between the Ottoman and the black troops led to rival factions seizing power in the Egyptian provinces and thus coming to control their revenues.[57] This in turn deprived the central government of much-needed income.

Al-shidda al-'uzma is often referred to as a seven-year crisis which started in 457/1064–5, and caused by low Niles that led to famine and epidemics. This, for example, is the explanation given by the late Mamluk historian Ibn Iyas (who died around 930/1523–4), who compares the *shidda* to the legendary famine that occurred during the time of the prophet Joseph.[58] This explanation has also been repeated in modern writings, such as those of Brockelmann and 'Abd al-Mun'im Majid.[59] It is clear that the foreign and domestic policy situation within the Fatimid state shows that the crisis was not the outcome of a natural disaster alone.

Records of Nilometer readings, if accurate, show that low Niles occurred only in 451/1059 and 460/1067.[60] Even these floods were not as low as those reported for the less serious famines under al-Hakim and al-Zahir. But the political situation, which was already deteriorating, heightened the crisis and brought about a disastrous famine and loss of life. This is Maqrizi's description:

> The lands remained uncultivated and fear prevailed. Land and sea routes became unsafe and travel became impossible without a large escort. Famine spread because of want of provisions ... So many dogs and cats were consumed that dogs became scarce ... Conditions worsened to the degree that people ate each other. People were constantly on their guard ... Ultimately, al-Mustansir was compelled to sell everything in his palace ... (then) he was unable to secure his own food.[61]

This time, there were no banquets at the palace. Al-Mustansir's two meals of crumbled bread were provided every day by the charity of a pious lady, al-Sharifa bint Sahib al-Sabil, as long as she could afford it.[62] The caliph could not manage to keep his family alive in Cairo, and had to send them abroad. Some of the wives and female members of the royal family could not make the planned trip to Iraq: they all fell at the gates of Cairo and died of starvation.[63] The caliph's sons however, managed to get to Syria.[64] Senior state officials and merchants also fled.[65]

Not only did the interfactional war produce a virtual collapse of the central government, but it was also extremely detrimental to agriculture. Effective agrarian management, as already mentioned, involved the administration at various stages. However, during the worst period of the *shidda*, government administration could not function.

This meant a lack of centralised co-ordination in the management of irrigation works and a severe shortage of seed corn. Thus, harvests were extremely low – even when the Nile levels returned to normal. Moreover, the wars carried on by the troop factions in the countryside had disastrous effects on the peasants, who were too terrified to go out and farm their lands. They were being killed in the war and dying of starvation.[66] According to Ibn Iyas, one-third of the population perished; others estimate that two-thirds of the population perished because, as often happened, famine and unrest were accompanied by epidemics.[67] Regardless of the accuracy of these estimates, it shows that there was a significant decimation of the population[68] which meant that much of the agricultural land was left uncultivated.[69] This naturally led to a severe decline in *kharaj* revenues[70] when the state had the power and the means to collect them.

The fighting also interrupted trade and communications between various Egyptian provinces and between Egypt and neighbouring states. This affected the economy in general, and the delivery of supplies and tax revenues to the capital in particular. The loss of control over Fatimid provinces in Egypt and Syria meant an interruption of trade routes that could have been used to secure grain imports to deal with the shortage. Grain trade with Byzantium had been in decline even before the *shidda*.[71] During the *shidda*, the Seljuks concluded a deal with the Byzantines which stipulated that the latter would not supply Egypt with grain.[72] Surviving sources say little about whether other alternative trade routes were used to supply Egypt with grain. Only one shipment of grain is reported to have reached Egypt from al-Andalus during the *shidda*.[73] In 464/1071–2, merchants were reported to have imported food from Sicily and al-Mahdiyya.[74] Even had the import of grain from abroad been possible, the treasury was already bankrupt and could not finance large orders.

Conclusion

The *shidda* was a manifestation of the collapse of centralised control which was essential for the management of a low Nile. It was the restoration of this control that was the real remedy for the crisis. In 466/1073, al-Mustansir sent for the loyal commander, Badr al-Gamali, military ruler of the Syrian provinces, to come to Cairo and assume the position of minister. Badr's decisive and tough measures restored law and order within a few years and conditions in Egypt quickly improved. With the help of his Armenian troops, Badr pacified the country, killing Ottoman and other warlords, as well as other corrupt administrators who had gained power during the *shidda*.[75] He also embarked on a reorganisation of the administrative system.[76]

The surviving chronicles say little about Badr's agrarian management. However, he is reported to have relieved the farmers from paying their land taxes for three years until their conditions improved.[77] This is further proof of how the *shidda* had hit farmers as well as residents of al-Qahira and Fustat. No major irrigation works were attributed to Badr, although he restored and maintained already existing ones.[78]

One of Badr's main titles is indicative of his power and of the new phase in Fatimid history. As *amir al-juyush*, Badr was first and foremost a soldier. His wazirate marks the beginning of a new age of military *wazirs* who rose to prominence during the twelfth century. Although, as a soldier, Badr's main tactic in restoring order was to control the army and kill off feuding troops, this was not the only area of his concern. If one takes Maqrizi's word, Badr encouraged trade, and agricultural revenues became even higher than before the *shidda*. The economy picked up under his management.

The study of *al-shidda al-'uzma* shows that the relationship between the Egyptian people and the Nile is not a simple or predetermined one. The Nile does fluctuate, and low Niles caused food shortages. However, good management of Egypt's agriculture by an effective central government could handle such natural disasters so as to minimise their impact on the state and the people. It was the lack of effective agrarian management which led to the catastrophic famine and disasters during the reign of Mustansir.

The terrible events reported to have happened during *al-shidda al-'uzma* make it seem to a modern reader an episode from horror fiction. Yet these events did happen. *Al-shidda al-'uzma* was not simply a 'natural' disaster, but one in which other social and political factors played a major role, in which conflicting interests of individuals and the collectivity could tip the balance.

Bibliography

Barrawi, Rashid al-, *Halat Misr al-iqtisadiyya fi 'ahd al-fatimiyin*, Cairo, Maktabat al-Nahda al-Misriyya, 1947.

Bianquis, Thierry, 'Une crise frumentaire dans l'Égypte fatimide', *Journal of the Economic and Social History of the Orient (JESHO)* 23, 1980, pp. 67–101.

Cahen, Claude, 'Contribution à l'étude des impôts dans l'Égypte médiévale', *JESHO* 5, December 1962, pp. 244–78.

Canard, M., 'Fatimids', *Encyclopedia of Islam*, second ed., Leiden, Brill, 1964, vol. 2, pp. 870–82.

Chapoutot-Remadi, Mounira, 'L'agriculture dans l'Empire amelouk au Moyen Âge d'après al-Nuwayri', *Cahiers de Tunisie* 22, 1974, pp. 23–45.

Cooper, Richard, 'The Assessment and Collection of Kharaj Tax in Medieval Egypt', *Journal of the American Oriental Society* 96, July–September 1976, pp. 365–82.

Frantz-Murphy, Gladys, *The Agrarian Administration of Egypt from the Arabs to the Ottomans*, Cairo, Institut Français d'Archéologie Orientale (IFAO), 1986.

Garcin, Jean-Claude, *Un centre musulman de la Haute-Egypte médiévale: Qus*, Cairo, IFAO, 1976.

Goitein, S.D., 'Mediterranean Trade in the Eleventh Century: Some Facts and Problems' in M.A. Cook (ed.), *Studies in the Economic History of the Middle East*, London/New York, Oxford University Press, 1970, pp. 51–62.

Herodotus, *Histories*, transl. George Rawlinson, Hertfordshire, Wordsworth Editions, 1996.

Ibn Iyas al-Hanafi, Muhammad b. Ahmad, *Bada'i' al-zuhur fi waqa' al-duhur*, ed. Muhammad Mustafa, Cairo, al-Hay'a al-Misriyya al-'Amma li'l-Kitab, 1982.

Ibn Mammati, al-As'ad, *Qawanin al-dawawin*, ed. 'Aziz Suryal 'Atiya, Cairo, Madbuli, 1991.

Ibn Manzur, *Lisan al-'Arab*, ed. 'Ali Shayri, Beirut, Dar Ihya' al-Turath al-'Arabi, 1988.

Ibn Muyasar, *Muhammad ibn 'Ali ibn Yusuf, al-Muntaqa min akhbar Misr: intaqahu Taqiyy al-Din Ahamd ibn 'Ali al-Maqrizi 814 AH, Textes arabes et études islamiques*, ed. Ayman Fu'ad Sayyid, Cairo, IFAO, 1981.

Lev, Yaacov, *State and Society in Fatimid Egypt*, Leiden/New York, Copenhagen and Cologne, Brill, 1991.

Makhzumi, Abul Hasan 'Ali b. 'Uthman al-, *Kitab al-Minhaj fi 'Ilm Kharaj Misr*, ed. Claude Cahen, Cairo, IFAO, 1986.

Maqrizi, Taqiyy al-Din Ahmad b. 'Ali al-, 'Ijhathat al-umma bi-kashf al-ghumma' in Adel Allouche (ed.), *Mamluk Economics: A Study and Translation of al-Maqrizi's Ighathah*, Salt Lake City, UT, University of Utah Press, 1994.

– *Itti'az al-hunafa bi-akhbar al-a'ima al-fatimiyin al-khulafa*, 3 vols, Cairo, al-Majli al-A'la li'l-Shu'un al-Islamiyya, 1996.

Munawi, Muhammad Hamdi al-, *al-Wizara wa'l-wuzara' fi 'l-'asr al-fatimi*, Cairo, Dar al-Ma'arif, 1970.

Musabbihi, al-Amir al-Mukhtar 'Izz al-Mulk Muhammad b., 'Ubayd Allah b. Ahmad al' in Ayman Fu'ad Sayyid and Thierry Bianquis (eds), *al-Juz' al-arba'un min akhbar Misr li'l-Musabbihi*, Cairo, IFAO, 1978.

Nasir-i Khusrau, *Book of Travels (Safarnama)*, transl. W.M. Thackston Jr, New York, The Persian Heritage Foundation, 1986.

Sami, Amin, *Taqwim al-Nil*, Cairo, al-Matba'a al-Amiriyyah, 1915.

Sawi, Ahmad al-Sayyid al-, *Maja'at Misr al-fatimiya: asbab wa-nata'ij*, Beirut, Dar al-Tadammun, 1988.

Sayyid, Ayman Fu'ad, *al-Dawla al-fatimiya fi Misr: tafsir jadid*, Cairo, al-Dar al-Misriyya al-Lubnaniyya, 1991.

Shoshan, Boaz, 'Fatimid Grain Policy and the Post of the Muhtasib', *International Journal of Middle East Studies* 13, 1981, pp. 181–9.

Notes on Chapter 4

1 Herodotus, 1996, p. 119.
2 Canard, 1964.
3 Ibn Mammati, 1991, p. 74.
4 *Ibid.*
5 *Ibid.*
6 *Ibid.*, pp. 217–9, 223–4, 235.
7 *Ibid.*, p. 232.
8 *Ibid.*, pp. 201–4; Makhzumi, 1986, pp. 58–9.
9 Cooper, 1976, pp. 366–7; Cahen, 1962, p. 258.
10 Chapoutot-Remadi, 1974, p. 28.
11 Bianquis, 1980, p. 72.
12 Lev, 1991, p. 162.
13 Barrawi, 1947, p. 81; Lev, 1991, p. 162.

14 Nasir-i Khusrau, 1986, p. 56.
15 Lev, 1991, p. 162.
16 Bianquis, 1980, pp. 72–3.
17 Maqrizi, 1996, vol. 2, p. 59.
18 *Ibid.*, vol. 2, p. 70.
19 *Ibid.*, vol. 2, p. 74.
20 *Ibid.*, vol. 2, p. 71.
21 *Ibid.*; Maqrizi, 1994, p. 32.
22 Maqrizi, 1994, p. 32.
23 Maqrizi, 1996, vol. 2, p. 74.
24 *Ibid.*, vol. 2, p. 76.
25 *Ibid.*, vol. 2, p. 77.
26 *Ibid.*, vol. 2, p. 79.
27 Ibn Iyas, 1982, vol. 1, p. 204. Ibn Iyas relates this anecdote quoting Musabbihi, the Fatimid bureaucrat and historian, who would have been an eyewitness to such an event. Unfortunately, this section of Musabbihi's own work does not survive and, as such, there is no way to confirm the sources used by Ibn Iyas.
28 Maqrizi, 1996, vol. 2, p. 134.
29 Musabbihi, 1978, p. 39; Maqrizi, 1996, vol. 2, p. 142.
30 Musabbihi, 1978, p. 74.
31 *Ibid.*, p.15.
32 Maqrizi, 1996, vol. 2, p. 165; Shoshan, 1981, p. 184.
33 Musabbihi, 1978, pp. 74, 76.
34 *Ibid.*, p. 75 ; Maqrizi, 1996, vol. 2, p. 166.
35 Barrawi, 1947, p. 101.
36 Shoshan, 1981, p. 184.
37 Maqrizi, 1994, p. 34.
38 Barrawi, 1947, pp. 100–1.
39 Lev, 1991, p. 163.
40 Maqrizi, 1996, vol. 2, p. 180.
41 See infra below.
42 Goitein, 1970, p. 57.
43 Lev, 1991, p. 163.
44 Sawi, 1988, p. 15.
45 Musabbihi, 1978, pp. 81–2; Maqrizi, 1996, vol. 2, pp. 166–7.
46 Musabbihi, 1978, p. 71; Maqrizi, 1996, vol. 2, pp. 162–3.
47 Musabbihi, 1978, p. 72.
48 The meanings of *shidda* in the famous lexicon, *Lisan al-'Arab*, include 'difficult times' and 'famine': Ibn Manzur, 1988, vol. 7, p. 55.
49 Maqrizi, 1996, vol. 2, p. 226.
50 Barrawi, 1947, p. 97.

51 Munawi, 1970, pp. 307–11.
52 Ibn Muyassar, 1981, pp. 15–7; Maqrizi, 1996, vol. 2, pp. 252–7.
53 Sayyid, 1991, p. 122; Lev, 1991, pp. 39–40.
54 Maqrizi, 1996, vol. 2, pp. 265–7.
55 *Ibid.*, vol. 2, pp. 265–7; Ibn Muyassar, 1981, pp. 24–6.
56 Maqrizi, 1996, vol. 2, p. 273; Ibn Muyassar, 1981, pp. 31–2.
57 Maqrizi, 1996, vol. 2, p. 275; Lev, 1991, p. 44.
58 Ibn Iyas, 1982, vol. 1, p. 216.
59 Cited in Sawi, 1988, vol. 1, p. 61.
60 The attached table has been compiled from Sami, 1988, vol. 1, pp. 92–6.
61 Maqrizi, 1994, pp. 37–8.
62 *Ibid.*, p. 38 ; Maqrizi, 1996, vol. 2, p. 298.
63 Maqrizi, 1996, vol. 2, p. 298.
64 *Ibid.*
65 *Ibid.*, vol. 2, p. 303.
66 Barrawi, 1947, p. 95.
67 *Ibid*; Sawi, 1988, pp. 68, 126.
68 Ibn Iyas, 1982, vol. 1, p. 218.
69 Lev, 1991, p. 45.
70 Sawi, 1988, p. 140.
71 In 446/1054, during the first low Nile in Mustansir's reign, the caliph contacted the Byzantine Emperor Constantine IX who agreed to supply Egypt with grain. When the Emperor died before the deal was terminated, his successor, the Empress Theodora, revoked the agreement because Mustansir refused to sign a defence pact with her. It seems that Egypt's imports of grain were not large or regular enough to warrant such a deal: Ibn Muyassar, 1981, p. 13; Barrawi, 1947, p. 101; Sawi, 1988, p. 63.
72 Sayyid, 1991, p. 127.
73 Lev, 1991, p. 163.
74 Maqrizi, 1996, vol. 2, p. 307.
75 Ibn Muyassar, 1981, pp. 40–1; Maqrizi, 1996, vol. 2, pp. 311–13; Lev, 1991, pp. 45, 96.
76 Garcin, 1976, p. 77.
77 Ibn Muyassar, 1981, p. 53 ; Maqrizi, 1996, vol. 2, p. 330.
78 Barrawi, 1947, p. 104.

CHAPTER 5

'Passive Revolution' as a Possible Model for Nineteenth-century Egyptian History

Peter Gran

Social and economic history made its great impact on the study of nineteenth-century Egypt in the 1970s and the early 1980s. In this period, it pushed aside the elite political and diplomatic history which had dominated up to this point. During this period, historians began to explore the historical agency of the wider urban class structure; some work on peasant structure appeared as well. After the early 1980s, history as a field fell into a rut; the history of nineteenth-century Egypt saw little more than elaboration of earlier work. This study surveys some of the main achievements in this field between 1970 and the present, and suggests that the adoption of a comparative history approach and a change in paradigm may be a way for the study of nineteenth-century Egypt to progress once again.

Nineteenth-century Egyptian history covers the period of the rise of the modern nation state and the birth of the modern culture of which today's Egypt is a part. Nineteenth-century historians must deal with these issues as well as with their relation to the eighteenth century, which is less studied. They must also study the relationship of the local ruling classes to those abroad, within the context of a growing world market. Last and most importantly, they must analyse changing power relations within Egypt.

It is within this last area that the field has registered its greatest successes. Several important historians have analysed the relationship between power and land ownership. Land ownership has been carefully studied from land registers in the national archives. Furthermore, it has been demonstrated from a variety of sources that, although there were several social classes owning some land, the large owners dominated the political scene. Class conflict too has been demonstrated. It took place not just between landlords and peasants, which was already assumed, but among landlords as well. Those who had acquired land early on – the original grandees from the Muhammad 'Ali period and the royal family – resisted the rise of a class of village notables. Furthermore, recent historical research has suggested that the class of village notables spearheaded modern Egyptian nationalism. Thus the 'Urabi revolt should be understood not only as a political act involving some officers, but also as an important social phenomenon to which different groups contributed.

On the margins of this research, there have been suggestions that violent clashes between the administration and the peasantry were common in the absentee estates of the royal family in places such as upper Egypt. The peasantry were capable of making their own social demands with or without a village shaykh to speak for them. Peasant and bedouin initiatives are especially documented for the period of the 'Urabi revolution. In short, the evolution of history as a field widened and deepened the picture of the past.

What has happened is no doubt rather more complicated than this simple outline suggests. It is not a matter of social history being added to the older political history, but rather of its disrupting it, pulling it and the dominant paradigm embedded in it asunder, yet doing so only half self-consciously. Indeed, for those who upheld the dominant paradigm – the oriental despotism and centralised power theory – social history was scarcely perceived as something new or threatening. For years, the two co-existed. Egypt was assumed to be highly centralised but, at the same time, it was slowly modernising, trying to become independent and escape from the periphery of the world market. However, as social history continued to develop, matters changed. For example, the position of the Cairo elite became less important. At this point, one can observe – after the fact at least – that the dominant paradigm had become an obstacle to the further development of history.

When, for example, should one now claim that modern Egypt 'started'? Prior to the opening up of these new perspectives by social historians, the advent of modern Egypt was based on important political dates and/or the rule of important individuals. As more emphasis on social classes emerged, dating became less clear. Instead of a single perspective, one now encountered a range of views, some clearly not congruent with one or another form of understanding history. Some writers believed that the critical date for the birth of modern Egypt was 1798, for others it was 1805, and yet again for a few others, it was 1863. Those choosing 1798 were mainly royalists or nationalists, and came from the previous generation of political historians. They attributed Egypt's ills to the Ottoman period. Historians such as Douin and Sammarco, who were employed by the king in the 1920s, belong to this school of thought. The coming of Napoleon was the earliest moment at which one can identify a break with the Middle Ages. Later, Egyptian historians concentrated on 1805 and the rise of Muhammad 'Ali. On the other hand, European historians have remained concerned with the 'rise of the West', and have continued to draw on the Napoleonic invasion as a critical moment when the West met the 'still sleeping East'. After 1952, Egyptian preoccupations shifted once again from Muhammad 'Ali's rise to power to a concern with what he did to build the state. Writers of that era began to concentrate on 1815 – on the new army, the new bureaucracy and the new health service.

After the 1952 revolution, three new problems confronted historians: the pronounced role of Europeans and the relative absence of Egyptians involved in carrying out the reforms, the fact that all the reforms eventually collapsed and had to be reinvented later in the nineteenth century, and the entry of social history into the field of Muhammad 'Ali studies, which brought to light the high level of discontent among the general population and did little to glamorise the birth of modern Egypt so conceived.[1]

Were there other options for the history profession? The choice of the age of Isma'il (1863–79) as a point of departure also had its proponents and its detractors but more of the latter than the former. After 1952, most historians avoided it as a take-off point since the ruler was so ineffective and because his mistakes and disasters led to the colonial takeover. Yet, as concerns capitalism and commercial law,[2] the development of professions[3] and government bureaucratic structure,[4] not to mention various areas of intellectual life, much can be gained from using the age of Isma'il as a point of departure for modernity, whatever one thinks of Isma'il himself.

Still, the choice – in this case 1863 – is not simple for a social historian, since many of the crucial issues stem from long-term trends that cannot be precisely dated. Work, for example, on the evolution of private property in land suggests a gradually unfolding tapestry of laws stretching through the nineteenth century. Likewise, descriptions of peasant strikes do not concentrate either in any one time or place. Trade statistics reflect the international cotton market, with its ups and downs, developing through the century; the year 1863 does not specifically stand out here either.

In sum, both for the traditional nationalist political historians and for the newer social historians, the age of Isma'il creates as many problems as solutions. Yet 1805 and 1863 remain the realistic choices for the birth of modern Egypt. The years of 1919, 1923 and 1952 – sometimes also proposed – all are far too recent to serve as a point from which to begin modern history.

What happens, however, when social history is pursued as comparative social history? At that point, the year 1863 becomes the clear choice for the birth of modern Egypt, such an approach overcoming most of the objections noted up to this point. The example of Italian history immediately comes to mind, and recourse to the example of Italian history clarifies what had been going on in an inchoate way in Egyptian history, that a paradigm shift was well underway (see below).

For the upholders of the traditional nationalist or oriental despot model of Egyptian history, the mention of Italy may be off-putting. It dimly reminds one of Taha Husayn's views on the future of culture in Egypt and on the rather conservative Mediterranean school of Egyptian historiography There are obvious differences between the two countries. This is correct. Of course, all countries differ, in fact and in self-representation. For example, Egypt has a long tradition of focusing on rule by foreigners, while Italy has no such tradition. But one might recall that the function of comparative history is to recognise and to articulate differences without allowing them to produce exaggerated uniquenesses. Eventually, the important thing is to determine the specificity of Egypt, not its uniqueness. Ultimately to overcome Egyptian exceptionalism, some kind of meaningful comparative framework is required. For the present generation, such a framework must come from social history, even when social historians have not provided it.

This leads to a concern. How adequate is the existing social history for purposes of comparative history? The existing social history on Egypt, still in the shadow of the older political history, is rather static. It continues to be, in fact, sociology. This 'social history' has generally portrayed the country's history as the outcome of autocratic rule as much as political history has done. Basically, the ruler and his entourage controlled the irrigation system of the Nile which brought water and thus the possibility of life to the peasants. Given this enormous leverage exercised by the ruler's control over the irrigation system, even 'social historians' have concluded that the Egyptian peasant, individually or collectively, has become a passive creature inured to hardship, someone who can be drawn into struggle only on the level of familial vendettas. Historians who adopt this approach – even social historians – feel justified in regarding the peasant as being outside history. There is little sense of the diffusion of power.

At their best, historians overcome these problems, but often one feels that whatever took place in Egypt is what makes Egyptian history whether or not it specifically involves large numbers of Egyptians. Take, for example, the campaign of General Rommel. Still, there are exceptions. For instance, F. Robert Hunter, author of one of the most important works on nineteenth-century Egyptian history, notes that the central government did not attempt to resolve irrigation matters on the village level until the twentieth century; consequently, there was not, in effect, during the formative years of the nineteenth century any oriental despotism. He also noted that until 1875 the Egyptian political elite regularly dealt with the European powers without letting them have any real power, but that in that year a power split occurred in which a number of officials went over to the idea of colonialism. Here, Hunter seems to be casting doubt on the thesis of the coming of the West as a long slow gradual process over which the Egyptian ruling class had no power. Shortly before Hunter published his work, the German historian Alexander Schölch published a series of articles on the background to the

'Urabi revolt, showing a wider range of Egyptian involvement in the historical dynamics of the period. He wrote, for example, on the role of the bedouin in the national struggle, on the role of the *'ulama* and last, perhaps most iconoclastically, he wrote about Europeans in Egypt as the 'men on the spot', participating in what became a rather new view of colonialism. What Schölch and several other writers had hit upon was the fact that Europeans in countries such as Egypt were pursuing their own interests and the interests of those with whom they were doing business – not those of the home country. If it was in their interest to manipulate the home country into an act of war and invasion, the Europeans in Egypt would do what they could to bring it about.[5]

If social history is to assume the passivity of the peasantry, then other social forces must be looked for to explain the course of history. A common solution was to concentrate on struggles within the elite around the state debt. It is a fact that Sa'id took terrible financial risks committing the Egyptian state to buy into the Suez Canal venture, and that Isma'il followed with many ruinous loans. In other words, the khedives dealt with European finance capital – so the argument goes – and what happened historically in Egypt followed from that fact.

This line of argument, while no doubt true, overlooks the political and social aspects of the debt situation. Looking at these aspects from the perspective of the royal family and other large landholders, one finds that the debt was not so onerous, since it was imposed as a flat tax per *feddan* of land on the entire society. Medium and small landholders were far more affected than large holders, some of the swing to nationalism among the village shaykhs and others who had been accumulating small and medium holdings stems from the politics of debt repayment. Other events coinciding with debt repayment seem worth emphasising, although less is known about them. They include the rise of the Egyptian village shaykhs up the power structure of the country and the increasing takeover by the state of what was termed 'uncultivated land', a term in need of further study. The two events may well be connected.

There are, however, features of this subject matter which bring out the contradictions between the newer social history and the bulk of the older work. Did, for example, Isma'il really make Egyptian history? Did he decide one day to outlaw slavery, and did the whole country acquiesce? Social history lays the groundwork for a different way of looking at the subject, one with implications for the whole larger paradigm for nineteenth-century Egypt. While one may grant that there is a correlation between the population growth of the middle decades of the nineteenth century, especially in the delta, and the improvement of government services in health, education and transportation in that area, is this going to prove that progress originating in the West trickled down from the elite to the masses in Egypt? The historian Reda Mowafi, author of a work on slavery in Egypt, concluded that, by the 1890s, population growth meant that neither slavery nor guilds were needed any longer. By this point, Egypt had a free labour market and increasing landlessness. Thus, a new mass of landless workers could perform the functions previously performed by slaves and guild workers. Furthermore, they required less care or attention than did slaves. It is thus a matter of some interest to analyse carefully what is meant by 'population growth'. Here, the research carried out in the dominant paradigm fails to clarify the matter, and Mowafi's work may be more to the point. It seems almost naive to suppose that slavery ended in Egypt because Isma'il decided to outlaw it one day, or to suppose that Isma'il outlawed slavery because Europe wanted it outlawed. There would have to have been interests behind such changes and, in all probability, the abolition of slavery must have helped solidify the power of the property-owning classes in Egypt. Whatever the case, by the 1880s, enough peasants had lost their land and were accepting any work out of desperation to eliminate the need for forced labour.[6]

With the rise of social history in Egyptian studies, a series of attempts have been made to incorporate wider segments of the population into the historical dynamic. While suggesting that this has not gone far enough, certainly the works of Ra'uf 'Abbas and 'Asim Dissuqi have studied and documented, from archival evidence, the fundamental linkages between the ruling bureaucrats and the land system. Henceforth, the old approach of terming this or that individual a military man, a Turk, an Armenian etc, started to become less useful in Egypt than knowing what an individual's claim to wealth was.

Complementing this work is the study of 'Ali Barakat, who argued that, prior to the 'Urabi revolt, the struggle of the peasants was largely spontaneous rather than political – a response to taxes and forced labour. He noted, for example, peasant flight from one village to another as an act which greatly vexed the government. Laws were passed to try to prevent it. In light of such references, it seems more than a little premature to dismiss the possibility of political significance embedded in such acts, especially given the consequences meted out in taxes and beatings for those who were caught. The burning or theft of crops may have appeared spontaneous but they may not have been.

'Ali Barakat's evidence, in any case, largely appears to fit the 'passive revolution' model proposed below, first used to describe Italy. In his description of the Battle of Fao in 1865 in upper Egypt, Barakat notes that the army crushed a large number of peasants, led by Ahmad al-Tayyib, who were protesting against forced labour, low wages and other hardships. The fact that Ahmad al-Tayyib used religion as a political tool scarcely negates the social and political dimensions of the struggle. The occurrence of this uprising and the way in which it was put down by the army with artillery reinforces another element of the model – regional inequality. No such event occurred in the delta.

In a similar vein, Barakat notes that while starvation was a general phenomenon in the countryside in 1877, so great was the devastation in 1879, that unburied bodies were visible throughout upper Egypt – a rare occurrence. That year, the same region witnessed a sharp outbreak in organised crime, increased clashes with the army and people fleeing to the mountains followed by social banditry.[7] This unrest did not end in the period of this study, as one may conclude from reading 'Abd al-Khaliq Lashin's work on Sa'd Zaghlul.[8]

The considerable extent of absentee land ownership in upper Egypt in this period contributes to an understanding of the region's social volatility. On close examination, it appears that the vast bulk of the Da'ira Saniyya lands (the royal family's absentee estate lands) were in middle and upper Egypt throughout this period. The royal family's holdings in the delta, the so-called domain lands, had been turned over to guarantee the Rothschild debt, leaving them only a few thousand *feddans* in the delta as *waqf.* Absentee land ownership, as studies of latifundism show, is well-known for its volatility; masses of unskilled farm workers are controlled by an often quite vindictive and uncaring managerial stratum. Latifundia seem as well to strengthen the preoccupation of some of the large landowners, such as the royal family, in blocking land reform up to the 1952 revolution.[9]

Additional evidence for the assumption of a more oppressed and more radical upper Egyptian peasantry emerges from certain events of the 'Urabi revolt. According to Barakat, the greatest political impact of peasant attacks on the wealthy classes was felt in al-Minya, where attacks were directed against the royal absentee estates of the Da'ira Saniyya. This land was owned by Isma'il, Sultan Pasha and Tal'at Pasha; here, spontaneous peasant land redistribution was the quickest and most radical, including even the appropriation of sugar factories located on the estates. Among other demands, the Minya peasants insisted on the abolition of their debts to the government. The local *'umda* was forced to demand that 'Urabi redistribute all the land in the country, giving it to the peasants and not to the Ottoman Turks.

By way of contrast, the struggle in the delta took on a more classical nationalist form, although there were land takeovers there too. However, the emphasis in the delta seemed to be more on confiscation than on redistribution, as practised in Asiyut and al-Minya.

Other work by social historians, such as that of Alan Richards and Gabriel Baer on the middle decades of the nineteenth century, focused on the rise both of a large landlord class and of a class of village shaykhs. This class steadily gained in power and was important in the nationalist movement spearheaded by Ahmad 'Urabi.[10] This fact has oriented a number of historians to find the causes of rural conflict on a higher as opposed to a lower level in the social structure of the country. The logic seems clear enough: the village shaykh was an Arabic-speaking Egyptian peasant, while the large landlord was Turkish and/or European. In other words, this was a classic case of nationalism.

Today, while one might still benefit from this line of interpretation, other elements also need to be considered. First, the evolution of the lower officialdom implied an attempt on the part of the state to control the peasantry more closely. Thus, the struggle between the peasants and the lower officials over customary rights surfaced as a very important arena of struggle in its own right, in addition to that between the village shaykhs and the large landlords. One outcome for the loser – often the peasant – was flight from the land. Such flight has rarely been interpreted as a part of a political struggle; historians have commonly found it to be an attempt to avoid the corvée, taxes or the draft, as noted above. Whatever the case, the relocation of population implied a lot of struggle and clearly had political repercussions. While flight to the hills around Luxor is mentioned repeatedly, it would seem logical to postulate that the state had more to fear from those peasants who definitively migrated to the cities or to the delta, and who had no steady employment.

Peasant struggles took place in the delta as well as in upper Egypt. The dynamics, however, appear different. When, for example, peasant struggle arose in the rice belt of the delta over the corvée in 1880, the village shaykhs sided with the peasants against the state and refused to impose the corvée requirement. Thus, the peasant struggle was channelled away from the anarchism and primitive socialism in upper Egypt towards nationalism and reformist Islam. 'Urabi seemed aware of this. He was struck by the magnitude of upper Egyptian self-sacrifice. At the same time, it was the delta peasantry who were more oriented to his nationalism.[11]

Gramsci's Theory of 'Passive Revolution'

This is an attempt to overcome the problem of historiographical stagnation, an attempt to confront the problem of Egyptian exceptionalism.

Antonio Gramsci, the Italian communist theorist, is not considered to have been a historian, but his theories of Italian history are those which largely shape the field of Italian historiography. The debates which he initiated persist to the present day.

The terrain of nineteenth-century history was important for Gramsci. One may surmise that Gramsci, as a southern Italian, wanted to show that the state had turned the south of Italy into a cheap labour export zone, that this system, based on gross regional inequality, persisted thereafter and that the dominant liberal historiography covered up this fact. The diligence of the northerners and the laziness of the southerners was stressed and the soil of the south was said to be poor.

For Gramsci, the modern Italian state, unlike the French one, was a case of failed northern capitalist development, the capitalist class being responsible for not progressing radically enough. In his view, Italian capitalists were too lazy. As a result, they failed to develop the internal market, leaving, as they did, the south essentially outside the market.

Gramsci characterises the lazy conservative approach to state formation as the 'passive revolution', a term which entered social thought from his writings and one which may apply to the study of nineteenth-century Egypt. For Gramsci, passive revolution meant, in the first place, the way that Italians achieved their modern state form in the *risorgimento* (national awakening). If other historians – especially liberals – saw the rise of modern Italy as the story of progress and freedom combined with the errors which led to its downfall and fascism – more or less how Anouar Abdel Malek or Louis Awad see the history of modern Egypt – Gramsci saw the rise of modern Italy in quite different terms.

For Gramsci, the original formation of the modern state came about as a result of the defeat caused by the irresolution and misjudgement of popular forces represented by Garibaldi and Mazzini, who were outmanoeuvred by the ever-pragmatic Cavour. Could one insert here the defeat of 'Urabi by the khedive and the British? And if so, as a side point, what was it that was so threatening about Egyptian nationalism that 'Urabi had to be exiled while Mazzini was not?

In Gramsci's terms, the heart of the idea of passive revolution was that the bourgeoisie pulled off a coup d'état without the involvement of the popular elements in society. They did this by striking a historic alliance with feudal elements in the south in return for their backing of the new state, which would be run primarily for the northern bourgeoisie. Some of the points that Gramsci drew from this framework serve equally as research hypotheses for the student of Egyptian history.

One of these points is that the newly formed Italian state came together as two unequal parts: the north dominated the south. The northern ruling class had the power to turn the southern working class into migrant labour at its beck and call. If one adopts the model, the Italian *bracciante* (seasonal migrants) would represent the Egyptian *tarahil*, the north becoming more capitalist while the south remained more pre-capitalist.

With the increase in class conflict following the deepening of private-property relations in land in the middle of the nineteenth century, rule was maintained by playing the northern worker off the southern peasant. Unnecessary southern peasants were forced to migrate abroad in search of work. The price that the northern ruling class paid for its control over the political and economic structure and its access to southern cheap labour was relinquishment of control over the cultural structure to the southern ruling class. To a degree, this would jibe with the present Egyptian situation, as large numbers of Egyptian writers are southerners. Rome, like Cairo, was a meeting-place of north and south, although it was not necessarily a melting-pot. One's family origin in the countryside or the location of one's land defined one in Cairo and in Rome, even after a generation or two.

Assuming this model of nation state rule for Egypt, one would tend to postulate resistance on the part of the Egyptian people, as Gramsci did for the Italian people. Was there important internal resistance to Egyptian hegemony, resistance which historians have not recognised? Were the political, legal and cultural reforms of the age of Isma'il, so often attributed to the influence of Europe, actually reactions to the struggles from below?

In this sense, it is important to reread what is known about peasant self-assertion. While the reports from primary sources almost invariably emphasise local or religious preoccupations, if not ordinary criminality, these sources tend to reflect the interests of the state. Moreover, the government employee of that day who wrote these reports would not see the events in the same way as today's social historian.

Here again, Gramsci's theory is of some use. In analysing the forms of consciousness in contexts marked by radically unequal power relations, Gramsci pioneered the idea that people become – or at least appear to be – massified. Prisoners, for example, start to repeat, in a simplified way, the language and value judgements of their captors (the Stockholm Effect); a so-called 'slave mentality' ensues. If religion or localism is expected, the oppressed will express it. However, as Gramsci points out, a change in power relations induced by struggle brings an explosion of clarity in the thoughts of the oppressed. It is as if the breakdown of the external oppression results in the breakdown of internal repression.

Therefore, what may be described as a local revolt in a chronicle might have had much wider significance lying slightly below the surface. This is not known for a fact, but one can note that such revolts were repressed by the Egyptian state with enormous brutality. One wonders why. If this was a local fight about a cow or an irrigation issue, would the state involve itself so heavy-handedly? One line of thought, close to Gramsci's, is that the local administrative strata had an intuitive understanding of where things might lead. If, after the event, they chronicled its occurrence in a belittling manner, this was simply one last attempt to bury their fears.

At this point the historian is advised to recall that who has a right to historical memory today is a contentious subject. Therefore, for the contemporary writer/reader, one suspects that any attempt to emancipate Egyptian social history from elite-oriented history goes hand in hand with a number of side issues, of which a political struggle over who owns memory may turn out to be one.

In countries such as India, the struggle over the meaning of sources and of memory is well underway, and Egyptian history has something to learn from this work as well. For the nineteenth-century rulers in India, dacoity was banditry. With the rise of social history in India in the past generation, dacoity took on class-conflict and anti-imperial dimensions. It was not dacoity but the land system and capitalism which were the problems – dacoity was simply one manifestation of this. Historians amassed much information about this. More recently, with the turn to the right in Indian historical writing – as, for example, in subaltern studies – the quest has become one of how to reinterpret what historians previously had found back into essentialist cultural terms. For reasons yet to be explored, Egyptian historiography has resisted moving from stage one to stage two. The idea of peasant struggle in Egypt is still best exemplified through literature, not history or literary theory; the best known example is 'Abd al-Rahman al-Sharqawi's novel, *al-Ard* (translated as *The Egyptian Earth*).

Conclusion

This research argues that the rise of social history has greatly benefited the study of nineteenth-century Egypt, but that it failed to achieve, in this context, what it achieved elsewhere – notably an articulation of the internal dynamic of struggle. To remedy the situation, the explicit use of a model of Italian history is proposed. Some evidence about upper and lower Egyptian social history appears to fit this model fairly securely. On the level of political history, much more work needs to be done to ascertain the type of thought which went into the formation of modern Egyptian hegemony. Was it similar to the *risorgimento* of Italy? In any case, what is known is that there certainly was a long-term affinity between the Egyptian royal family and its Italian counterpart, virtually from the nineteenth century to the 1952 revolution.

Bibliography

'Abbas Hamid, Ra'uf, 'Historiography in Egypt in the twentieth century', *Cairo Papers in the Social Sciences* 18, 1995, pp. 18–40.

Baer, Gabriel, *A History of Land ownership in Modern Egypt*, 1800–1950, London, Oxford University Press, 1962.

Barakat, 'Ali, *Tatawwur al-milkiyya al-zira'iyya fi Misr 1813–1914 wa Atharuha 'ala al-haraka al-siyasiyya*, Cairo, Dar al-Thaqafa al-Jadida, 1977.

Eissa, Hossam M., *Capitalisme et sociétés anonymes en Egypte*, Paris, R. Pichon, 1970.

Frank, André Gunder, *Global Economy in the Asian Age*, Berkeley, CA, University of California Press, 1998.

Gran, Peter, *Beyond Eurocentrism: A New View of Modern World History*, Syracuse, NY, Syracuse University Press, 1996, especially chapters 4–6 (on Gramsci and associated ideas).

Hunter, F. Robert, *Egypt Under the Khedives*, Pittsburgh, PA, Pittsburgh University Press, 1984.

Lashin, 'Abd al-Khaliq, *Sa'd Zaghlul wa-dawruhu fi 'l-siyasa al-misriyya*, Cairo, Madbuli, 1975.

Lawson, Fred H., *The Social Origins of Egyptian Expansionism During the Muhammad 'Ali Period*, New York, Columbia University Press, 1992.

Mowafi, Reda, *Slavery, Slave Trade and Abolition Attempts in Egypt and the Sudan, 1820–1882*, Malmo, Lund, 1981.

Reid, Donald M., 'Cromer and the Classics: Imperialism, Nationalism and the Greco–Roman Past in Modern Egypt', *Middle East Studies* 32, 1996, pp. 1–29.

Raziq, Younan Labib, 'The Development of the Ministerial System in Egypt, 1878–1923' in Nelly Hanna (ed.), *The State and Its Servants*, Cairo, American University in Cairo Press, 1995, pp. 88–97.

Richards, Alan, *Egypt's Agricultural Development, 1800–1980*, Boulder, CA, Westview Press, 1982.

Schölch, Alexander, *Egypt for the Egyptians!*, London, Ithaca, 1981.

Notes on Chapter 5

1   Lawson, 1992. In general terms, the Oriental despotism and the older political and economic history fit the modernisation thesis of social scientists, while social history tends towards political economy. For a thorough discussion of trends in Egyptian historiography, see 'Abbas Hamid, 1995.

2   Eissa, 1970.

3   See, for example, Reid, 1996.

4   Hunter, 1984; Raziq, 1995.

5   Hunter, 1984, pp. 4, 35, 233, note 4; Schölch, 1981, especially p. 372. The role of internal dynamics as a part of history remains surprisingly controversial. A major current opponent is the Annales school, which proves that neither the state nor social dynamics matter, what matters is the world market which has been around for centuries. Hence the willingness to go beyond Eurocentrism and argue for an Asian world market seemingly to preserve the argument that what people do politically does not matter: Frank, 1998.

6   Mowafi, 1981, p. 98; Barakat, 1977, pp. 313–14, 408.

7   Barakat, 1977, pp. 385–96.

8   Lashin, 1975.

9   Baer, 1962, pp. 41–4.

10 Richards, 1982, pp. 329, 432.

11 Some of this regional differentiation appears earlier in Fred Lawson's account of Muhammad 'Ali's Hijaz campaign: Barakat, 1977, p. 397.

Part Two:
CRAFTS AND TRADES

CHAPTER 6

Making a Living or Making a Fortune in Ottoman Syria

Abdul-Karim Rafeq

The conditions for making a living or a fortune in Ottoman Syria varied across time. When the administration was strong and corruption was minimal, the chances of making a fortune through illegal means were limited. Earning a living and even making big money through legal means were, however, possible through individual initiative and collective effort at all times, provided that neither the state nor influential groups, such as the military, intervened. External factors also played a role in the ways which individuals used to make a living or a fortune. Mercantilist and industrial Europe as instrumental in shaping the economies and societies of Syria and the Middle East as a whole. The importation of specie from the New World through Spain in the sixteenth century, for example, caused a price revolution in Europe and brought about a devaluation of Ottoman silver currency. In the 1560s, inflation occurred in the Arab provinces and salaried troops rose in revolt in Yemen, Egypt, Syria and Iraq, when the state tried to stop them from imposing illegal taxes on the people to make up for the falling value of their pay.[1]

Chronicles, biographical works, travel accounts, court records and reports by Europeans stationed in Syria describe the hardships that the majority of the population suffered in urban and rural regions. The sources indicate that poverty was widespread, as shown by the jamming of bakeries by restless crowds. The main reason was not the drought, which people accepted as fate, but the hoarding of food supplies by merchants in complicity with top officials, who were anxious to make a fortune by raising price. Professional creditors usually offered credit at excessive rates. A class tension of sorts frequently occurred between the haves and the have-nots. This paper will focus on such issues as guilds, loans and credit, and the renting and abuse of *waqf* land, which had a great impact on the lives and fortunes of individuals and groups.

The Egalitarian Aspect of the Guilds

Introduced into Syria by the Ottomans,[2] the guilds constituted the backbone of the country's economy. They upheld the division of labour and controlled the three major activities of production, services and marketing. Guilds were autonomous organisations which enacted their own regulations, set the prices of their own products and monitored the quality of work of their members. They merged with each other, separated from each other and even dissolved themselves according to their own interest. They also chose and dismissed their heads (shaykhs) by majority vote, without government intervention. Guilds were useful to the authorities because they regulated economic activity and, more importantly, collected taxes for the government from their members. Since taxes were collectively imposed on each guild, the head of the guild, with the help of an identifier (*mu'arrif*), specified the amount of tax that each member had to pay, according to his economic situation.[3]

Craftsmen earned their living from their work within guilds, according to the professional rank that they held as apprentices, journeymen or masters. The apprentice joined the guild as a beginner to learn the craft; the master who taught him gave him a stipend that took care of his meals, clothing and other expenses. A contract was signed between the apprentice and the master that detailed the conditions of employment. If the apprentice was a minor, a guardian would sign the contract on his behalf. In 1722, for example, a cloth printer (*tabba'*), Sayyid Muhammad al-Halabi, employed (*ista'jara*) his adult nephew, 'Abd al-Rahman, for six years, according to a contract approved by the Shafi'i judge in Damascus. 'Abd al-Rahman's daily pay was six silver misriyyas (40 misriyyas equalled 1 piastre), four of which were to be retained by the employer to cover 'Abd al-Rahman's expenses for food, clothing and other necessities; the remaining two misriyyas were given to 'Abd al-Rahman. The contract was signed in the presence of 'Abd al-Rahman's father.[4] The apprentice was usually an adult, but there are examples of apprentices who were minors. The number of apprentices that a master could employ in his workshop varied according to the type of craft and the size of workshop. Apprenticeship within a craft was a precondition for practising the craft and for promotion within its ranks. An outsider was not allowed to practise the craft, no matter how expert he may have been in the profession. He had to join the guild as an apprentice and rise within its ranks upon satisfactory performance. A court injunction in Damascus in 1707 forbade outsiders from practising crafts (*al-ajnabi bi'l-kar la yashtaghil*). The prohibition was still valid in 1845 when the Higher Consultative Council (Majlis Shura al-Sham al-'Ali) in Damascus made the same statement in a dispute within the guild of weighers (*qabbana*).[5] This was primarily intended to ensure a better quality of work under the supervision of the shaykh of the guild. It also limited the number of guild members, prevented outside competition and ensured an equitable distribution of collective taxes among the members.

When an apprentice learned the craft, he was promoted to the rank of journeyman (*sani'*). The journeyman received his pay either on a daily or a weekly basis. The weekly pay is referred to as *usbu'iyya*. In certain crafts, such as those dealing with textiles, a journeyman was paid upon the completion of a piece of cloth. Master craftsmen (the Persian word, *ustadh*, was abbreviated to *usta*; in Arabic, the word used was *mu'allim*) required an independent workshop and had to employ journeymen and apprentices. Many journeymen thus preferred to remain at this level, because of the expenses involved in becoming masters, and the number of years that a journeyman stayed at this level had no limit. The master would also delay the promotion of the journeyman, because this would make the latter a potential rival to him. Another consideration for delaying the promotion of journeymen was the absence of openings, that is the number of licenses at master level. These were connected with the number of *gedik* and *khilu* – the number of licenses and authorised workshops in any craft. However, with the decline of the guild system in the nineteenth century under the impact of industrial Europe, the rules governing promotion within guilds were relaxed. According to the contemporary Damascene, Ilyas Qoudsi, some apprentices were promoted to the ranks of journeyman and master on the same day.[6]

Gedik, a Turkish word rendered in Arabic as *kadak*, was the equipment in a workshop, such as looms in a textile shop. A court document from Damascus in 1855 refers to *gedik* as all the equipment in the shop (*jami' 'uddat al-dukkan al-mu'abbar 'anha bi'l-kadak*).[7] *Gedik* was owned, sold and inherited as a whole or in portions measured by the *qirat* (one unit of 24). The first function of *gedik* in Istanbul was 'to limit and control the location of the craft or trade and to prevent its dispersion' and 'the limitation of guild members'.[8] (This was also the case in Albania, where *gedik* was used to limit the number of corporation members in an attempt to keep aliens, such as non-artisans and peasants, from penetrating the guilds.[9]) When the Arabic word *khilu*, meaning the price paid to use a shop, is mentioned together with *gedik* in a sale transaction, this refers to the equipment and the right to use the shop that had been sold. However, the use of either term could implicitly include the other, as was the case in Aleppo. Investment in *gedik* and *khilu* by people who did not belong to a profession indicates the economic value of these facilities. The *khilu* of shops located in key markets is still very highly priced in Middle Eastern cities.[10]

While guilds provided work for all qualified people, there existed variations in wealth among guild members. These variations depended on the type of craft, the size of workshop, the amount of capital invested and the profit generated by the products. But within the same guild, there were no major variations in the wealth of members, because the price of their products was fixed by the guild, the quality of work was supervised by the shaykh and the raw materials were supplied to guild members by quota. Partnership (*sharaka*) among masters within a craft, for the purpose of maintaining a monopoly over a product and increasing its price, was prevented by guild regulations and discouraged by the judicial authorities. In one case, a judge in Damascus ordered the saddlers (*sarrajun*) to work independently, each in a separate workshop, and not to resort to partnership because it was harmful to the Muslims ('yashtaghil kullu wahid minhum fi dukkan mustaqill wa-la yashtarikun fi 'l-'amal li-anna fihi dararan li'l-muslimin').[11] The guild members themselves pledged not to resort to partnership, but to work independently.[12]

Given their large number among the population, Muslims constituted the majority in guilds, but non-Muslims were also integrated with them in the same guilds. In mixed guilds, all members were given equal opportunities for work. The members of the guild of cloth bleachers (*qassarin*) in Aleppo, for example, which included Muslims and Christians, agreed among themselves on 19 July 1627 to divide the cloth that they received for bleaching into six parts: four parts were to be given to Muslim members and two parts to Christians. The agreement had the approval of both the shaykh and the judge. Three months later, on 16 October, however, the same members decided to divide the cloth equally among themselves.[13] In Aleppo in 1631 a similar arrangement for an equitable distribution of linen among the members of the guild of linen printers (*tabba'in*), which included Muslims and Christians, was agreed upon.[14] Thus, the guilds integrated all craftsmen within their ranks, irrespective of their religious affiliation.[15] An example may be found in the major guild appointment of the person responsible for the safety of public and private buildings, with the nomination by the Higher Consultative Council in Damascus in 1845 of an expert Christian master builder, *mu'allim* Ibrahim Barbara, as aide to the Muslim *mi'mar bashi* (shaykh of the guild of builders).[16]

Since businesses were small and the prices of commodities were fixed by guilds, a master craftsman feeling economic strain would either withhold any increase in the wages of his journeymen, or decrease the wages. Such actions were subjects for litigation in court. In 1588, the journeymen manufacturing Aleppine cotton cloth appealed to a judge, protesting against their payment of 30 silver pieces (*qit'a*) for manufacturing a cotton garment (*thawb*), a figure short of the legitimate wage (*ujrat al-mithl*). Upon the recommendation of a number of knowledgeable professional people, the judge ordered the masters to increase the wage to 32 silver pieces.[17]

During the seventeenth and the eighteenth centuries, when the guilds became fully established in the local economy and society, some influential guilds began to challenge the traditional regulations that limited their resources and consequently prevented the expansion of their businesses. Those guilds began to attach to themselves smaller but related guilds through a relationship called *yamak* in Turkish. This term, which means 'attached to', is occasionally substituted in the court records by the Arabic word *tabi'in*. The *yamak–tabi'in* relationship fell short of a merger between the two guilds, but it ensured additional resources to the major guild by having the junior guild work and market its by-products and participate in the payment of its taxes. The guild of makers of headgear (*tawaqiyya*), for instance, was *yamak* to the guild of tailors (*khayyatin*). The *khayyatin* supplied the *tawaqiyya* with cloth for headgear and made them share in the payment of their taxes. Through the *yamak* relationship, the dependent guild could also supply the major guild with raw materials, as in the case of the guild of the slaughterers (*masalkhiyya*) which was *yamak* to the guild of butchers (*qassabin*) and which supplied the latter with meat. Disputes arose as to which guild should follow another guild. The guild of merchants in Suq Jaqmaq in Damascus, for example, wanted to attach the guild of the sellers of small wares (*ta'ifat al-khurdajiyya*) to itself, for the purpose of making the latter share in the payment of taxes with the merchants. The *khurdajiyya* objected to this request and established in court that they were attached to (*tabi'in*) the guild of the makers of swords (*siyufiyya*).[18] Whatever the case, the control of a dependent guild by a major guild through the *yamak–tabi'in* relationship is an example of an advanced economic organisation, indicating the formation of a capitalist system of sorts long before capitalist Europe exercised its influence on Middle Eastern economies and societies in the nineteenth century.

Prior to the nineteenth century, mercantilist Europe co-existed with Middle Eastern economies and societies because its major interest was to promote its trade. Competition among the European mercantilist states and rivalry between their commercial companies, even within the same state, damaged their interests abroad. The English Levant Company, which was established in Aleppo in 1581, for example, suffered from the Russian occupation of the silk-producing territories in northern Iran in the early 1720s during the rule of Peter the Great, which diminished the flow of Iranian silk to Aleppo. The Levant

Company also suffered from the competition of the English East India Company, which was chartered in 1600. By contrast, the French were able to promote their trade in southern Syria by virtue of the economic policy known as colbertism, named after Jean Baptiste Colbert (1661–83), the finance minister of Louis XIV, whose expansionist policy promoted French trade with Syria. French economic involvement in Ottoman Syria dates back to the early 1540s, after the Ottomans granted economic privileges known as capitulations to France in 1535, during the rule of the French king Francis I.

The attempt by industrial Europe to control the markets of Syria in the nineteenth century damaged the guild system and the majority of craftsmen involved in the textile industry. European goods were transported by steamship to the expanded seaport of Beirut and from there were sent into the interior along the carriage road, inaugurated in 1863, that linked Beirut with Damascus and, later on, by railway. Local textiles could not compete with European textiles, which were of better quality, more appealing to local taste and better suited to Western fashions then spreading in Syria. They eventually dominated the local markets. The guilds involved in the production of textiles suffered tremendously because of this competition. Local looms were put on sale more frequently than before, and their prices went down. To make up for their loss, the masters of textile workshops tried to lower the wages of their journeymen. This triggered revolts within the guilds.[19] Bankruptcies among merchants retailing local goods multiplied, and in the 1840s impoverished manufacturers sent petitions to the Higher Consultative Council of Damascus declaring their inability to honour their debts.[20] A tax farmer charged with the collection of taxes from textile guilds reported their inability to pay their taxes. He blamed the flooding of the market with European goods (*al-badai' al-afranjiyya*) as the main cause for their economic strains.[21]

The disparity in wealth between impoverished craftsmen and the emerging class of local middlemen and entrepreneurs who were promoting the sale of European goods created social tension among the parties. The middlemen included a majority of Christians – mostly Catholics – as well as Jews and Muslims. But only the rich Christians were targeted by the mob, in what came to be known as the 'event' (*haditha*), a term used for the riots that occurred in Aleppo in 1850 and in Damascus in 1860. The rich Christians were quick to display their wealth publicly, which antagonised the poor Muslims, whereas the few rich Jews usually kept a low profile. Other factors also contributed to the riots, such as the declaration by the Ottomans of equality among all subjects, the conscription of Muslims to the exclusion of non-Muslims, the drive by the state towards centralisation, the complicity of top Ottoman officials and the growing involvement of European powers in protecting the minorities. A number of Ottoman officials were executed by the state for the roles they played in the riots.[22]

The guild regulations and culture – which discouraged partnership and monopolies, fixed prices of commodities and integrated the diverse religious communities – began to founder. By contrast, the emerging local bourgeoisie resorted to partnerships and the pooling of resources across the religious divide to promote their economic interests. They also imported European machinery, notably the Jacquard loom, in a bid to imitate European goods and measure up to the challenge. Muslims, Christians and Jews were represented in the commercial tribunals that were established in Aleppo and Damascus in the 1850s.[23] Arab national consciousness began to take shape at the time, a consciousness especially promoted by Christians anxious to legitimise their growing role in society and the economy; this movement was also supported by Muslim intellectuals.

Loans and Credit

Loans and credit were at the core of financial dealings in Ottoman Syria. They helped people manage their businesses and carry on with their lives. They carried no social stigma and were condoned by Islam as long as they were free of interest. All people, in fact, were engaged in lending and borrowing money, regardless of race, creed, gender and social status. Most estates of deceased people – whether men or women, Muslims, Christians or Jews – that were reported in the probate inventories (*sijillat al-mukhallafat* or *al-tarikat*) included debts, owed by the deceased to others, owed by others to the deceased or both. The term used in the judicial records for indebtedness was *bi-dhimmatihi* – 'he owes money'. When a debt was paid, the judicial records used the term *ada' dayn*. If the debt was not paid, the records say that the debtor still owed the debt to the creditor (*bi-dhimmatihi lahu* or *lahu bi-dhimmatihi*).

The earliest court records from Hama, dating back to 1535–6 (942 AH) abound with information about financial dealings among the people. Four types of financial transactions authorised by Islamic law were in use in Hama at the time: *qard* (loan), *dayn* (debt), *bay' bi'l-dayn* (delayed payment for commodities sold or selling on the money) and *salam* (a sale with delivery to be in the future). Out of 429 credit transactions mentioned in the first register of Hama, which covers the period between 18 Jumada I 942 and 1 Rabi' I 943 (14 November 1535 and 18 August 1536), 18 were *salam*, 43 were *dayn*, 96 were *qard* and 272 were *bay' bi'l-dayn*.

Salam transactions were lesser in number apparently because they were the most exploitative. In a *salam* transaction, an investor, usually an urban creditor or a foreign merchant, bought crops in advance at a price much lower than the one that they would sell for during the season. The investor-buyer took advantage of the peasants' need for cash before the season to provide for their living expenses, pay for their taxes and arrange for other urgent needs. The nineteenth-century Syrian jurist, Muhammad b. 'Abidin, blamed *salam* for causing the ruin of villages.[24]

Dayn was very often described in the court records as *shar'i*, that is, conforming to Islamic law and involving no interest. Big debts usually required a mortgage (*rahn*) as security for their payment. More often than not *dayn*, however, included interest in a very subtle way, as will be shown later. The *dayn* transactions in the Hama register constituted only 10.02 per cent of all the financial transactions and their value was a mere 7.46 per cent. Selling on credit (*bay' bi'l-dayn*), on the other hand, was and still is very popular. In fact, the largest number of all the financial transactions in the Hama register fell under this category. There were 272 transactions for selling on credit, which constituted 63.40 per cent of the total transactions reported in the register. The sums of money invested in these transactions were large, totalling 1,155,550 Aleppo dinars, 71.11 per cent of the total. By contrast, *qard* transactions amounted to 22.38 per cent, their cash value constituting 15.50 per cent of the total.[25]

The most meritorious of the credit transactions was the *qard*, because it did not include interest, had no time limit, did not need security and was usually offered to a person in need. As such, *qard* was very often described in the juridical books and among the people as *hasan*, that is a good and fair act intended as a friendly gesture to relieve a person in need.

The estates that carry debts did not usually refer to the type of debt involved in them. When such debts occurred in an estate, creditors had the priority over heirs in the payment of their debts, after all the necessary expenses relating to the funeral and the payment of the delayed portion of the wife's bride price (*mu'akhkhar mahr*) had been made. The probate inventories gave the names of both creditors and debtors, and the amounts of the debts. The religious affiliation and sometimes the occupation of the creditors and the debtors may have been known from the probate inventories. Such information was important for establishing the identity of who borrowed from whom and the extent to which social and religious groups interacted with each other in the financial market. The following examples illustrate those dealings.

The estate of Hajj Muhammad b. Ahmad al-Rihawi, known as al-Qabuni, who was a cloth merchant in Damascus, was reviewed by the *qassam* judge (divider of inheritance) on 7 Dhu 'l-Hijja 1096 (25 September 1686). Two sisters and three cousins succeeded al-Qabuni. His estate included local cloth (*baladi*), imported cloth (*majlub*), cloth from Asiyut (*asyuti*), English gold coins and copper misriyyas, a total equivalent to 963 piastres. His share in a house amounted to 156 piastres. The total value of the estate was 1119 piastres, of which 205 piastres were used for expenses, leaving 914 to the heirs. Money totalling 4179 piastres was owed to Hajj Muhammad by 129 people. The debts were legalised either by a *tadhkira* (certificate) or a *hijja* (court document) and were contracted over a period extending between Ramadan 1088 (October 1677) and Dhu 'l-Hijja 1096 (October 1685). The average debt per person was 32.39 piastres. The debtors were mostly single individuals, including five Christians identified by the word *walad* (son of), at the time a term reserved for Christians, along with the title *nasrani*. The total debts owed to Hajj Muhammad were equal to 4.57 times his assets, which indicates the extent to which people involved themselves in debts as both creditors and debtors.[26]

The estate of Hajj 'Ali b. Husayn al-Makari, which was reviewed by the *qassam* in 1687, included cash (English and Venetian coins and silver asadi piastres) valued at 64 piastres, goods worth 734 piastres and home belongings priced at 449 piastres with the total amounting to 1247 piastres. A wife and a minor son succeeded al-Makari. After deducting expenses, the sum left for the heirs was 959 piastres. Al-Makari was owed 7368 piastres by 21 people. Of this sum, 2944 piastres represented the price of goods dispatched to Hasan al-Nahri in Dumyat, Egypt. Among others indebted to al-Makari were Khawaja Claude al-Afranji (the European), who owed al-Makari 2000 piastres, and al-Khawaja Klein, who owed him 1000 piastres. Only two local Christians were indebted to al-Makari, for a total of 46 piastres.[27] If the three large debts totalling 5944 piastres are deducted from the total of the 7368 piastres which were owed to al-Makari, the average debt per person for the remaining 25 debtors is 56.96 piastres. The average debt in al-Qabuni's estate was 32.39 piastres.

The fact that a large number of people owed money to individual creditors, who were mostly professional money-lenders, clearly shows that credit played a major role in society at the time: debtors were engaged in it to carry on with their lives and creditors to accumulate wealth. The geographical extent of debt can be illustrated by a case from the end of the eleventh/ seventeenth century. In 1688, Hajj Murad al-Rifa'i, a prominent merchant trading in textiles and soap, died in Ramle, but his estate was referred to the *qassam* in Damascus, where he apparently lived with his wife and six children. His estate included 5765 piastres in cash, 12,167 piastres in goods and home belongings, while 6021 piastres in debts were paid to his estate apparently after his death. The total worth of the estate was 23,953 piastres. Expenses and payment of debts owed by al-Rifa'i totalled 14,731 piastres. The remaining sum of 9222 piastres was given to his heirs. Al-Rifa'i still owned property in Damascus, quantities of soap in Ramle and Dumyat and two and a quarter *qintars* of iron, which his heirs were to inherit. He also had debts totalling 8588 piastres owed to him by 210 people from Damascus, Jerusalem, Nablus and Ramle. Among those indebted to him were six Christians whose debt was 1085 piastres, and six Jews, whose debt was 344 piastres.[28]

The small debts owed by Christians and Jews to Muslim creditors in the above samples demonstrate that, like the Muslims, they needed to contract debts in order to ensure their living. As the probate inventories indicate, Christians and Jews of the time were generally not well-off compared to their Muslim compatriots. In 1687, the estate of Jurjus b. Ibrahim al-Nasrani, a coppersmith in Damascus who was survived by a wife, two minor children, an unborn child and a father, was valued at 109 piastres, of which 34.25 were deducted for the expenses of his funeral. The remaining sum of 74.75 piastres was distributed among his 12 creditors, 8 of whom were Muslims and 4 Christians, including his wife, to whom he owed 80 piastres, and his father, to whom he owed 8 piastres. Since his total debt of 205 piastres was much bigger than his net estate, the creditors were paid about 36 per cent of their debts in equal proportion.[29] Heirs were not held responsible for the remaining portions of debts. The estate of another Christian, Mas'ad b. Musa al-Bunduqji, a repairer of or dealer in rifles (*bunduqiyyas*), who was survived by a sister, was valued at 142 piastres. Expenses for the funeral amounted to 32 piastres and the remaining sum of 110 piastres was distributed among nine creditors, one of whom was a Christian. Each creditor received about 38 per cent of the debt.[30]

In 1730, the estate of a *yerliyya* (local) janissary from Damascus, Sayyid 'Ali b. Nassar Bashsha, a grandson of Shaykh Sulayman, who was survived by a wife, two sisters and an uncle, was evaluated at 425 piastres. The expenses were 202 piastres. The surplus of 223 piastres was to be distributed among 65 creditors, to whom Sayyid Nassar owed 3730 piastres. The creditors included 40 Muslim men, 3 Muslim women, 2 Jews and 20 Christians. Being a military man and a *sayyid* (a descendant of the Prophet), 'Ali Bashsha seems to have used his prestige to buy on credit and to borrow money. His total debt amounted to about 17 times the value of his estate.[31]

Women were active in the credit market. In 1730, the estate of Saliha bint al-Hajj Bakri consisted of personal belongings estimated at 216 piastres. A husband, a minor daughter from a former husband and two sisters survived her. The expenses totalled 64 piastres and included the payment of six debts, two of which belonged to women. The remaining sum of 142 piastres was given to her heirs. Saliha also had 14 debts totalling 164 piastres owed to her by eight Muslim women, two Muslim men, two Muslim couples, a Jewish woman and a Jewish couple. The debts equalled 75.92 per cent of her gross estate. The average amount per debt was 11.71 piastres, which again indicates the smallness of debts and people's need to borrow.[32]

The largest estate in our sample belongs to Sayyid 'Abd Allah Efendi b. Sayyid 'Abbas Efendi 'Ajlani. The *qassam* reviewed the estate records in 1828. At that time, the 'Ajlani family monopolised the high office of *naqib al-ashraf* (head of the ashraf) in Damascus. Sayyid 'Abd Allah was survived by two wives and six children. His belongings consisted of his clothing, house cutlery and books, all valued at 57,419 piastres. His expenses, which included the payment of 132 debts, amounted to 26,966 piastres. The remaining sum of 30,453 piastres was divided among his heirs. Sayyid 'Abd Allah also had property as well as 45 unredeemed debts. These debts amounted to 6727 piastres and, together with the price of the property, the total was 10,340 piastres. Many villagers figured among his debtors as well as among his creditors. Among the 132 creditors, there were 5 Christians and 24 women who included his 2 wives and 2 sisters, the 4 of them had the highest debts.[33]

Loans and credit, like guilds, crossed religious barriers. Muslims borrowed from Christians and Jews and vice versa. The interaction among religious communities in the workplace and in financial dealings reflects their co-existence and co-operation with each other.

In compliance with Islamic law, which forbids interest, the debts quoted in the court records do not refer to any interest attached to them. Only in two cases does Islamic law allow a profit to be made, *murabaha* – the investment of money belonging to orphan minors – and *waqf*. Examples of guardians investing minors' money for profit abound in the probate inventories. A guardian had to report annually to the *qassam* on the finances and expenses of the minors in his custody. The report was given the title of *muhasaba* (accountability) in the *qassam* register. The *muhasaba* report filed in court on 20 Jumada I 1209 (13 December 1794) by Sayyid 'Abd al-Ghani Chelebi gives details about the finances of two minors, Ahmad and Khadija, who were under his guardianship during the year ending on 30 Muharram 1209

(27 August 1794). The amount of money that Chelebi invested on behalf of the minors totalled 1118 piastres; the profit that it accumulated within one year was 112 piastres, the rate of profit being 10 per cent. Ahmad and Khadija also had an additional income of 41 piastres from debts and a shop's rent and an inheritance of 125 piastres. Their money totalled 1396 piastres. The expenses of the two minors for one year were 90 piastres. The guardian then pledged himself in court that the minors' remaining money of 1306 piastres would become 1423 piastres upon investment for another year, beginning on 22 Muharram 1209 (19 August 1794). A *murabaha* of 117 piastres was guaranteed by the guardian for that year, and was listed in the court records as the price of a *farjiyya* (robe),[34] a term used as a substitute for profit, which was, in effect, interest.[35]

The investment of *waqf* money for profit and the borrowing of money at a profit for the benefit of *waqf* are reported less in the judicial records than the investment of minors' money. One reason, it seems, is that *waqfs* had a special department to look after them. More importantly, however, *waqfs* usually suffered from abuse that left them little or no money for investment. The *mutawalli* (administrator) of the *waqf* of Bab al-Barid's prison in Damascus, for example, was authorised by the court on 10 Jumada I 1101 (19 February 1690) to borrow 69 silver piastres at legal profit (*bi-murabaha shar'iyya*) for buying bread and soup for the prisoners, because the *waqf* had no more money for these offerings. The 69 piastres equalled 2760 misriyyas, which was enough to buy bread and soup for seven months and 20 days at the rate of 12 misriyyas per day.[36]

While 'profit' money in the case of minors and *waqfs* was legally allowed in the Islamic court, the investment of large amounts of money by professional money-lenders at usurious rates was camouflaged in legal contracts as the price of soap. In the nineteenth century, the price of a ringing wall clock (*sa'a daqqaqa*) was used as well as soap as a cover for interest.

The attitude of the Ottoman state and the Islamic courts in Syria towards interest was one of expediency. The Islamic courts in Anatolian towns, for example, overtly applied interest in debts with the approval of the state.[37] The Syrian juridical works and the court records refer to orders issued by the Ottoman sultan sanctioning interest.[38] Economic considerations no doubt

Please add my name to your mailing list to receive details of books in the following subject areas

Middle East ☐
Islamic Studies ☐
Iran ☐
Jewish Studies ☐
Women's Studies ☐

Archaeology & Ancient History ☐
Art & Architecture ☐
Film / Media / Visual Culture ☐
Politics, Intl. Relations & Defence ☐
Russia & Former Soviet Union ☐

Asian Studies ☐
Central Asia ☐
Human Geography ☐
Modern History ☐
African Studies ☐

My other areas of interest are:..

Name...

Address..

....

....

Postcode.................... Email address........................ Date............

Your requests can also be directed to marketing@ibtauris.com

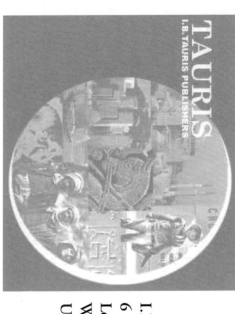

TAURIS
I.B. TAURIS PUBLISHERS

I.B. Tauris & Co Ltd
6 Salem Road
London
W2 4BU
United Kingdom

necessitated the application of interest in the Ottoman Empire.[39] A case from the Islamic court in Aleppo in 1585 refers to a villager from the region of Jabal Sam'an, west of Aleppo, who owed money to a creditor from Aleppo. The debt was 126 dinars, which were to be paid back after eight months at the rate of eleven-and-a-half dinars for every ten dinars owed, 'according to the noble order of the sultan' (*bi-mujib al-amr al-sharif al-sultani*), in relation to the debt contract.[40] Interest, in this case, amounted to 15 per cent. Anxious to absolve himself, his court and the Islamic *shari'a* from the responsibility for charging interest, the Aleppo judge laid its responsibility squarely with the Ottoman sultan.

Soap was the primary commodity used in the courts in Syria in the seventeenth and the eighteenth centuries to indicate interest. Villagers in need of money to pay their debts and provide for their needs approached urban professional money-lenders who lent them large amounts of money and, in the same contract, 'sold' them a quantity of soap whose value apparently equalled the interest that was secretly agreed upon by the parties. Villagers were held collectively responsible for their debts, and the shaykh and elders of the village pledged themselves as guarantors for debts. In a case from the court in Damascus dated 29 Shawwal 1180 (30 March 1767) and approved by the official Hanafi judge, 18 people from the village of Darayya al-Kubra, on the outskirts of Damascus, borrowed money from the *daftardar* of Damascus, Muhammad b. Husayn Efendi Farrukhzada, who was the holder of several *malikanes* (tax farms for life) and administrator of the *waqf* of Sultan Sulayman the Magnificent.[41] He lent the villagers 2200 piastres for a period of six months, in an official contract registered in court before the Hanafi judge. Three hundred and fifty-eight piastres of this sum were the price of an unspecified quantity (*miqdar*) of soap 'sold' to the villagers; the remaining amount – 1842 piastres – was the debt. Interest in this case amounted to 19.43 per cent.[42] In his report to Paris in 1852, the French consul in Damascus gave a vivid account about the use of soap as a cover-up for interest: 'Vous seriez etonné, Monsieur le Ministre, si vous voyiez l'usure en action en ce pays... (le savon joue un grand role dans ces sortes de transaction)'.[43]

Professional money-lenders were composed largely of urban notables, including merchants, local janissaries (*yerliyya*), religious dignitaries who possessed *malikanes* or who acted as administrators of *waqfs*, and feudal lords in control of land grants (*iqta'*) in the countryside. Notables made fortunes from lending large sums of money, mostly to needy villagers. The extortionate attitude on the part of urban money-lenders towards poor villagers deepened the feeling of mistrust between them. This lack of trust was further strengthened when the urban notables abused the rent on *waqf* agricultural land, which damaged the interests of the peasants.

The Abuse of *Waqf* Land

Most of the agricultural land in Ottoman Syria belonged either to the state (*miri*, from *amiri*) or to *waqf*. Private ownership of land was limited to the urban areas and villages and their immediate neighbourhoods. State land was the responsibility of the state and its agents, but *waqf* land, which was under the control of a *mutawalli* and a *nazir* (supervisor), could be abused by powerful notables and military men, who occasionally colluded with administrators and supervisors. This situation led to the amassing of large fortunes by the lessees of *waqf* land at the expense of the *waqf* and its beneficiaries. The legal process by which this was done was for the lessee to avoid renting *waqf* land with the official Hanafi judge. Instead, he first referred the lease contract either to the Shafi'i judge or, less often, to the Hanbali judge – each one of whom authorised lease contracts for long duration.

According to the Hanafi *madhhab*, school of jurisprudence, *waqf* land, like *miri* land and land belonging to orphan minors, could not be rented for more than three years.[44] In his juridical work dealing with the four Sunni *madhhabs*, 'Abd al-Rahman al-Jaziri mentions that, according to Hanafi law, the rent should not exceed three years for *waqf* agricultural land, and only one year for houses and shops, unless the interest of the *waqf* necessitated a longer period. A recent juridical work by Wahba al-Zuhayli concurs with these time periods according to Hanafi law.[45] In a case from Damascus, dated 29 Jumada II 1112 (11 December 1700), the Hanafi judge annulled a rent contract of *waqf* land for six years that had been approved by the Shafi'i judge, because its length contravened the three-year period and violated the terms of the Hanafi *madhhab* ('wa'arrafahuma [the Hanafi judge addressing the two lessees] anna al-ijara fi ard al-waqf la tasuhhu illa fi thalath sinin wa-inna ijarat ma zada 'alayha ghayr sahih wa-abtala ijarat al-mudda al-za'ida 'ala al-thalath sinin li-'annaha lam tusadif mahallan shar'iyyan').[46] The three-year limit for a rent contract (*'aqd*) according to the Hanafi *madhhab*, was more often substituted for by the word *'aqd*. Thus, a lease period for two *'aqds* usually meant a lease for six years. A two-year period for the *'aqd* was used very rarely.

The rationale behind the three-year period was to revisit the lease contract before or after its expiry and readjust the rate of the rent for the benefit of the *waqf*. The readjustment became all the more necessary in the second half of the sixteenth century when the value of the Ottoman silver currency, the akçe, dropped due to the importation of specie from the New World to Europe.

When the Ottoman Empire was at the peak of its power in the sixteenth century, the Hanafi *madhhab* was rigidly applied in the lease contracts of *waqf* land.[47] Corruption soon crept into the system, and influential people were able to lease *waqf* land for several *'aqds*. There were leases in the eighteenth century which extended over a period of 40 *'aqds*, that is over 120 years.[48] These leases were first approved by either the Shafi'i or the Hanbali judge and then legalised and executed by the official Hanafi judge. The legalisation of these contracts, however, was not always possible, because the Hanafi judge occasionally blocked leases exceeding three years.[49]

The leasing of *waqf* agricultural land for long periods was beneficial to the lessee, not to the *waqf*. According to a clause in the lease contract known as *mugharasa* or *munasaba* (plantation), the lessee was authorised to plant plantations on *waqf* land and own one-third to three-quarters of what he planted as freehold. The same rule applied to the buildings that the lessee built on the land. Another clause in the contract known as *musaqat* (irrigation) entrusted the lessee with looking after the plantations belonging to the *waqf*, and granted 999 of 1000 shares (*sahm*) of their produce. The remaining one share went to the *waqf*.[50]

By claiming for themselves most of the revenue of *waqf* land, influential lessees deprived the charitable institutions of most of their resources. Many mosques, madrasas and shrines fell into ruin because they lost their resources. The twentieth-century Damascene Hanbali 'alim Shaykh 'Abd al-Qadir Badran visited the ruins of many religious establishments in Damascus and their environs, lamenting on the damage done to them by those who laid their hands on the revenue of their *waqfs*. He described his grief at the sight of the ruined buildings in a work entitled *Munadamat al-atlal wa-musamarat al-khayal* (*Speaking to the Ruins and Chatting with Phantoms*).[51] Many *'ulama* earned their living from the offices that they held and the jobs that they performed in the religious establishments.[52] When these establishments lost their *waqfs* and fell into ruin, the *'ulama* who were employed in them subsequently lost their incomes.

Conclusion

As a postscript to this study, it is important to note that, in addition to their dealings in the financial market, women in Ottoman Syria earned their living from a variety of sources. They were entitled to inherit from their parents, albeit at half the share of the male. A married woman received the deferred portion (*mu'akhkhar*) of her dower (*mahr*) when she was divorced or when her husband died. Women also owned houses and invested in the property market. Rural women frequently came in person and unveiled to court in matters of litigation. Legal agents usually represented veiled urban women in court. Although women did not figure in the guilds in Ottoman Syria, they worked in the privacy of their homes as mat makers, cotton spinners, needleworkers and seamstresses.[53]

Male children were considered an economic asset to the family. They worked at an early age and contributed to the living expenses of their parents. They also took care of their parents in old age. According to samples from the probate inventories of Damascus in the eighteenth and the nineteenth centuries, the largest number of children, six to seven children per family, belonged to either wealthy or poor families.[54] Wealthy families could afford to raise a large number of children, and considered male children to be a source of power and social prestige. The poor, on the other hand, welcomed male children as a source of income. Given the reduced lifespan in Syria during the Ottoman period due to high mortality caused by plagues and other problems, most families encountered difficulties in earning a living. Minors outnumbered adults in most households, adding to the financial burden of the head of the family.

With improved sanitation and the introduction of the quarantine into Syria in the nineteenth century, high mortality rates diminished and the lifespan increased. The expanding population, however, became a major threat to public order, as social tension between the poor majority and the rich minority increased in the nineteenth century in the wake of the integration of the Syrian economy into the world market.

Bibliography

Primary Sources

Affaires Etrangères (Paris), Correspondance Commerciale, Damas.

Markaz al-Watha'iq al-Tarikhiyya (Directorate of Historical Documents), Damascus; Damascus Law Court Records (LCR); Majlis Shura al-Sham al-A'li (The Higher Consultative Council of Damascus) (HCCD).

Published Studies

Badran, 'Abd al-Qadir, *Munadamat al-Atlal wa-Musamarat al-Khayal*, Damascus, Al-Maktab al-Islami, 1379/1960.

Baer, Gabriel, *Fellah and Townsman in the Middle East*, London, Frank Cass, 1982.

Cahen, Claude, 'Y-a-t-il eu des corporations professionelles dans le monde musulman classique?' in Albert H. Hourani and Samuel E. Stern (eds), *The Islamic City*, Oxford, Cassirer, 1970, pp. 51–63.

Dozy, R., *Supplément aux Dictionnaires Arabes*, 2 vols, Leiden, Brill, 1881, new ed., Beirut, Librairie du Liban, 1981.

Ibn 'Abidin, *Muhamamd Amin, Radd al-muhtar 'ala al-durr al-mukhtar (better known as Hashiyat Ibn 'Abidin)*, 5 vols, Cairo, Bulaq, 1272 AH, reprinted in Beirut, Dar al-Ihya al-Turath al-'Arabi, 1407/1987.

— *al-'Uqud al-duriyya fi tanqih al-fatawa al-hamidiyya*, 2 vols, Cairo, Bulaq, 1301 AH, reprinted, 2 vols, Beirut, Dar al-Ma'rifa, n.d.

Jaziri, 'Abd al-Rahman al-, *al-Fiqh 'ala al-madhahib al-arba'a*, 5 vols, Beirut, Dar Ihya' al-Turath al-'Arabi, 1986.

Jennings, Ronald C., 'Loans and credit in early 17th century Ottoman judicial records, the Sharia court of Anatolian Kayseri', *Journal of the Economic and Social History of the Orient* XVI, 1975, parts 2–3, pp. 168–216.

Masters, Bruce, 'The 1850 events in Aleppo: An aftermath of Syria's incorporation into the capitalist world system', *International Journal of Middle East Studies* 22, February, 1990, pp. 3–20.

Muradi, Muhammad Khalil al-, *Silk al-durar fi a'yan al-qarn al-thani 'ashar*, 4 vols, Cairo, Bulaq, 1301 AH, reprinted in 2 vols, Baghdad, Maktabat al-Muthanna, n.d.

Qoudsi, Ilyas 'Abduh, 'Nubdha Tarikhiyya fi'l-Hiraf al-Dimashqiyya' in Carlo Landberg (ed.), *Actes du VIe Congrès des Orientalistes*, Leiden, 1885, pp. 27–34.

Rafeq, Abdul-Karim, 'Economic relations between Damascus and the dependent countryside, 1743-71' in A.L. Udovitch (ed.), *The Islamic Middle East, 700-1900: Studies in Economic and Social History*, Princeton, NJ, The Darwin Press, 1981, pp. 653–85.

— 'Aspects of land tenure in Syria in the early 1580s', in Abdeljelil Temimi (dir.), *Les Provinces Arabes à l'Époque Ottomane*, Zaghouan, 1987, pp.153–63.

— 'New light on the 1860 riots in Ottoman Damascus', *Die Welt des Islams* 28, 1988a, pp. 412–30.

— 'The social and economic structure of Bab al-Musalla (al-Midan), Damascus, 1825–1875' in George N. Atiyeh and Ibrahim M. Oweiss (ed.), *Arab Civilization, Challenges and Responses: Studies in Honor of Constantine K. Zurayk*, Albany, NY, State University of New York Press, 1988b, pp. 272–311.

— 'Craft organization, work ethics, and the strains of change in Ottoman Syria', *Journal of the American Oriental Society* 111/3, 1991, pp. 495–511.

— 'City and countryside in a traditional setting: the case of Damascus in the first quarter of the eighteenth century' in Thomas Philipp (ed.), *The Syrian Land in the 18th and 19th Centuries*, Stuttgart, Franz Steiner Verlag, 1992, pp. 295–32

— 'Craft organizations and religious communities in Ottoman Syria (XVI–XIX Centuries)', *La Shia Nell'Impero Ottomano*, Rome, Academia Nazionalae Dei Lincei, 1993, pp. 25–56.

— 'The Syrian 'Ulama, Ottoman Law, and Islamic Shari'a', *Turcica, Revue d'Etudes Turques* 26, 1994a, pp. 9–32

— 'Registers of succession (*Mukhallafat*) and their importance for socio-economic history: Two samples from Damascus and Aleppo, 1277 Ah./1861 AD' VII. *CIEPO Sempozyumu'ndan Ayribasim*, Ankara, Turk Tarih Kurumu, 1994b, pp. 479–91.

Rafiq, 'Abd al-Karim, 'Thawrat al-'asakir fi 'l-Qahira fi 'l-rub' al-Aakhir min al-qarn al-sadis 'ashar wa'l-'aqd al-awwal min al-qarn al-sabi' 'ashar wa-maghzaha' in 'Abd al-Karim Rafiq, *Buhuth fi 'l-tarikh al-'iqtisadi wa'l-Iitima'i li-bilad al-Sham fi'l-'asr al-hadith*, Damascus, 1985, pp. 97–129.

— 'Mazahir iqtisadiyya wa-'ijtima'iyya min liwa' Hamah, 942–3 AH (1535–6)', *Dirasat Tarikhiyya (Damascus University)*, vols 31–2, March–June 1989, pp. 17–66.

— al-'Arab wa'l-'uthmaniyyun, 1516–1916, 2nd ed., Damascus, Atlas, 1993.

Shkodra, Zija, *Esnafet Shqiptare* (Shek. XV–XX), Akademia e Shkencave E. R. P, të Shqipërisë, Instituti i Historisë, Tirane, Shtypur ne Nish Shtypshkronjave, Mihal Duri, 1973.

Zuhayli, Wahba al-, *al-Fiqh al-islami wa-adillatuhu*, 8 vols, 3rd ed., Damascus, Dar al-Fikr, 1989.

Notes on Chapter 6

1 Rafiq, 1985; *ibid.*, 1993, pp. 124–48.
2 See, for example, Cahen, 1970.
3 For more details about these aspects of the guilds: Rafeq, 1991.
4 Law Court Records (LCR), Damascus, vol. 50, p. 28 (50:28), case dated 25 Dhu 'l-Hijja 1134 (6 October 1722).
5 *LCR*, Damascus, 33:80, case dated 23 Sha'ban 1119 (19 November 1707); Majlis Shura al-Sham al-A'li (HCCD), 1258–1261 (1852–1845), one volume in Markaz al-Watha'iq al-Tarikhiyya, Damascus, p. 112, case dated 17 Muharram 1261 (26 January 1845) in which the Council stated 'al-ajnabi bi'l-kar la yashtaghil'.
6 Qoudsi, 1885, p. 28.
7 LCR, Damascus, 472:131, case dated 14 Safar 1272 (26 October 1855).
8 Baer, 1982, p. 185.
9 Shkodra, 1973, pp. 376–7.
10 For more information about the *gedik* and the *khilu*: Rafeq, 1991, pp. 503–4.
11 LCR, Aleppo, 22:248, case dated 14 Ramadan 1049 (8 January 1640).
12 LCR, Aleppo, 15:809, case dated 2 Safar 1046 (6 July 1636).
13 LCR, Aleppo, 15:208, case dated 6 Dhu 'l-Qa'da 1036 (19 July 1627), p. 239; case dated 5 Safar 1037 (6 October 1627).
14 LCR, Aleppo, 15:571, case dated 21 Safar 1041 (18 September 1631).
15 See Rafeq, 1993.
16 HCCD, pp. 8–9, case dated 12 Shawwal 1260 (25 October 1844), pp.122–3; case dated 24 Muharram 1261 (2 February 1845).

17 LCR, Aleppo, 6:166, case dated 3 Safar 996 (3 January 1588).

18 See Rafeq, 1991, pp. 504–5; see also *LCR*, Damascus, 29:174, case dated 23 Muharram 1120 (14 April 1708).

19 Qoudsi, 1885, p. 15.

20 For copies of these petitions, see *HCCD*, pp. 205–6, 211–12, Appendices 2, 3.

21 *Ibid.*, pp. 99–100.

22 For these riots, see Masters, 1990; Rafeq, 1988a, 1988b.

23 See Rafeq, 1991, pp. 510–1.

24 Ibn 'Abidin, 1987, vol. 4, p. 176.

25 For more details about these financial practices: Rafiq, 1989, p. 19; Rafeq, 1994a, pp. 14–15.

26 LCR, Damascus, 15:3–6, case dated 7 Dhu 'l-Qa'da 1097 (25 September 1686).

27 LCR, Damascus, 15:79–85, case dated 20 Shawwal 1098 (29 August 1687).

28 LCR, Damascus, 15:114–23, case dated 1 Rabi' I 1099 (5 January 1688).

29 LCR, Damascus, 15:104–5, case dated 25 Safar 1099 (31 December 1687).

30 LCR, Damascus, 15:207, case dated 5 Sha'ban 1100 (25 May 1689).

31 LCR, Damascus, 68:190–3, case dated 24 Rajab 1142 (12 February 1730).

32 LCR, Damascus, 68:190–1, case dated 19 Rajab 1142 (7 February 1730).

33 LCR, Damascus, 314:26–36, case dated 6 Rabi' II 1244 (16 October 1828).

34 Dozy, 1981, vol. 1, p. 248, explains *farjiyya* as 'robe flottante, faite ordinairement de drap, à manches amples et longues qui dépassent un peu l'extremite des doigts, et qui ne sont point fendues'.

35 LCR, Damascus, 224:179, case dated 20 Jumada I 1209 (13 December 1794, an error occurs in this document in the date of 1208, which should be 1207).

36 LCR, Damascus, 117:193, case dated 10 Jumada I 1101 (19 February 1690).

37 Jennings, 1975.

38 See, for example, Ibn 'Abidin,1987, vol. 4, p. 175; vol. 2, p. 204.

39 For more details: Rafeq, 1994a, pp.13–4, 17–20.

40 LCR, Aleppo, 6:107, case dated 2 Muharram 994 (24 December 1585).

41 For the biography of Muhammad b. Husayn Farrukhzada: al-Muradi, n.d., vol. 4, p. 38.

42 LCR, Damascus, 178:46, case dated 29 Shawwal 1180 (30 March 1767).

43 'You would be surprised, Mr Minister, to see how usury is used in this country... (soap plays a large part in this sort of transaction)'. For more details about the report sent by the French consul in Damascus to his superiors in Paris: *Affaires Etrangeres* (Paris), Correspondance Commerciale, Damas, vol. 3 dépêche du 12 janvier 1852. The consul's description is given in Rafeq, 1994a, p. 21.

44 See Ibn 'Abidin, n.d., vol. 2, pp. 92–3.

45 Al-Jaziri, 1986, vol. 3, p. 102; see also Zuhayli, 1989, vol. 8, pp. 228, 233–4.

46 *LCR*, Damascus, 25:54, case dated 29 Jumada II 1112 (11 December 1700).

47 See Rafeq, 1987.

48 See Rafeq, 1981, p. 670.

49 *LCR*, Damascus, 25:54, case dated 29 Jumada II 1112 (11 December 1700).

50 For more details about these clauses in the lease contract: Rafeq, 1992, pp. 312–23.

51 Badran, 1960, pp. 53, 145.

52 For the jobs that the '*ulama* performed in the religious establishments in Damascus: for example, *LCR*, Damascus, 36:31, two cases dated 1 Rajab 1130 (31 May 1718).

53 See Rafeq, 1991, p. 508.

54 See Rafeq, 1994b.

CHAPTER 7

Manufacturing Myths:
Al-Khurunfish, A Case Study

Pascale Ghazaleh

Myth and Mystery

The categories used to speak of industrialisation or a proto-industrial mode of production are often too categorical. This study will try to show that, in the case of Egypt, at least, the introduction of new ways of producing often combined very different systems that are usually thought of as diachronically and conceptually separate. Indeed, the available models, many of which were elaborated on the basis of an abstracted European experience, simply do not fit the processes taking place in Egypt in the first half of the nineteenth century.

Al-Khurunfish was the first of the manufactories established by Muhammad 'Ali[1] and, judging from secondary sources, it seems to have been a controversial innovation, one which aroused curiosity, admiration, condescension and censure in equal amounts.

Contemporary observers of al-Khurunfish and the other manufactories were divided in opinion as to their productivity and efficiency. Several European consuls expressed the conviction that Egypt was destined to remain an agricultural economy; any attempts to industrialise were futile and presumptuous. In vague remarks, published in 1823, about two manufactories, one at Bulaq and the other in 'the interior of Cairo', Mengin expressed some contempt at the *wali*'s efforts, noting that:

Since all types of industry have come under the viceroy's control, the products of the manufactories are much less highly esteemed; they are considered to suffer from negligence in preparation and workmanship. The servitude which has come to replace ownership has destroyed emulation; the worker labours without worrying if his piece is well or badly executed; what is important for him is to receive the agreed-upon price.[2]

Mengin's condemnation of state ownership is, perhaps ironically, almost identical to present-day criticisms of public-sector enterprises. The standards of liberty, private property and free enterprise formed his opinions of the manufactories, which did not conform to the free-market ideology developing in Europe at the time.

Al-Khurunfish will be examined not as a one-off case, but as a case study of the manufactories established in the first part of the nineteenth century. Some scholars have explained that Muhammad 'Ali's 'industrialisation experiment' was doomed to failure for various reasons. According to some, Egyptian workers were unsuited to factory work, either because they were lazy or simply incapable of coping with relatively sophisticated equipment. According to others, the lack of primary products – especially fuel – made the efforts to launch an industrial revolution in Egypt futile. In fact, the very terms in which the manufactories were perceived – as an 'experiment in industrialisation' or as the '*wali*'s factories' – imply that they were essentially alien creations imposed by an overambitious ruler on hostile or, at best, inhospitable soil. Theoretically, they have been made to represent modernity's incursion into the sphere of traditional craft production.

From one perspective, the manufactories heralded the transformation of the Egyptian economy and the beginnings of its industrialisation: they introduced new work ethics, transformed labour organisation and ushered Egypt into the modern age. But not all scholars adopt this view. To claims that industry allegedly transformed the 'way of production', removed restrictions on industrial liberty and transformed masters and artisans into wage workers, some scholars reply that the number of guild members far exceeded the number of factory workers. The industries set up by Muhammad 'Ali opened up new branches of production, and therefore presented no competition to traditional economic activities: artisans were often rejected from the factories because of their working habits. Muhammad 'Ali's experiment was too short to bring about a wholesale transformation of urban society[3] and was intended mainly to supply his army with necessary equipment.

These two different sets of perceptions both echo the impressions of European travellers. In this respect, they are also influenced by ideas that held sway in Europe at the time of the industrial revolution and have shaped our understanding of the processes that constitute or 'should' constitute industrialisation. But are these perceptions – or the premises on which they are based – correct?

Very little is known about al-Khurunfish and the other *fawriqat* or *fabrikat* (manufactories) because, until this day, most analyses have been based on the eyewitness accounts of travellers and consuls, not on administrative records issued by the government or accounts kept by the managers of the manufactories themselves. Even those historians who did rely on primary sources based their analyses mainly on brief translations of documents, overwhelmingly in Turkish, relating to the administration of the manufactories. For this reason, even the date on which al-Khurunfish was established is uncertain.[4] This uncertainty seems to stem primarily from the fact that most accounts are based on the same few sources. Al-Jabarti, perhaps, gives the most reliable account of its establishment.[5]

The area from which the manufactory originally took its name seems to have been known as al-Khurushtuf. According to Maqrizi, at the time of the Fatimid caliphs al-Khurushtuf had been a large *maydan* (square) near the Western Palace and the al-Kafuri gardens, but when the caliphate fell a number of residences and a street market were built there. Maqrizi explains the area's name with a cryptic reference to the caliph al-Mu'izz, who built stables there. These stables provided the fuel for heating the water of the public baths in the vicinity.[6]

By the sixteenth century, al-Khurushtuf had undergone another transformation. The stables were once again replaced by houses which were among the most expensive in Cairo at the time. This wealthy residential area was dotted with large palaces.[7] Al-Khurushtuf changed yet again under Muhammad 'Ali. Perhaps its change in name was due to a mispronunciation which became common usage; the area (and, presumably by extension, the manufactory) was being referred to as al-Khurunfish by the second decade of the nineteenth century.

Having undergone such marked changes in the span of several centuries, which characteristics prompted the choice of al-Khurunfish as the site for a new manufactory? Its proximity to centres of artisanal production and trade may well have played a part, but this cannot suffice as an explanation, especially given that many of the workers were, at various times, army recruits from the countryside or prisoners. Since the manufactories did not necessarily draw on a pool of skilled labour from the surrounding area, the reasons for the selection of al-Khurunfish and other sites on which the manufactories were built remain unknown. The 1846 census may yet reveal the impact which the establishment of the manufactories had in terms of the industrialisation of the population: by mid-century, were most of the inhabitants of al-Khurunfish engaged in professions linked to the manufactories? Answering this question will open new avenues of investigation.

Ironically, the available information for this more recent period is far vaguer than that available for earlier centuries. During the nineteenth century, descriptions of the manufactory at al-Khurunfish were riddled with uncertainties, repetitions and myth, stemming in large part from personal convictions and interests of contemporary writers, upon whose accounts one still relies today for information. Mengin's second description of the Egyptian manufactories, published in 1839, is identical, word for word, to the report written in the same year by Bowring on the state of industry. Bowring, in turn, had borrowed most of his information from Campbell, the British consul. Little has changed since then. Through repetition, the same conclusions have come to acquire legitimacy even in the eyes of twentieth-century scholars, many of whom accepted the apparent absence of reliable primary sources. In a very limited way, this study seeks to fill the gap left in descriptions and analyses of the manufactories.

The Documents

The main primary source used for this research is a register of accounts for the manufactory at al-Khurunfish and its subsidiary branch at Sayyida Zaynab, which covers the months from Muharram to Rabi' al-Akhar 1239/1823. While, by necessity, a comparison between the different months covers only a short time span, it provides interesting information as to possible variations in daily wages, monthly salaries, the prices of goods produced by subcontractors and monthly bonuses received by some groups. Since it also contains information on the branch at Sayyida Zaynab, the register could be useful for comparing respective volumes of output and labour employed, as well as salaries.

Al-Khurunfish seems to have been set up initially for the production of silk. In his relatively detailed account of 1839, Mengin speaks of a few workers brought from Florence around 1816 to spin silk threads into velvet and light satin cloths.[8] Thereafter, al-Khurunfish, according to the same source, was converted to the production of cotton and other textiles under the supervision of Jumel; Mengin notes that the looms used to spin silk and velvet 'were transported to another establishment', while looms for cotton cloth were installed in their place. The register in question, however, concerns another aspect of production at the manufactory. Although it does mention weavers of *bafta* (a light, cheap cotton cloth), *fattalin* (plaiters), *qattana* (weavers of cotton) and *haririyya* (silk weavers) among the textile workers, the majority of workshops listed are involved in the production of capital goods – looms for weavers and equipment which would then be used in the manufacture of cloth. 'Apart from the spinning and weaving looms', writes Mengin, 'there are at Khorounfech workshops of blacksmiths, filers, turners of metal and wood and carpenters to fix the machines and create new pieces'.[9] In the register, these workers are listed in detail: their names, the numbers of workers in each workshop, the number of days that they worked each month, the salaries that they received and the number and type of pieces they produced. The actual organisation of this department of the manufactory emerges quite clearly from the register, which is divided into several sections. New sources – such as this register – may allow for the development of a new theoretical model of industrialisation, combining a variety of processes, and help us to understand the impact of these processes on the urban economy.

Organisation of Labour

One of the puzzling questions regarding the manufactories in general relates to the recruitment of workers. While it would seem logical that artisans provided the pool from which labour for the manufactories was drawn, some scholars have contested this idea with the argument that Egyptian workers were not qualified to work in modern industry.[10] Workers were, in fact, brought to Cairo from the countryside or vice versa, in many cases, according to the needs of the new institutions. The recruitment process, in general, seems to have been directed and implemented by the state to a large extent. In other words, the workers employed in the manufactories were not necessarily landless peasants 'freed' from agricultural labour by sweeping expropriations, as was the case in England at one time.

At any rate, some of the craftsmen or young apprentices recruited for work in the manufactories were not always willing to go. The recruitment of workers took place as follows.[11] In the case of Cairo and Bulaq, lists were drawn up of the workers needed, in co-operation with the *thumn*[12] in which these individuals were found. Then, they were rounded up with the assistance of the shaykhs of the *hara* (neighbourhood quarter) and the *thumn*. Care was taken that the workers were permanent residents of Cairo and not 'vagabonds or thieves' (*al-aghrab al-marrin bi'l-turuq wa'l-fulatiyya*) and guarantees were obtained from the workers' close relatives. If the heads of the *athman* were unable to carry out this operation themselves, they received military assistance, 'as long as this measure did not cause any distress'. These measures were apparently necessitated by the workers' dislike of the manufactories, demonstrated by their tendency to run away. Obtaining guarantees from close relatives – an effective form of blackmail – was replaced or supplemented a few years later with the practice of obtaining guarantees from the shaykhs under whose jurisdiction the recruits fell.[13] Still, to judge from the number of complaints and orders for their arrest, workers continued to resist recruitment. Prisoners were also put to work in the manufactories,[14] which suggests that manufactory work was used as a form of punishment, at least after the end of Muhammad 'Ali's reign.

Judging from the register, labour at al-Khurunfish was divided into three main categories: day workers (*bi'l-yawmiyya*), those who received a monthly salary (*al-mahiyat al-shahri*), most of whom were not artisans or manual workers but bureaucrats and piece-workers (*bi'l-qita'*), including the subcontractors (*bi'l-muqawala*) who produced wooden looms. Both within and between these large categories, however, there were profound differences which show the extent to which the manufactory adopted and integrated both the guild system and other forms of labour organisation – subcontracting and day labour – pressing these into sometimes uneasy forms of co-existence. Classified according to their average daily wage, the different groups of craftsmen clearly did not present a homogeneous mass. There were sharp differences in pay levels. The best-paid among them, the European carpenters (*najjarin ifrink*), received approximately 360 paras a day,[15] while the worst-off among them, those working in the lathe shop (*maghlaq al-makharit*), were paid a comparative pittance of 40 paras a day. The piece-workers, on the other hand, of which there were 75 in all,[16] were remunerated on the basis of the number of pieces that they had produced.

The Day Workers

There were a considerable number of day workers and apprentices at al-Khurunfish and Sayyida Zaynab. Around 2000 workers are listed in all for the month of Muharram while the number for Safar is slightly smaller, at 1188 workers. For the month of Safar, the following contains a few examples of the numbers of workers in each workshop: 28 ironsmiths (*haddadin*), 113 fitters (*barradin*), 41 iron-turners (*kharratin hadid*), 28 lathe-makers (*maghlaq al-makharit*), 22 European carpenters (*najjarin ifrink*, whose names reveal, for the most part, that they were Greek or Italian), 19 Turkish carpenters (*najjarin arwam*), 93 Egyptian carpenters (*najjarin baladi*), 4 carpenters specialised in the production of silk looms, 28 turners (*kharratin*), 1 turner working specifically on the silk looms (*ihtiyaj anwal al-harir*), 766 sawyers (*nashsharin*), 7 saddle-makers (*surujiya*, possibly hired to make saddles for the horses which turned the lathes), 12 tinsmiths (*samkariyya*), 1 coal-siever (*mugharbil fahm*), 1 painter (*naqqash*), 7 carders (*imshatiyya*), 1 smelter (*sabbak*), 6 plaiters (*fattalin*) and 10 makers of beams or girders (*qamaratiyya*). The numbers at Sayyida Zaynab were far smaller and, in most cases, each workshop contained only two or three workers.

As can be seen, most of the workers were organised into groups of varying size according to their trade. The sawyers, whose number far exceeded that of any other group of workers in the manufactory,[17] were something of an aberration. They seem to have been hired in teams of two, each consisting of a teacher or specialist (*mu'allim*) and an apprentice or follower (*tabi'*). Each group only worked, on average, for approximately two days. Each *mu'allim* received the same day wage (80 paras), while their apprentices received exactly half this sum. While they outnumbered the other workers by far, they are not taken into account in the total numbers of workers calculated (*ijmaliyat*), suggesting that they were not formally considered employees of the manufactory.

The other day workers paradoxically seem to have been hired on a monthly basis. The theoretical number of days that they were to work and the days on which they actually worked are both listed. Many of them, hired for 30 days, actually worked 25 or 28 days. It is unclear whether references to 'days of unemployment' (*ayam al-batala*) mean the days that they were absent from the manufactory or the days on which there was no work for them. Their salaries, at any rate, were calculated on a *per diem* basis. Some of the European carpenters received a bonus at the end of the month equivalent to an extra day's work. They are the only workers to have enjoyed this privilege, along with a few of the apprentices, who sometimes also received an additional day's salary with their total for the month.

While the day workers were classified into groups reminiscent of the guilds – local Turkish (*rumi*)[18] and foreign (*ifrink*) carpenters, sawyers, turners, fitters, smelters, rope-makers etc – they and the other workers were closely supervised by a body of officials primarily defined not according to the goods that they produced but by their affiliation with the manufactory as an institution closely connected to the state. In this body were the general supervisor of the manufactories (*nazir umum al-fawriqat*), the supervisor of al-Khurunfish, the inspector (*mufattish*), the storehouse keepers (*makhzanji*), the guards and doormen (*bawabin wa-ghafara*), the secretaries (*kuttab*) etc. This set-up is described by Foucault in his analysis of the surveillance techniques applied in the manufactories of France before these were replaced by the process of constant supervision characteristic of the modern factory, school, hospital or prison. Foucault notes that the surveillance practised in the 'regimes of the manufactories ... had been carried out from the outside by inspectors, entrusted with the task of applying the regulations'. Both this system and that applied in the factories differed from 'the domestic supervision of the master who was present beside his workers and apprentices'.[19] But at al-Khurunfish, three systems[20] overlapped: the guild framework within which the master (*mu'allim* or *ra'is 'ala al-ashghal*) supervised his apprentices, the government officials who supervised the work such as the inspector, the director and the overseer, and the 'specialized personnel ... constantly present and distinct from the workers',[21] made up of soldiers ready to enforce discipline at any time.

At al-Khurunfish, the administrative, supervisory and disciplinary personnel amounted to a total of around 75 individuals on the payroll. Several of the high-ranking workshop heads seem to have been specially imported, such as the ironsmith brought from Istanbul, and '*al-khawaja* Monciaud'. These officials were differentiated from the workers not only in terms of duties but also in that they received a monthly – not a daily or piece-work – salary.

These few remarks indicate that it would be difficult to classify al-Khurunfish within one specific category. Like its counterparts in Europe, it drew on 'pre-modern' forms of labour organisation (the workshops were classified by profession, similar to the guild system) while inserting them within a system characterised by 'modern industrial' modes of surveillance (the staff whose sole task was to supervise the workers). The whole was closely tied to the state, which determined the volume of output, the goods to be produced and the standard of the final product. The manufactory also depended on the 'putting-out' system of which more or less sophisticated forms had been used by the guilds, and which consisted in the distribution of various tasks among a group of piece-workers, who delivered parts of the machinery or worked on a subcontractual basis. Therefore, assertions that the monopolies and the manufactories were transformed in favour of the putting-out system[22] are more categorical than was actually the case. The accounts of al-Khurunfish show that putting-out work was an integral part of the manufactory system itself. This situation seems similar in some respects to that prevailing in Europe and, more specifically, in England, where some scholars estimate that, under George IV (1820–30), the putting-out system was still the predominant form of capitalist industry.[23]

Al-Khurunfish: An Uncertain Fate

It is unclear when and why the manufactory at al-Khurunfish was closed down. It is too facile to conclude, as Toledano did, that 'the Old Pasha and his son Ibrahim ... benevolently allowed the edifice of industry to fall into disrepair' due to the disappearance of a captive market, the lack of funds and the absence of motivation.[24] Far too little is still known about the manufactories to speculate about their decline. Some of the questions that must be considered include how much the manufactories produced, whom they supplied, their effect on the guilds and the traditional system of production, how a permanent labourforce was recruited and trained, whether the putting-out system proved less risky and more productive, and whether the artisans were successful in resisting proletarianisation.

At any rate, it would seem that several ideas were floated for the conversion of al-Khurunfish, among other manufactories, from the production of machinery and textiles. In 1856, Viceroy Sa'id issued an order to the governor of Cairo (dated 17 Jumada Akhar /24 February) for the buildings which had housed the workshops to be transformed into a hospital replacing that at Qasr al-'Aini. This order was taken on Clot Bey's advice.[25]

It is clear, however, that this order was never implemented. Already in 'Ali Mubarak's time, the manufactory at al-Khurunfish had been transformed – not into a hospital, but into the Dar al-Kiswa where the covering for the *Ka'ba*, manufactured in Egypt and sent to Mecca each year with the pilgrims' caravan, was produced.[26] Today, the words 'Dar al-Kiswa' are still written above the entrance portal.

Conclusion

The social organisation of labour in the Egyptian manufactories was inspired by the guilds in many ways. The manufactories did not transform the production process from within; they adopted the hierarchies and apprenticeship processes of the guilds. Al-Khurunfish, in fact, may be seen as a group of guilds working on the same premises. But these guilds were supervised by government officials and produced goods which all contributed to the creation of one final product – textiles. The state also decided on the quantities to be produced, approved the quality of the product and took charge of marketing and sales – duties which had previously been the task of guilds. This does not imply that craftsmen were transformed into wage labourers: wage labour had always existed and many of those working in the manufactories were not originally craftsmen. Nor does it mean that the artisans were alienated from their means of production: during the Ottoman period, many artisans rented their tools as well as their workplaces.[27] One might say that the craftsmen were at one remove from the final product: not entirely alienated, but hardly in complete control of all aspects of its production.

What impact did all this have on the individual worker? A study of the probate inventories of manufactory workers helps to discover whether they died more impoverished than their counterparts who did not leave the guilds. In general, however, one might suggest that the manufactories did not actually transform the guild system, but drew on and co-operated with it. The state often relied on the shaykhs of the guilds for assistance in recovering workers who had run away from the manufactories. This meant that while workers may have moved between the two systems, they were subjected to the authority of both.

Large chunks of the history of the manufactories – crucial to the understanding of the developments which took place in the nineteenth century – are still missing. The register used for the present research and other documents of this nature will help dispel some of the myths still mired in nineteenth-century beliefs, interests and ideologies.

Bibliography

Primary Sources

Bitaqat al-dar,[28] 'Ummal 282, 28 Rabi' Awwal 1252/1836, from the Bashmu'awin Janab Dawri to Mahmud Afandi, general inspector of manufactories, Awamir register 10, series 181, 61.

Bitaqat al-dar, Ihsa' 4, 24 Dhu 'l-Qa'da 1276/1860, from the Ma'iyya to the Railway and Transport Authority, register 1646, Sadir Ma'iyya 'Arabi, series 33, 39.

Daftar al-Mutasarrif bi-Karakhanat al-Khurunfish Ujrat al-Shaghala al-ladhi bi'l-Yawmiyya wa-l-ladhi bi-l-Muqawala wa-l-Mahiyat al-Shahri, register 7253, series 5122, old no 7599, new no 12, Muharram to Rabi' Akhar 1239/1823.

Diwan Majlis Ahkam Misr S7/33/1, Daftar Majmu' Umur Idariyya wa-Ijra'at, old register no 178, new no 1 (various dates).

Published Studies

Baer, Gabriel, *Egyptian Guilds in Modern Times*, Jerusalem, Israel Oriental Society, 1964.

Dockès, Pierre and Bernard Rosier, *L'histoire ambiguë: croissance et développement en question*, Paris, Presses Universitaires de France, 1988.

Foucault, Michel, *Discipline and Punish: The Birth of the Prison*, transl. A. Sheridan, London, Penguin Books, 1991.

Hanna, Nelly, *Habiter au Caire aux XVIIe et XVIII siècles*, Cairo, IFAO, 1991.

Hassan, Fayza, 'The pilgrims' prospects', *al-Ahram Weekly* newspaper, 17–23 April 1997, pp. 12–13.

Isma'il, Muhammad Husam al-Din, *Madinat al-Qahira min wilayat Muhammad 'Ali ila Isma'il, 1805–1879*, Cairo, Dar al-afaq al-arabiyya, 1997.

Maqrizi, Taqiyy al-Din al-, *Kitab al-mawa'iz wa'l-i'tibar bi-dhikr al-khitat wa'l-athar*, 2 vols, Cairo, Maktabat al-thaqafa al-diniyya, n.d.

Marsot, Afaf Lutfi al-Sayyid, *Egypt in the Reign of Muhammad 'Ali*, Cambridge, Cambridge University Press, 1984.

Mengin, Félix, *Histoire de l'Égypte sous le gouvernement de Mohammed-Aly, ou récit des évènements politiques et militaires qui ont eu lieu depuis le départ des Français jusqu'en 1823*, 2 vols, Paris, Arthur Bertraud, 1823.

— *Histoire sommaire de l'Égypte sous le gouvernement de Mohammed-Aly, ou récit des principaux évènements qui ont eu lieu de l'an 1825 à l'an 1838*, Paris, Librarie de Firmin Didot Frères, 1839.

Mubarak, 'Ali Pasha, *al-Khitat al-tawfiqiyya al-jadida li-Misr al-Qahira wa-muduniha wa-biladiha al-qadima wa'l-shahira*, Cairo, General Egyptian Book Organisation, 1994.

Raymond, André, *Artisans et commerçants au Caire au XVIIIe siècle*, 2 vols, Damascus, Institut français de Damascus, 1973–4.

Sami, Amin Pasha, *Taqwim al-Nil*, vol. 2, Cairo, Dar al-kutub al-misriyya, 1928.

Toledano, Ehud, *State and Society in Mid-nineteenth Century Egypt*, Cambridge, Cambridge University Press, 1990.

Notes on Chapter 7

1   According to Sami, Muhammad 'Ali ordered the creation of the manufactories at al-Khurunfish and Bulaq on 5 Rabi' Awwal 1234/1818: Sami, 1928, vol. 2, p. 276.

2   Mengin, 1823, pp. 375–6.

3   Baer, 1964, pp. 130–3.

4   While Amin Sami maintains that it was set up in 1818, Mengin claims that it was established in 1816. Other authors contend that it was established in 1816, but converted from silk to cotton production in 1818.

5   According to Jabarti, al-Khurunfish was built 'in the month of Dhu 'l-Hijja 1233 [1816–17] in Harat al-Nasara, also known as [Harat] Khamis al-'Ads, which leads towards al-Khurunfish, upon the recommendation of some of the Christian foreigners. They spent some time making the original machines, like anvils, iron lathes, *tizajat*, hammers, saws and other things of this sort. They assigned a place to each craft and trade, containing looms and machines and strange tools for the production of cotton and different types of silk and textiles embroidered in gold (*al-aqmisha al-muqassaba*) and other things.' Mubarak, 1994, vol. 3, p. 138.

6   Maqrizi, n.d., vol. 2, p. 27.

7   Hanna, 1991, pp. 208–9.

8   Mengin, 1823, p. 195.

9   *Ibid.*, p. 198.

10   Baer, 1964, p. 131.

11   Diwan Majlis Ahkam Misr, p. 317. Summary from the Majlis al-Milkiyya, 22 Rabi' Akhar 1245/1829 no 7, listed no 371.

12 An administrative sector (pl. *athman*).

13 Bitaqat al-dar, 'Ummal 282. Similar orders were issued throughout the country to ensure that the workers who were recruited for work in the manufactories were guaranteed by their shaykhs in a bid to prevent them from running away.

14 Bitaqat al-dar, Ihsa' 4.

15 In some cases, these day wages were augmented by an end-of-month bonus equal to the worker's wage for the whole month. The European carpenters were the only group to receive this benefit, which pushed their salaries far above the overall average.

16 There were 15 ironsmiths, 44 fitters, 15 lathe-makers and 1 smelter.

17 The sawyers are not included in the manufactory's general accounts, presumably since they were hired only for very limited periods of time – from one to six days.

18 The exact meaning of the term *rumi* is a matter of some contention. While some scholars translate it as Greek Catholic or Eastern non-Coptic Christian, the general consensus holds that *rumi* signifies Turkish as opposed to, for instance, *awlad 'arab* (native Egyptians) or *'urban* (bedouin).

19 Foucault, 1991, p. 174.

20 In retrospect, these may be seen as three consecutive 'stages of industrialisation' which co-existed in the manufactory system of al-Khurunfish.

21 Foucault, 1991, p. 174.

22 'Rather than continue running the mills through direct government supervision, the government merely supplied the entrepreneurs with the raw materials and received the finished product...the pasha had found a way of making more money out of the factories and textiles by putting out.' Marsot, 1984, pp. 173–4.

23 Dockès and Rosier, 1988, p. 128.

24 Toledano, 1990, p. 13

25 According to Sami, the order was worded as follows: 'Clot Bey has explained to us that the location of the two manufactories at al-Khurunfish [presumably, the viceroy meant the manufactories for the production of textiles, on one hand, and machinery, on the other – not the subsidiary branch of al-Khurunfish at Sayyida Zaynab] is appropriate for the hospital which will replace Qasr al-'Aini. Therefore, it is necessary that you go there with whomever is necessary to inspect the two aforementioned manufactories. Take action rapidly according to what you find you need for their reparation and restoration. When something is removed from its place, the transfer should be carried out as you go along, so that the

transfer of the royal and military hospital from Qasr al-'Aini to the two manufactories in the aforementioned location may take place in the shortest possible delay.' Cited in Isma'il, 1997, p. 129.

26 Hassan, 1997.

27 Raymond, 1973–4, pp. 226–7. Numerous examples of rent are provided by the Qisma 'Askariyya registers, in which the legacies of many artisans and merchants may be found.

28 The *bitaqat al-dar* are cards classified according to subject, containing translations in Arabic of Turkish documents.

CHAPTER 8

The Private Papers of an Armenian Merchant Family in the Ottoman Empire, 1912–14

Armin Kredian

The business correspondence of Hagop Kheretian and Misak Chokarian (the fathers of the author's paternal grandparents) will be examined in this study. The business that they established involved the production of woollen shawls in Gurin (Anatolia) and the distribution of these shawls, both locally and in neighbouring regions. A discussion of these private papers, which are incomplete and uncatalogued, nevertheless shows how one can understand certain aspects concerning the historical development of the concerned region, and of the textile industry in particular, through the study of individual trajectories. Thus, one sees the family develop its textile production in Anatolia and in Syria at a time of severe political and economic crisis in the Ottoman world. One also sees how these developments affected the destinies of different family members.

Gurin was the main provincial town in the *kaza* of Gurin, located in the *sanjak* of Sivas (Sebastia) within the *vilayet* of Sivas (Sebastia) which, together with five other Armenian *vilayets* of eastern Anatolia, formed Ottoman Armenia. The Armenian townspeople in the *vilayet* of Sivas were engaged mainly in printing cotton hangings, painting and dyeing, textile weaving, sewing, belt-making, carpet-making, shoe-making and watch-repairing; they also worked as blacksmiths, carpenters and masons.[1] Armenians in Gurin had a school and a church. On the eve of the First World War, the town numbered 3000 household; until June 1915, 1550 of these were Armenian.[2]

Sources and Background

The sources for the present research are both oral and written. The source for background information on this business is the family oral history which has come down to me through my uncle. The latter, in turn, had learned it from his father, Yeghia Kredian, one of the partners in the enterprise and its representative in Aleppo. Although containing many gaps, this oral history provides enough information to make sense of the written correspondence which has been preserved. It has been particularly useful in identifying the names that appear in the letters and in determining the family ties of merchants mentioned. The written material verifies and filters this oral legacy, in addition to providing details – through bills and account sheets – of trade transactions that are impossible to transmit orally.

On the basis of oral history, the process of production and distribution of the business goods can be reconstructed as follows: the founders of the enterprise were originally two friends, Misak Chokarian and Hagop Kheretian, natives of Gurin. Exactly when this business was started and when it was expanded into a network is unknown. My grandfather's autobiographical notes show that, by 1904, the enterprise had been extended, and it had a branch in Kayseri, where Chokarian had moved to expand the sphere of the distribution of the shawls. In 1910, the two original business partners became 'family' when Hagop's son married Misak's daughter. Whether or not this marriage (which lasted for 54 years) involved an element of romance cannot be verified. In any case, it represents a common pattern found in Middle Eastern and other societies: reinforcing business ties with matrimonial links.

Eventually, at an unknown date, the enterprise was named Misak Chokarian and Hagop Kheretian and Sons. By 1912, this company, still based in Gurin, had branches in Kayseri, Adana, Konya and, from 1912, in Aleppo. In 1915, the entire trading network collapsed as a consequence of the massacres and deportation of the Armenians in the Ottoman Empire.[3] From the day of the company's establishment until 1915, Gurin remained the only town in which shawls were manufactured. The branches in the other cities and towns were involved in the sale of the shawls, in purchasing raw materials (the Aleppo branch) and sending them to Gurin and in the trade of various goods which the company purchased wholesale – mainly from Aleppo. In other words, a network was established in which each town fulfilled a particular function.

Imported British wool yarn was purchased on the domestic market. Family members did not import the wool from England themselves, and it is not clear from whom or where precisely they acquired the needed wool in the initial stages of the enterprise. Later, when a branch was established by my grandfather in Aleppo, the imported British wool was purchased there and sent to Gurin. The wool yarns were dyed in different colours in Gurin. The dyed wool yarns were then distributed to households which had weaving machines. These machines (Jacquard looms) had been introduced in Gurin by an Armenian named Titizian, nicknamed *khelok emin* (smart uncle), for their novelty. The weavers were also given the flowery patterns of the shawls that they were required to weave. According to a specific time limit, the shawls were handed over and the maker received the agreed-upon wage for her or his workmanship.

Initially, the shawls were sold locally in Gurin and the surrounding area. The main purchasers of these shawls were Kurds, who used them as belts. As mentioned above, from at least as early as 1904, they were also sent to Kayseri, thus expanding the scope of distribution. Once the children of the original partners were old enough and experienced, other branches were to follow. Thus, the Adana branch was run by Misak's son, Mihran, while the Aleppo branch was managed by Hagop's son, Yeghia (my grandfather). The business representative in Konya was Misak's brother, Hapet.

The written documents that have survived are mainly letters.[4] They are obviously the business files of the Aleppo branch, as they include the originals of letters sent to Aleppo and copies of letters sent from Aleppo. Hence, the periodisation of this branch may be established, as the Aleppo section was founded in 1912 and came to an end in the early months of 1915. The files of the other branches have not been preserved, limiting not only the periodisation of this research but also its geographical setting as the family network's transactions outside the sphere of the Aleppo branch remain unknown.

The preserved documents can be categorised into three sections. Firstly, two folders, one entitled the 'House of Gurin', the other the 'House of Kayseri', consisting of letters written between 1912 and 1914. The former includes letters sent from Gurin to the branch in Aleppo, while the latter includes letters sent from the branch in Kayseri to the branch in Aleppo. The original reply letters sent from Aleppo to Gurin and Kayseri have not been preserved. Secondly, a hardcover bound volume includes almost illegible copies of handwritten letters from August 1913 to August 1914 by the author's grandfather sent from Aleppo to the different branches of the network and to various customer merchants. Occasionally, the letters sent to these merchants were accompanied with bills, the copies of which are also found in the bound volume. Thirdly, a few scattered bits and pieces of documents concerning business forms, auto-biographical notes, business transactions and financial accounts.

Most of the letters and the few preserved bills and accounting documents are in Armenian (for the semi-official internal company documents). The Armenian accounts and bills use a number of Ottoman Turkish words for quantity (*okha*, *shiwal*) and prices. Sometimes even the names of certain items are in Ottoman Turkish. Ottoman Turkish is used for a few letters and bills to non-Armenian merchants (all in copies). There is also an Arabic current account balance sheet bearing an official stamp, probably for official use in Aleppo in case of a breach of faith.

The difference in the language and the spelling between the letters written by my grandfather and his father makes it clear that the latter had had little or no schooling and had learned to read and write in a rather homely manner. The language in his letters is nothing but an application of the Armenian alphabet to the locally spoken Armenian dialect without any application of spelling or grammatical rules; Yeghia's letters have only a few traces of the local Armenian dialect of Gurin and almost no spelling or grammatical mistakes. According to my grandfather's autobiographical notes, he had attended the local Armenian school in Gurin, graduating at the age of sixteen. This gives an idea of the high level of instruction of the Armenian language in provincial towns in Ottoman Armenia at the end of the nineteenth century.

As stated, most of the letters are in Armenian. The letters written by my grandfather's father are in the local Armenian dialect of Gurin and might prove to be a source of some importance for Armenian linguists. Of particular linguistic interest is my grandfather's correspondence with an Armenian merchant by the name Keshishian in Damascus. The letters in this correspondence were written in Ottoman Turkish using Armenian characters.[5]

From the perspective of different members of the family, the present work, based on a preliminary examination of this merchant family's papers, explores some aspects of regional trade within the Ottoman Empire at the beginning of the twentieth century, a field of study almost totally neglected by historians preoccupied with the empire's international trade. On the basis of the private Kredian papers, this research focuses on the production and trade in textiles and analyses modes of production and distribution, patterns of transactions among merchants, ethnicity and division of labour, local and foreign competition etc. It then touches upon the importance of these documents as a source for social and linguistic issues in the region. Finally, the research concludes with conceptual issues related to these documents.

Trade Patterns

Scope of Business

At this stage in the study, the scope of the business remains vague in terms of capital, manpower and production. With further research, the few preserved bills and account sheets may shed light on some of these aspects. Even then, due to the loss of the documents of the branches outside Aleppo, as well as the illegibility of some of the existing ones, it will not be possible to determine the scope of the business in these terms.

There are, however, hints on the capacity of production. For example, an order by a merchant from Diyarbakir for 100 shawls is considered a 'large order' and the merchant is advised that it would take two months to fulfil.[6] Of course, this does not mean that it took two months to prepare 100 shawls for, at the same time, the network provided shawls for at least 10 merchants known to us from the letters.

Cottage Industry Mode of Production

As described above, the wool yarns for the production of the shawls was provided by the merchant-entrepreneur who, in this case, dyed the yarns at home. Interestingly, a notebook was found in which the recipes for dyeing 17 different colours and tints were written down. The process of dyeing was undertaken at home in large copper cauldrons. The notes detail the amount of dye, acid and fixer (sulphate) that was used for the eight colours and the combinations used for the nine tints.

After dyeing, the yarns were distributed to the peasants who wove the shawls. The machines were owned by the weavers, who were paid by piece. Thus, the mode of production can be categorised as cottage industry. Whether or not it was also part of rural industry defined as 'the activity of households engaged in both industry and agriculture partly for the market, partly for home consumption'[7] is not clear.

In terms of capital, this mode of production is an example of the pre-factory where, as Franklin Mendels points out, 'the principal form of capital was circulating capital', as opposed to fixed capital in the ownership of factory and machines by the industrialist merchants.[8] In fact, once this family business grew into a network, the limitations of cottage industry were felt and prospects to found a factory in Aleppo begin to appear in the letters.

Letters written in 1913 reveal intentions to change the mode of production because of a number of difficulties. First, because of growing demand, Gurin was not able to produce enough shawls to supply all branches in the networks.[9] Second, fear of losing ground in face of the local competition with a rival Armenian family, Minassian, is explicitly mentioned in the letters.[10] Third, the quality of the Gurin production was unable to compete with that of European shawls in Aleppo, though the latter were more expensive.[11]

As a result, attempts were made to introduce novelties in the kind and style of the production. 'Double-face shawls are in fashion now', reported the Aleppo branch to Gurin, 'we have to order a machine. It's in our interest to produce this new kind. There is great profit in it.'[12] It seems that the company succeeded, to a certain extent, as one of the letters states that it was taking longer than usual to produce 'the new kind' of shawl that had been ordered due to the lack of skilled weavers for it.[13]

As a long-term solution to the problems faced by the company, the Aleppo branch proposed opening a mechanised workshop in Aleppo, which would use modern European machinery. In fact, certain steps were taken in that direction in the spring of 1914. Machine experts were contacted, and a down-payment was even made to buy machines from Germany.[14]

The entire prospect was, however, frozen at the outbreak of the First World War, when a general atmosphere of instability and uncertainty prevailed and the attitude of merchants became one of 'wait and see'. The Company was already facing a financial crisis in September 1914, due to circumstances created by the mobilisation of the Ottoman army. A letter from Konya stated that the roads were inactive because there were neither horses nor carriages, while the trains were transporting only army troops. It was impossible to collect money from debtors.[15]

The news arriving from Gurin to Aleppo was even more discouraging. Great quantities of merchandise had been taken away from the shop by government officials. 'We are still able to secure our daily bread', wrote Hagop to his son, 'do not worry about us, we will somehow pull through these difficulties. Just know the value of life.'[16] Today, one knows that he was too optimistic. The business never recovered from the crisis, and during the massacres and deportations of the Armenians which started in early 1915, family members in all branches except Aleppo suffered both of these fates.[17]

Here, taking into consideration the pre-war mechanisation prospects of the company, one sees how the process of mechanisation – had it worked out – was brutally or abruptly interrupted. The development from a craft to an industry came in stages and, like in England, the first textile-factory builders were former merchants because, as Mendels explains, merchants were the ones who had accumulated capital during proto-industrialisation.[18]

Distribution

The location of the cities and towns where the family had branches or markets indicates that the geographical scope of the business was quite large, taking into consideration the fact that the trade was run by members of one family and was only a regional business and not part of international trade. The documents reveal that, whereas all the branches were involved in the sale of shawl-belts produced in Gurin, the Aleppo branch was also involved in the wholesale trade of various items listed in the bills sent to merchants.[19]

There is no evidence to indicate that family members were involved in retail in all the branches of the network. Reference to a shop owned by Hagop Kheretian in Gurin indicates that, in that town, they were engaged in both retail and wholesale.[20] Similar information on the other cities and towns in which they had branches remains to be verified. As for wholesale trade, the letters and account sheets reveal that in each city or town where trade was conducted, there was only one merchant who purchased goods as retail and sold to retailers. Apart from in the branches in which the network representatives were family members and partners, merchandise was sent to merchants in Damascus (referred to as Sham in the letters) and Beirut (where the same Damascus merchant moved later), Iskanderun, Kilis, Ayntab and even Istanbul – though trade with the latter was minimal.

Another method for distribution of merchandise was through commissioners, though only one such transaction of this type has surfaced so far: an Armenian from Van came to Aleppo to take merchandise to Van to sell on commission. Because of the insecurity of the roads, however, he was stranded in Aleppo.[21]

This raises the question of the regional infrastructure of the business. The geographically large scope of distribution is unavoidably linked with important issues related to regional trade networks, primarily that of communication and transportation which, in this case, was over mountainous terrain.

Communication

The existing documents containing data on communication among the partners in different branches and merchants in different towns consist mainly of letters, although there are also a few postcards and telegrams. Most letters went to and from Aleppo by post, the services of which seem to have been quite regular between 1912 and 1914. The letters are dated; moreover, all of them refer to the date of the last letter received, so that one can estimate the time that it took to receive a letter sent from one branch to another. For example, a letter from Kayseri to Aleppo took between 12 and 15 days to arrive.

Three postcards sent from Ayntab to Aleppo have been preserved. One of them bears the seal of both the Ayntab and the Aleppo post offices. The dates on these seals (Ayntab: 27 October 1914, Aleppo: 28 October 1914) indicate that it took the postcard only one day to reach Aleppo from Ayntab. The seals were marked both by Christian and Hijri dates. These postcards are also the only ones which mention the address of the branch in Aleppo, which was in the Sabunkhana[22] (the Khan al-Sabun), one of the older *khans* or commercial warehouses of the city, which still survives. In the Ottoman period, this *khan* specialised in the sale of soap.

Some of the letters were hand delivered via the transporters of the merchandise dispatched from town to town, mostly by mule-drivers or coachmen, who were referred to in the letters as *'arabaji*.[23]

Transportation of Merchandise

As mentioned above, the Aleppo files reveal that, in addition to the business branches in five cities, family trade encompassed at least seven other cities, in which there were regular merchant-customers.

A look at a 1918 railway map of the region reveals the total absence of railway lines in Ottoman Armenia, at least up to this time. This meant that the branches were not linked to Gurin, the production centre, by railway lines. As mentioned in the letters – which often contain references to mule-drivers and coach-men who were entrusted with merchandise to be delivered from Aleppo to Iskenderoun, Gurin and Ayntab – goods were transported by mules and coaches. When Mihran, the family representative in Adana, became sick, the company suggested to my grandfather that he run both the Aleppo and Adana branches, but he refused, saying, 'I cannot agree until the railway line in Aleppo is linked with Adana'.[24] Obviously, until August 1913, the railway line linking Aleppo with Adana had not yet been completed.

Ayntab was a transit point on the road between Aleppo and Gurin,[25] where the business contact was an Armenian merchant by the name of Kevork Horomian. Wool yarns and various other items were sent to Ayntab by the Aleppo branch. Horomian took the part of the merchandise that he had ordered and re-dispatched the rest to Gurin. Similarly, the dispatch of shawls from Gurin to Aleppo was via Ayntab, from where, after taking the quantity of shawls that he needed for the market, Horomian re-dispatched the rest to Aleppo.[26]

The transporters were paid by the recipient of the merchandise. The dispatcher of the goods sent a letter with the transporter, who determined how much money the latter should be paid if he delivered the goods undamaged. In the case of damage, the transporter was fined by the merchant. Transportation fees were standard and were determined on the basis of distance and the weight of the merchandise. For example, the transportation cost from Ayntab to Aleppo for a parcel weighing 200 *ukhas* was 75 qirsh[27] (1 *ukha* equalled 1.3kg; 200 *ukhas* equalled 260kg).[28]

Patterns of Transactions among Merchants

The documents include a number of bills addressed to merchants in different cities. They present a rich source of information, as they include a detailed list of the quantity, kind and price of goods. The bills were either sent following the dispatch of merchandise or accompanying it. In some letters, nothing indicates that a down-payment had been made by the purchasing merchant prior to the reception of goods. Obviously, the element of trust was crucial in this kind of transaction.

Trust was often based on the reputation of a merchant. Therefore, inquiries were made on the reputation of a new client before starting a trade transaction. For example, before concluding a deal involving a large quantity of merchandise with an Armenian merchant in Damascus, the Aleppo branch asked for information from the Adana branch about the reputation of this merchant as the latter was a native of Adana and was currently based in Damascus.[29] Transactions in which trust played a crucial role were those made by unofficial personal letters. For example, a handwritten letter (in Armenian), signed by two merchants, concludes the following deal: a merchant in Aleppo owed a certain amount of money to a merchant in Konya. The merchant in Aleppo delivered goods for the amount concerned to a merchant in Ayntab and instructed him to pay the amount to the merchant in Konya after 31 days following the date of the agreement. The transaction was signed by both merchants.[30] In today's terminology, this letter would be called a post-dated, re-endorsed cheque.

Though reputation and trust played a major role in trade transactions among merchants, they were not the only guarantees for protection against dishonesty. The letters often refer to *kimbiyalat*,[31] which had widespread circulation. Unfortunately, no sample of a *kimbiyala* has been preserved. Yet, in this regard, an extremely interesting and informative document has been found. This is the balance sheet of a 1914 current account of the Chokarian–Kheretian enterprise and an Armenian merchant in Aleppo by the name of Nigoghos Ter Mesrob al-'Ajami, written in Arabic and bearing an official stamp. This document indicates, among other things, that in addition to *kimbiyalat* being signed in return for delivered goods, many *kimbiyalat* were re-endorsed, so that a *kimbiyala* signed by a merchant in favour of another one would be accepted by a third merchant, either to be cashed or as a guarantee for future payment. The total amount of money involved in this transaction was 77,701 qirsh (equalling 777 Ottoman pounds [liras]), a substantial amount of money for the period.[32]

Ethnicity and Division of Labour

Unfortunately, at this stage of the study, it has not been possible to determine, on the basis of the information in the documents, the ethnicity and sex of the peasant workers involved in weaving in Gurin. Outside sources provide only vague – sometimes contradictory – notions, on the basis of which it is not possible to divide labour along ethnic lines. For example, among the major occupations of the Armenians in Sivas province listed above, Krikorian mentions textile weaving.[33] This by no means asserts that weavers were predominantly or exclusively Armenians. It does, however, bring into question the credibility of theories of ethnic divisibility of labour on the basis of which Kasaba asserts that 'historically, Muslims were more identified with crafts such as tanning, saddling, shoe-making, wool and silk weaving and dyeing; Armenians worked more as tinsmiths, lock-smiths, silversmiths, goldsmiths and construction workers'.[34] Repeating 'historically identified' notions may sometimes be misleading. Kasaba's assertion does not apply at all to Armenians in Ottoman Armenia. As Kasaba claims to be dealing with western Anatolia, one may assume that his statement on the ethnic division of labour involved western Anatolia only, where labour patterns could have been different from Ottoman Armenia. Even so, Kasaba's statement is vague inasmuch as he neither defines the specific regions in western Anatolia to which his statement applies nor determines the borders of western Anatolia.

The merchants with whom the family network did business were, judging from their names, of different ethnicities and religions. Though mainly Armenian, the names of a number of non-Armenian merchants also appear in the letters and account sheets preserved. Out of the 10 merchants with whom the Aleppo branch transacted, two were Muslims and one was a non-Armenian Christian. Their names reveal their religion but not their ethnicity. There are also two merchants who had signed *kimbiyalat* who have mixed Armenian and non-Armenian names: Selim Vartan and Stepan Qarajah. The letters of business transactions with non-Armenians are in Ottoman Turkish.

From the above, it can be concluded that this particular Armenian family of merchants tended to trade more with members of their community. On the other hand, they did not limit their trade transactions to Armenian merchants. Whether this was a common trend among Armenian merchants or merchants of different ethnicities in the Ottoman Empire remains to be verified.

The names of the same mule-driver and coachman repeatedly appear connected with dispatches on the same route. Merchandise was sent from Aleppo to Ayntab by coach, and the coachman was an Armenian. From Aleppo to Iskenderoun, a mule-driver called Ghasim transported the merchandise on mules. Judging from his name, he could have been a Turk, a Kurd or an Arab. 'Arabaji Ahmad Agha delivered the goods sent from Ayntab to Aleppo.[35] Obviously, as far as the transportation of goods is concerned, these documents point in the direction that there were no divisions along ethnic lines for this sector. For a region as socio-economically understudied as Ottoman Armenia, it would be premature to try and apply theories of ethnic division of labour.

Family Business Ties

The letters reveal that the author's grandfather had a very responsible and crucial function in the network. Yet, he did not have the right or power to take any major financial decision without the consent of his father and father-in-law. The latter seems to have been the wealthier partner and the one who had a firm hold on the capital. In 1914, my grandfather, a married man of 28 years of age and the father of a three-year-old son, was paid, sometimes irregularly, as an employee by his father-in-law. In case of business disagreements, his father-in-law kept him short of cash as a pressure lever to have his word implemented.

Matrimonial ties played an essential role in expanding the network. All the business branches were run by the two founders or their brothers, their sons or their sons-in-law. The letters also reveal that the decision for the marriage of any female member of the family lay strictly in the hands of the male head of the family. To all appearances, as in most Middle Eastern societies, male seniority had a dominant role in social relations. As in most Middle Eastern societies, too, the significant yet invisible role of females remains to be unveiled.

Conclusion: Assessment of the Importance of Documents of this Kind for Historiography

A number of questions are raised by these sources. The documents provide answers to some of the questions related to trade patterns, social issues, ethnic relations and linguistic aspects.

On the other hand, the documents also raise some questions without offering any answers.

Case studies are critical, especially when historians attempt to derive unsubstantiated generalisations based on a few examples. On the other hand, in addition to the information that they provide, case studies can play a crucial role in questioning existing generalisations. The developments of the period have frequently been analysed in terms of incorporation theory which examines European penetration of the Ottoman or Middle Eastern world. According to this theory, the European core is conceived as a dynamic economic force which dominates a passive periphery. The study of the textile establishment developed by this particular family at a time when incorporation was very strong shows some of the weaknesses of this theory. My conclusions therefore support the research undertaken by Donald Quataert, who studied the means by which Ottoman industry in the nineteenth century faced the challenge of European competition by modifying some of its methods of production in order to cope with new conditions.[36]

Firstly, rather than being adversely affected by European penetration, both local competition in Gurin and European competition in Aleppo moved this merchant family towards taking steps in expanding and modernising its production.

Secondly, this Armenian merchant family was not involved in a 'peripheral network' as 'non-Muslim intermediaries'.[37] Nor were they 'beneficiaries of the peripheralisation of the Ottoman Empire',[38] as is often asserted in the case of non-Muslim merchants. They neither benefited from the capitulations nor enjoyed the protection of any foreign power. Therefore, before making conclusions on the 'decline' of Muslim merchants, further research is needed on Arab and Turkish merchants engaged in regional trade networks who, as in the case at hand, probably remained untouched by European penetration in the Ottoman Empire even as late as the twentieth century. Accordingly, one can question the validity of Kasaba's assertion that the 'textile-related occupations – where Muslims were especially well represented – faced particularly fierce competition and declined rapidly after the middle decades of the nineteenth century'.[39]

Therefore, although one cannot generalise on the basis of a single case, studying such data can help determine the extent of the applicability of certain models. It can also help pinpoint directions for further study. In this particular case, it becomes obvious that research has yet to be undertaken on Ottoman local trade, particularly in regions of the empire where European penetration was either minimal or totally absent, as was the case of Ottoman Armenia. The internal dynamics of such regions has, so far, been neglected by Ottoman historiography.

The reasons for the major difficulties faced by this study are inherent in the politics of the region. The periodisation of this study (1912–14) was limited by the preserved documents, as because of the massacres and deportation of the family members in the other branches, only the Aleppo documents have survived. Another major drawback is the absence of socio-economic studies on the region, against the background of which this case study could have been examined.

The socio-economic historiography of Ottoman Armenia, today's eastern Turkey, remains underdeveloped for a number of mainly political reasons, such as the lack of available material as a result of political events (war, massacre, deportation),[40] the intentional destruction of documents as part of the secretive nature of the Young Turks' genocidal policy against the Armenians, the preoccupation of some academics affiliated to the Turkish government to deny the genocide of the Armenians in the Ottoman Empire[41] and the time and effort shed by historians proving the falsity of the denials at the expense of socio-economic studies on the region.

As in the case of Ottoman Armenia, the destruction of valuable material during wars, massacres and deportation in entire regions may be tantamount to wiping out the social history of nations simultaneously with the physical liquidation of the population of a region. Today, in line with their policy of denial of the Armenian genocide, the Turkish authorities seek to 'Turkify' the history of eastern Anatolia. Ironically, social history as a movement to liberate historiography from the clutches of political history is faced with the ever-frustrating reality of the omnipresence of politics.

Bibliography

Unpublished Sources

Family Papers, Cairo.

Published Primary Studies

Archives du génocide des Arméniens: recueil de documents diplomatiques allemands, extraits de Deutschland und Armenien (1914–1918), compiled and presented par Johannes Lepsius, transl. from German by Marie-France Letenoux, Paris, Fayard, 1986.

Les Grandes Puissances, l'Empire ottoman et les Arméniens dans les archives françaises (1914–1918), compiled and presented by Arthur Bevlerian, Paris, Publications de la Sorbonne, 1983.

United States Official Documents on the Armenian Genocide, compiled and introduced by Ara Sarafian, MA, Armenian Review, 1993.

Published Studies

Aghayan, Y., *Arti Hayereni Batsatrakan Bararan (Dictionary of Modern Armenian)*, Yerevan, Armenia Publishing House, 1976.

'Gurin' (no author mentioned), *Armenian Soviet Encyclopedia*, vol. 5, Yerevan, 1979, p. 494.

Hovannisian, Richard G., *The Armenian Holocaust: A Bibliography Relating to the Deportations, Massacres, and Dispersion of the Armenian People, 1915–1923*, MA, Armenian Heritage Press, 1980.

Kasaba, Resat, *The Ottoman Empire and the World Economy: The Nineteenth Century*, New York, State University of New York Press, 1988.

Krikorian, Mesrob, *Armenians in the Service of the Ottoman Empire 1860–1908*, London, Routledge and Kegan Paul, 1978.

Mendels, Franklin, 'Proto-industrialization: The first phase of the industrialization process', *Journal of Economic History* 32/1, March 1972, pp. 241–61.

Quataert, Donald, 'Ottoman Manufacturing in the Nineteenth Century' in Donald Quataert (ed.), *Manufacturing in the Ottoman Empire and Turkey, 1500-1950*, New York, State University of New York Press, 1994, pp. 87–122.

Smith, Roger W., Eric Markusen and Robert Jay Lifton (eds), *Professional Ethics and the Denial of the Armenian Genocide*, Oxford, Oxford University Press, 1995.

Notes on Chapter 8

1 Krikorian, 1978, p. 55.

2 'Gurin', 1979. According to my grandfather's report on the massacres and deportation of the Armenians of Gurin: in 1915, prior to their mass deportation, the town had 2000 Armenian households and 10,000 Armenian individuals, of whom only 250 reached Aleppo.

3 For a bibliography of Armenian and non-Armenian sources on the Armenian Genocide, including lists of Armenian, Austria-Hungarian, French, German, British and American archival material: Hovannisian, 1980; for published German documents: Archives du génocide des Arméniens, 1986; for published American official documents: United States Official Documents on the Armenian Genocide, 1993; for published French official documents: *Les Grandes Puissances*, 1983.

4 All original documents used in this article are in the possession of the family in Cairo, henceforth referred to as Family Papers.

5 In the nineteenth century there existed a number of Armenian publications of this kind: namely, books in Ottoman Turkish printed with Armenian letters. Here, in Cairo, I have found a dozen books published in this manner, the oldest of which dates back to 1819. Some of these were published in Istanbul, others in Venice and Vienna by Armenian-owned publishing houses. Their publication indicates that there was a considerable number of Armenians in the Ottoman Empire who knew the spoken Ottoman language but could not read or write it. At the same time, these people knew the Armenian alphabet but did not understand the Armenian language.

6 Family Papers.

7 Mendels, 1972, p. 258.

8 *Ibid.*, 1972, pp. 255–6.

9 Family Papers.

10 *Ibid.*

11 *Ibid.*, letter dated 18/31 August 1913, written by Yeghia Kheretian in Aleppo to the company in Kayseri.

12 *Ibid.*

13 *Ibid.*

14 *Ibid.*

15 *Ibid.*, letter dated 10/23 September 1914, written by Ghazaros Kharmantaian in Konya to Yeghia Kheretian in Aleppo.

16 *Ibid.*, letter dated 24/7 September 1914, written by Hagop Kheretian in Gurin to Yeghia Kheretian in Aleppo.

17 According to my grandfather's autobiographical notes, the family members in Kayseri were deported to Aleppo on 15 July 1915.

18 Mendels, 1972, p. 244.

19 Family Papers.

20 *Ibid.*, letter dated 24/7 September 1914, written by Hagop Kheretian in Gurin to Yeghia Kheretian in Aleppo.

21 *Ibid.*

22 *Ibid.*

23 *Ibid.*

24 *Ibid.*, letter dated 18/31 August 1913, written by Yeghia Kheretian in Aleppo to the company in Kayseri.

25 In his report on the Gurin massacres and deportation, my grandfather mentions that it was an eight-day journey on foot between Gurin and Ayntab.

26 Family Papers.

27 *Ibid.*

28 Aghayan, 1976, p. 1587.

29 *Ibid.*

30 *Ibid.*

31 The plural of *kimbiyala*, which is a promissory note for payment.

32 Family Papers.

33 Krikorian, 1978, p. 55.

34 Kasaba, 1988, p. 104.

35 *Ibid.*

36 Quataert, 1994.

37 Kasaba, 1988, p. 114.

38 *Ibid.*

39 *Ibid.*, pp. 104–5.

40 For example, J.B. Jackson, the US Consul in Aleppo, who left the city in May 1917, wrote: 'Hundreds of inquires were received by the Consulate in reference to the families of Armenians then living in the United States, and which families had been deported to Aleppo or the vicinity. Practically all of Vice Consul George W. Young's time was occupied in securing the information necessary to prepare the replies thereto, but many of these and much other valuable information, including copies of military and political reports, and details of massacres and racial disturbances, were burned before my departure from Aleppo, following the instructions from the Department transmitted through the Embassy.' United States Official Documents, 1993, document 70, pp. 154–5.

41 Smith, Markusen and Lifton, 1995.

CHAPTER 9

The *Rasa'il Ikhwan al-Safa'* and the Controversy about the Origin of Craft Guilds in Early Medieval Islam

Abbas Hamdani

The *Rasa'il Ikhwan al-Safa'* (*The Epistles of the Brethren of Purity*) is a well-known encyclopedia of medieval Islam composed by a religio-political secret society.[1] Its 52 epistles are grouped into four parts: mathematical sciences, physics, psychology and religion and politics. It is followed by an epistle called *al-Jami'a*, which makes more explicit that which is implied in the main text. It was written by the same authors, simultaneously with the main *Rasa'il*, but as a separate work.[2] A *Risalat Jami'at al-Jami'a*, a much later summary of *al-Jami'a*, found in Syrian collections, edited by 'Arif Tamir (Beirut, 1959), is not an integral part of the original composition of the encyclopedia.

The encyclopedia covers almost all topics of the sciences known to the classical period of Islam. They are presented in a popular manner, with a religious and political purpose, which was to bring in the rule of a new state in place of the Abbasid caliphate, in whose domain it was composed. The epistles are written with an eclectic sweep of Pythagorean and Nichomachian arithmetic, numerology and music, Hermetic and Indo-Persian magic and astrology, Aristotelian logic and physics, Gnostic esotericism, neo-Platonic cosmology, theory of emanations and metaphysics, Biblical and Qu'ranic prophetology, Platonic concepts of law and leadership, and Buddhist, Zoroastrian and Manichaen wisdom and allegory. This synthesis and the writers' theory and preference for a descendent of 'Ali to lead the community indicate generally a Shi'ite and, more particularly, an Isma'ili or Fatimid affiliation.

There is a general consensus among scholars that the epistles were composed sometime between the mid-third/ninth century to the late fourth/tenth century, that is during the period of classical Islam, and that they are of Shi'ite Isma'ili persuasion.[3] Although other theories also exist, they are not relevant to the purpose of the present work. In several of my own studies, I have maintained that they were composed in a period just prior to the establishment of the Fatimid caliphate in 297/909.[4] Even if one considers the *Rasa'il* to be a later composition, it would not have been written later than the second half of the tenth century.[5]

For the discussion here, these epistles are of relevance and importance, as they are the first in Islamic history to describe the various manual crafts and to emphasise the dignity of human labour. The epistle on manual crafts is number eight in the first part on mathematical sciences, that is after seven other epistles on numbers, geometry, astronomy, geography, music, numerology and intellectual crafts.

In an article written in 1943,[6] Bernard Lewis summarised the contents of this epistle on manual crafts. In an earlier article on Islamic guilds,[7] he had used this epistle to provide inferential evidence for the existence of guilds in classical Islam. He was following Louis Massignon's contention, which went far deeper in asserting the existence of these guilds and their connection with the Isma'ili/Qarmatian movement.[8] Later, Yves Marquet described the role of labour in the *Rasa'il*, relying on the theory of Massignon stated above.[9] His emphasis, however, was on the philosophical classification of crafts as derived from the Isma'ili cosmological doctrines. Before discussing the controversy between those asserting and those denying such an existence, a survey of views concerning the *Rasa'il* is enlightening.

This eighth *risala* is couched in philosophical terms. In Lewis's words, 'Crafts, we are told, are of two kinds, intellectual and practical. The latter... deal with their matter, their essence, their quantities and their qualities and the quality of the manifestation of their craftsmanship on the materials allotted to them.'[10] Then, the brethren describe the various products in terms of the four elements and the animal, vegetable and mineral kingdoms. From water, there are sailors and water-carriers; from earth, there are miners and diggers of wells, rivers, canals and graves; from fire, there are torch-bearers, stokers and naphtha extractors; from air, there are pipers and trumpeters; from water and earth, there are potters, porcelain makers, pot-sellers and milk-beaters; from minerals, there are ironsmiths, copper-smiths, goldsmiths, lead-workers, glaziers; from vegetable material, there are carpenters, basket-makers, mat-sellers, flax-spinners, hemp-workers, paper-workers, flour dealers, pressers, rice dealers and seed dealers; from animals, there are hunters, shepherds, cowherds, grooms, furriers, bird-keepers, butchers, roasters, cooks, tanners, shoemakers, cobblers and other leather-workers; from evaluating quantities of things, there are weighers, measurers, money-changers, brokers, evaluators; in relation to human bodies, there are physicians, barbers, etc.

Human professions are also classified: preachers, poets, judges, readers, sentinels, watchmen, weavers, dancers, mourners and swimmers. Then, depending on the tools which are used, there are pipers, trumpeters, drummers, tailors, scribes, messen-gers, surveyors, garment-menders, carders, rice-grinders and water-wheel movers.

There is, then, a more practical classification of crafts: primary crafts, such as weaving of different kinds, ancillary crafts, such as those connected with agriculture, and luxuries, such as dealers of silk, brocade, perfumes etc.

Crafts are, therefore, divided according to their nobility and level of required skill, as well as according to their public utility. The market-sweepers are considered higher in nobility than perfumers because, although the former may be poorer, they are of more social service than the latter.

The epistle describes many more professions, but the above list should be sufficient to illustrate the diversity of economic life in the early medieval Islamic city.

A Persian king, Ardeshir, is quoted commending the transmission of a craft from father to son. Among the concluding remarks, the following is interesting:

> And know, ô, brother, that every human craftsman requires a teacher (*ustadh*) from whom he learns his craft or his science and that his teacher in turn requires a teacher before him and so on until one is reached whose knowledge does not derive from any

human being. And this can be in one of two ways – we can say, as do the philosophers, that he invented it himself by the powers of his own soul, thought, vision and effort or we can say, as do the Prophets, that he inherited it from one who was not human.[11]

From the above description, we can infer several things: that by the late ninth or early tenth century, there was a proliferation of professions and crafts with a system of apprenticeship, preferably within families, that each craft developed so distinctly that the acquisition of its know-how depended on an organisation of teaching and learning and, finally, that the nobility of a craft depended on its degree of service to the society.

Other passages from the *Rasa'il* state the depth of the presence of the brethren among various classes of people. For example:

Know, ô brother, may God aid you and us with His spirit, that we have brethren and friends among the noble and gracious people, spread out in different places. Among them is a group of the sons of kings, *amirs*, *wazirs*, secretaries [*kuttab*] and governors [*'ummal*]; among them are the sons of notables, the *dihqans*, small property holders [*tunna'*] and merchants [*tujjar*] and among them is a group of the sons of '*ulama*', men of letters [*udaba'*], jurists [*fuqaha'*] and religious men and among them is a group of the sons of craftsmen [*sunna'*], local headmen [*mutasarrifin*] and leaders of crafts and professions [*umana' al-nass*]. We have delegated to each group of them a brother from our brethren, whose knowledge and insight we approve, to represent us in their service by counselling them with fellow-feeling [*rifq*], kindness [*rahma*] and affection [*shafaqa*].[12]

The reference to *sunna'* and *umana' al-nass* is noteworthy. The brethren ascribe their influence and instruction among them which could imply their organising those crafts in the service of their own political aims. The expression 'sons of...' refers to 'groups of...'.

Another sort of influence which the brethren seek is among the youth groups. They say:

It behoves our good and eminent Brethren, may God guide them and us with His spirit, to follow the example of the philosopher in wisely choosing [i.e. seeking] the company of the *ahdath* and *fityan* [members of youth groups] who are good and noble, well-mannered and cultured, understanding and intelligent, for sustaining our knowledge and the secrets of our wisdom, following the tradition of God. This is because He does not send a prophet who is not young nor does he give wisdom to any devotee who is not young [*hadath*] from among the youth fraternities [*fityan*].[13]

The same brethren working among the crafts are also working among the *futuwwa* groups, suggesting that there was a certain organisational overlap and convergence. The young craftsmen, particularly the apprentices, could be the link.[14]

On the level of youth and 'working-class' solidarity, religious differences disappear and a certain inter-confessional and liberal attitude develops:

> Do not occupy yourself with the reforming of men who have kept since their childhood false ideas, bad habits, and evil qualities, for they will weary you and will not be changed. If they do change, it would be very little and of no avail. Your concern is with young men of sound heart who incline towards letters, begin to study the sciences, seek the path of truth and the other world, believe in the day of reckoning, make use of the religious codes of the Prophets, study the secrets of their books, renounce passion and polemic and are not fanatical in matters of doctrine.[15]

And:

> Know that truth is found in every religion [*din*] and is current in every tongue. What you should do, however, is to take the best and to transfer yourself to it. Do not ever occupy yourself with imputing defects to the religions of people; rather try to see whether your religion is free from them.[16]

The Brethren of Purity were political activists with an intellectual appeal. If they worked among the craft and youth fraternities, they also wanted to unite them by *mithaq* of *'ahd*, (covenant of initiation), which itself is an attribute of an organisational structure. This is what they say:

> Know that the government of the People of Good begins, firstly by their gathering in a place [which may mean a professional or fraternal quarter] of good and noble people and by agreeing on one opinion, one faith and one religion and by binding themselves together by a *'ahd* and *mithaq* to help each other and not avoid each other; to co-operate with each other and not to withdraw from such co-operation.[17]

From many other writings in the *Rasa'il*, it is clear that the brethren were part of the Isma'ili Fatimid Da'wa, a well-knit organisation with a hierarchy under an *imam, bab, hujja* and *da'i,* reaching down to the believer (*mu'min*) and even the *mustajib* (a candidate member).[18] The lines about *'ahd* and *mithaq* quoted above are addressed to a *mustajib.*[19] This organisation had a system of initiation and a concern for training and teaching, for passing on its ideology and its own internal secrecy and discipline. If it worked in the crafts and professions (*hiraf, asnaf*) or youth organisations (*futuwwa*) or Sufi orders, it was bound to replicate its organisational structure in them. They could not be immune from their organisation nor from their politics.

Concerning the controversy over the origin of craft guilds, scholars had several problems in mind, both in affirming and denying the existence of corporate institutions in early Islam. Firstly, they referred to the ancient Greco–Roman society in which the city-state was the best example of a corporate entity, with its *agora* (marketplace), where various crafts and their organisations practised. Then, over a span of several centuries, Italian cities developed, along with a rise in municipal institutions and European universities. The question was whether there was any continuity in terms of craft organisation. Byzantine occupation and rule over Syria, Egypt and North Africa was the obvious link to which Massignon referred. He asserted early Islamic origin of guilds and their association with Shi'ite, particularly Isma'ili/Qarmatian, Sufi and youth movements. He even went so far as to say that they influenced the rise of European institutions.[20] Lewis followed him in this assertion.[21] The two maintained that, under Fatimid rule, not only was al-Azhar established as an independent university, but that the tolerance of independent commercial life led to the proliferation of guilds. Among later writers, Ashtor-Strauss used the *hisba* (a market inspection) literature to point out that professions and crafts had their *'arifs* (assistants) or heads, which denoted their autonomy.[22] He was followed by Elisséeff, who had studied the corporations of Damascus under Nur al-Din in Syria.[23] In his *Handelsgeschichte*, Subhi Labib gave examples of *ra'is al-atibba* (chief of the physicians), *kahhalin* (chief of the oculists) and *jarrahin* (chief of the surgeons) to denote the organisation of these professions.[24] Similarly L.A. Semenova, basing herself on Ibn Furat's history, wrote about the *ru'asa ahl sanayihim* (heads of the craftsmen).[25]

On the contrary, other scholars asserted just the opposite. S.M. Stern led a vicious attack on Massignon's ideas,[26] referring to his 'fancies',[27] his 'whim', his 'reckless theory, wild speculations, opacity of thought and expression, figment of an unbridled imagination',[28] as well as his 'bogus argument' and 'pell-mell collection of false logic'.[29] Stern's attack was so severe that he inhibited future fair discussion of the subject, tilting it against the existence of autonomous guilds. Stern seemed to think that accepting such an autonomy of professional life would mean an autonomy of municipal institutions in early Islamic cities which would, in turn, mean some credit to early Islam for the rise of similar institutions in Western Europe. He could not see a continuity from early Greco–Roman times to Renaissance Europe via medieval Islam.[30]

According to Stern, medieval Byzantine autonomy, as evidenced in the *Book of the Prefect* with regulations for crafts and professions of Constantinople, degenerated to such an extent that there was nothing for Islam to inherit.[31] He claimed that, since early Islam was averse to any type of organisation in general, later Western European institutions had nothing to take from it.[32] Stern claimed that he, Claude Cahen and S.D. Goitein arrived at similar conclusions independently.[33] This, however, is an overstatement. Although the other two scholars have grave doubts about the existence of craft guilds in early Islam, their attitude is not so drastic. Cahen talks about autonomous popular movements[34] and Goitein conditions his denial in relation to time, implying that loose organisations could have existed in early Islam until the twelfth century.[35] Lapidus[36] and Gabriel Baer,[37] who summarised the controversy, merely followed the new scholarly trend of that time, which denied organisation of crafts in early Islam.

Yet, Stern had to admit several points, but he did so using his own caveats. He admitted that great cities were created in early Islam, but that they neither inherited municipal institutions nor developed any of their own.[38] He claimed that market inspectors (*muhtasibs*) regulated the markets with the help of *'arifs* from different professions, but that these *'arifs* were only agents for policing and not true representatives of the professions.[39] In the same way, Stern admitted that there were *waqfs* (religious endowments) with juristic personality, but that this was only an exception.[40] He says that there were examples of *qadis* (judges) leading their cities' autonomy against larger empires, but these attempts were only 'abortive'.[41] Stern again admits that 'it is true, however, that, in the later Middle Ages, the organisation of crafts seems to become more articulate, especially by adopting the ideology of the *futuwwa*', but 'these details are, however, not of immediate relevance to our problem'.[42] Why not? Probably because they may indicate a continuity from early Islamic times.

Two sources are relevant here. First, there is the *hisba* manual, *Kitab nihayat al-rutba fi talab al-hisba* of 'Abd al-Rahman al-Shayzari, who died in 589/1193, just 20 years after the fall of the Fatimid caliphate. He says this about the *'arifs*:

> And when it is not possible to control the activity in the market by the *muhtasib*, he should recognise, for every craft, an *'arif* from the best of its members, knowledgeable about their craft, cognisant of their cheating and deceptions, well-known for his reliability and honesty, making him an overseer of their affairs.[43]

Here, one finds the *'arif* as an assistant of the *muhtasib*, but also as a representative of the craft, otherwise he could not have been described in this manner.

Another source is the *Kitab al-futuwwa* by the thirteenth-century Hanbalite shaykh Ibn Mi'mar (died in 642/1244)[44] whose sixth chapter describes the *futuwwa* organisation. Each lodge was called a *bayt*. The *futuwwa* had a genealogy of predecessors (*nisba*), that is a pedigree of masters, as well as branches (*ahzab*). Each lodge had a syndic (*kabir*, *shaykh* or *naqib*), whose relation to the members or comrades (*rafiqs*) and their assistants, apprentices or journeymen (*masabil*), was a paternal one. The syndic was the intermediary (*wasita*) for the youth (*fityan*) and their ideologue (*khatib*). The *futuwwa* members were bound by a covenant of initiation (*'ahd*), which was symbolised by the insignia of a belt (*shadd*), trousers (*sarawil*), a drink (*sharb*) and salt (*malh*). The *futuwwa* had their own rules, judicial procedures, manners and etiquette. Mustafa Jawad's edition of this work attaches an appendix which contains the text of an earlier *futuwwa* manual of Ibn al-Sa'i (circa 604/1207). It is quite likely that there were earlier *futuwwa* groups that reflected craft organisations.[45] It is interesting that, even if these organisations were Sunni in later times, their *isnad* (oral references to an authoritative source), going back to Salman al-Farisi and 'Ali ibn Abi Talib, indicate that their origins were in a Shi'ite milieu.[46]

In his introduction, Mustafa Jawad, the learned editor of the *Kitab al-futuwwa*, explains that such an organisation goes back a long way.[47] For example, Jawad mentions that Ibn al-Athir reported that, in the tenth century (361/971), in the Karkh suburb of Baghdad, there was a *naqib* of the merchants by the name of Abu Ahmad al-Musawi, who was the father of Sharif al-Radi. Similarly, the historian Muhammad ibn al-Najjar al-Baghdadi said that Abu al-Fatik ibn Ahmad al-Daylami was the judge of *fityan*, a militia organised by guild members, or *qadi al-fityan* in third/ninth century Karkh. A *hadith* (a tradition of the Prophet) is reported from the eighth century Shi'ite Imam Ja'far al-Sadiq that among the 10 qualities which the Prophet Muhammad attributed to the *fityan*, one was called *ikthar al-sana'a* (the increase of crafts). Mustafa Jawad also discussed the Shi'ite *futuwwa* orders of the tenth century, one of which is one mentioned by Ibn Mi'mar, namely, the *nabawiyya*.

Albert Hourani has pointed out[48] that the Western qualifications for the rise of modern industrial society depended upon urban entities that had autonomous associations, government and law with markets and fortifications; a necessary characteristic was also the existence of craft organisations with juristic personality as 'corporations' distinct from the individuals who composed it. In this narrow sense, the autonomous cities of Europe, the harbingers of craft and industry, were not the norm but an exception to the cities of the world. The fault does not lie with the assertion that guilds existed in early Islamic history; it lies with the requirement of conformity with a very limited European model. Behind it all was the notion that the Islamic world, unlike the West, was generally incapable of organisation. To quote Stern again, ' ... both the tendency towards municipal independence and the ultimate sterility of this tendency are phenomena characteristic of the Islamic world as a whole'.[49]

A couple of points should be noted on the question of terminology. In Arabic, the terms *sinf*, *hirfa* and *tariqa* signify both a profession and a professional organisation. Similarly, the term *da'wa* is 'a call', 'a propaganda', 'an invitation', 'a missionary purpose' and 'a well-knit organisation'. The term sultan denotes both authority in the abstract as well as a person, the head of a ruling institution. The term *futuwwa* itself means the quality of youthfulness in the abstract, and has also been applied to organisations. At the present time, an *Ittihad al-Mahamiyyin* is not just a unity of lawyers, but also an organised union. The use of the term *naqib* (syndic) in all fraternities – crafts, sects, Sufi and youth groups – suggests an overlap which serves to strengthen the organisational aspect.

Keeping this in mind, one should avoid a very narrow definition of the term 'guild'. If one calls it a corporation, complete with a juristic personality and having total or nearly complete autonomy, it is necessary to point out that such an organisation did not exist in the Islamic world or in Europe until the thirteenth century. Rather, a guild should be called a professional organisation or association. This would be true not only for manual crafts, but also for cities whose municipal functions necessarily had to be organised. If not, how would great cities such as Baghdad, Cairo, Damascus or Cordoba carry out their work? The logic of collective action is behind such an assumption.

The confusion arose, in the first place, from Massignon's use of the term 'corporation' to refer to a professional organisation or association or, at times, a labour union. Cahen, taking up the term 'corporation', as emphasised by Massignon, who strongly compared it with the European model of a specific period, began to doubt and not altogether reject the inference of guild structure as articulated by Massignon.[50] Stern, on the other hand, applying the French usage of the term 'corporation', went even further than Massignon. In Stern's words,

> Now guilds are corporations (does not the French term, corporation, mean guild?). And so the thesis about the absence of corporative institutions in Islam would run into difficulties. Moreover, it could be rightly observed that if guilds flourished in Muslim cities, it is even more surprising that no municipal institutions did evolve, since the guilds would have been a natural basis for them.[51]

This is a convoluted argument based on the presumption of the absence of municipal institutions that is supposed to prove the absence of guild structures which, in turn, must allegedly conform to the French usage of the term 'corporation', implying that such an organisation must have juristic personality and autonomy.

Conclusion

The likelihood of the presence of professional organisations in early medieval Islam is strong – it is irrelevant whether the structure of such organisations was loose. To summarise, the present inquiry began with the text of the *Rasa'il Ikhwan al-Safa'*. It examined the critique by Cahen of Massignon's assumption that the *Rasa'il* was evidence of Isma'ili penetration in the professional organisations. He does not, however, contest the Isma'ili character of the *Rasa'il*. Cahen points out that there was also a Hanbalite penetration in the professional organisations, as in the case of Ibn Wahshiyya's movement.[52] However, even if there were a later Hanbalite influence in some movements and organisations, it would not necessarily mean that there was not an Isma'ili influence in earlier ones. The quotations from the *Rasa'il* cited at the beginning of this article had most probably escaped Cahen's attention.

The *Rasa'il* was not the only work which described the proliferation of the professions in early medieval times. In his article on the professional organisations in tenth-century Baghdad, T. Fahd studied Abu Said Nasr ibn Ya'qub al-Dinawari's book, *al-Qadiri fi 'l-ta'bir*, written in 397/1006, pointing out that al-Dinawari, in chapter 12 of this book, mentions 200 manual crafts. In chapter eight, al-Dinawari gives the nomenclature for the religious hierarchies of the three monotheistic religions, and in chapter nine he presents the list of the *califal* court's functionaries. On the basis of this information, Fahd observes, '...a lively image of the Islamic medieval city overflowing with merchants, artisans, brokers and those in the caravan trade. All seemed to have been well organised. The commerce was well divided up.'[53]

With such a proliferation of crafts and professions, early Islamic urban life could not in any way be considered devoid of an organisational principle, if only for training and for the continuity of craftsmanship. In this connection, it is worthwhile to step out of the field of Islamic history into modern economic theory of groups and organisations. One of the most prominent works on the subject was written by Mancur Olson,[54] who concludes firstly that the proliferation of professional groups and their specialisation would suggest an organisation. Secondly, Olson contends that the smaller the group, the more cohesive and organised it is.[55] Thirdly, he asserts that one group's collective action benefits larger groups.[56] Olson affirms that 'groups cannot get infinitesimally small quantities of a formal organization or even of an informal group agreement; a group with a given number of members must have a certain minimal amount of organization or agreement, if it is to have any at all'.[57]

Lastly, the overlapping of goals – religious, economic or political – produced further cohesion and drive towards collective action. If one applies these principles to the situation of Islamic cities in the ninth and tenth centuries, one finds that the Fatimid Da'wa, or Brethren of Purity, had a 'small group' cohesion and that they had interest in the collective action of other autonomous larger groups, whether professional, political, religious or youth, such as the various crafts (*asnaf* or *hiraf*) in the quarters of the cities' youth groups (the *futuwwa*) or Sufi orders. This is exactly what the *Rasa'il Ikhwan al-Safa'* describes.

Bibliography

Ali, Zahid, *Tarikhi fatimiyyin-i-misr* (in Urdu), Hyderabad, Deccan, 1948.

Amin, Ahmad and Ahmad al-Zayn (eds), *Kitab al-imta' wa'l-mu'anasa*, 3 vols in 1 vol., Beirut, 2nd ed., al-Maktaba al-Asriyya, 1953.

Ashtor-Strauss, E., 'L'administration urbaine en Syrie medievale', *Rivista degli Studi Orientali (RSO)* 31, 1956, pp. 71–128.

— 'L'urbanisme syrien à la basse-époque', *RSO* 33, 1958, pp. 181–209.

Baer, Gabriel, 'Guilds in Middle Eastern History' in M.A. Cook (ed.), *Studies in the Economic History of the Middle East*, London, Oxford University Press, 1970, pp. 11–30.

Boak, E.R., 'The organization of guilds in Greco–Roman Egypt', *American Philological Association: Transactions* 68, 1937, pp. 212–20.

Breebaart, D.A., 'The Futuvvet name-i-Kebir: A manual of Turkish guilds', *Journal of the Economic and Social History of the Orient* 15, 1972, pp. 203–15.

Bustani, Butrus (ed.), *Rasa'il Ikhwan al-Safa'*, Beirut, Dar Sadir, 4 vols, 1957.

Cahen, Claude, 'Mouvements populaires et autonomisme urbain dans l'Asie musulmane de Moyen Âge', *Arabica* 5, 1958, pp. 225–50; *Arabica* 6 1959a, pp. 25–56; *Arabica* 6, 1959b, pp. 233–65.

— 'Y a-t-il eu des corporations professionelles dans la monde musulmane classique?' in A.H. Hourani and S.M. Stern (eds), *The Islamic City*, Oxford, Bruno Cassirer/University of Pennsylvania Press, 1970, pp. 51–63.

— 'Futuwwa', *Encyclopedia of Islam*, 2nd ed., Brill, 1983, pp. 961–9.

Elisséeff, N., 'Les 'corporations' de Damas sous Nur al-Din', *Arabica* 3, 1956, pp. 61–79.

Fahd, T., 'Les corps de métiers au IV/Xe siècle à Baghdad', *Journal of Economic and Social History of the Orient* 8, ii, November 1965, pp. 186–212.

Goitein, S.D., 'The working people of the Mediterranean during the high middle ages' in S.D. Goitein (ed.), *Studies in Islamic History and Institutions*, Leiden, Brill, 1966, pp. 255–78.

— 'The working people' in S.D. Goitein (ed.), *A Mediterranean Society*, Berkeley and Los Angeles, CA, University of California Press, 1967, I, pp. 77–99.

Hamdani, Husayn, '*Rasa'il Ikhwan al-Safa*' in the literature of the Isma'ili Tayibi Da'wat', *Der Islam* 20, 1932, pp. 281–300.

Hamdani, Abbas, 'Evolution of the organizational structure of the Fatimi Da'wah', *Arabian Studies*, Cambridge University, 3, 1976, pp. 84–114.

— 'Abu Hayyan al-Tawhidi and the Brethren of Purity', *The International Journal of Middle Eastern Studies* 9, 1978, pp. 343–53.

— 'An early Fatimid source on the time and authorship of the *Rasa'il Ihwan al-Safa*", *Arabica* 26, 1979, pp. 62–75.

— 'Shades of Shi'ism in the tracts of the Brethren of Purity' in *Traditions in Contact and Change*, Waterloo (Ontario), Wilfred Laurier University Press, 1983, pp. 447–60, 726–28.

— 'The arrangement of the *Rasa'il Ikhwan al-Safa*' and the problem of interpolations', *Journal of Semitic Studies* 29, 1984, pp. 97–110.

Hourani, Albert, 'The Islamic city in the light of recent research' in A.H. Hourani and S.M. Stern (eds), *The Islamic City*, Oxford, Bruno Cassirer/University of Pennsylvania Press, 1970, pp. 9–24.

Ibn Mi'mar (Abu 'Abd Allah Muhammad ibn Abi 'l-Makarim al-Baghdadi al-Hanbali), *Kitab al-futuwwa*, eds Mustafa Jawad, Muhammad al-Hilali *et al.*, with an introduction by Mustafa Jawad, Baghdad, Maktabat al-Muthanna, 1958.

Labib, Subhi Y., *Handelgeschichte Agyptens im Spatmittelalter (1171–1517)*, Wiesbaden, F. Steiner, 1965.

Lapidus, Ira, *Muslim Cities in Later Middle Ages*, Cambridge, MA, Harvard University Press, 1967.

Lewis, Bernard, 'The Islamic guilds', *Economic History Review* 8, London, 1937–8, pp. 20–37.

– *Origins of Isma'ilism*, Cambridge, Heffer and Sons, 1940.

– 'An epistle on manual crafts', *Islamic Culture*, Hyderabad, Deccan, 27, 1943, pp. 142–52.

Marquet, Yves, 'La place du travail dans la hiérarchie Isma'ilienne d'après *l'Encyclopédie des Frères de la Pureté*', *Arabica* 8, September 1961, pp. 225–37.

– 'Ikhwan al-Safa'', *Encyclopedia of Islam*, 2nd ed., 1986, pp. 1071–6.

Massignon, Louis, 'Les corps de métiers et la cité islamique', *Revue Internationale de Sociologie*, 28, 1920, pp. 473–89.

– 'La Futuwwa, ou pacte d'honneur artisanale entre les travailleurs musulmans au Moyen Âge', *Nouvelle Clio*, Brussels, 1952, pp. 171–98.

– 'Karmatian', *Encyclopedia of Islam* (1st ed.), reprint 1987a, pp. 767–72.

– 'Sinf', *Encyclopedia of Islam* (1st ed.), reprint 1987b, pp. 436–7.

Nasr, Syed Hosein, *An Introduction to Islamic Cosmological Doctrines: Conceptions of Nature and Methods Used for its Study by the Ikhwan al-Safa, al-Biruni, and Ibn Sina*, Boulder, CO, Shambhala, 1978.

Olson, Mancur, *The Logic of Collective Action: Public Goods and the Theory of Groups*, vol. 124, Cambridge, MA, Harvard University Press, Harvard Economic Studies, 1965.

Semenova, L.A., *Salah ad-din i mamluki v Egipte*, Moscow, Izd vo 'Nauka' Glav red. Vosrochnoi lit-ry, 1966.

Shayzari, 'Abd al-Rahman ibn Nasr al- (d. 589/1193), *Kitab nihayat al-rutba fi talab al-hisba, ed. al-Sayyid al-Baz al-Arini*, Beirut, Dar al-Thaqafa, n.d. (after 1946).

Stern, S.M. 'The authorship of the Epistles of the *Ikhwan al-Safa*'', *Islamic Culture* 20, October 1946, pp. 367–72.

– 'Addendum to the authorship of the Epistles of the *Ikhwan al-Safa*'', *Islamic Culture* 21, October 1947, pp. 403–4.

– 'New information about the authors of the Epistles of Sincere Brethren', *Islamic Studies* 3, 1964, pp. 405–28.

– 'The constitution of the Islamic city' in A.H. Hourani and S.M. Stern (eds), *The Islamic City*, Oxford, Bruno Cassirer/University of Pennsylvania Press, 1970, pp. 25–49.

Thropp, Sylvia L., 'Guilds', *International Encyclopaedia of the Social Sciences*, London/New York, MacMillan, 1972, pp. 184–7.

Tibawi, A.L., 'Ikhwan al-Safa' and their *Rasa'il*: a critical review of a century and a half of research', *Islamic Quarterly*, 1955, pp. 28–46.

Vryonis, Spero, 'Byzantine HMOKPATIA and the guilds in the eleventh century', *Dumbarton Oaks Papers*, Washington, DC, 1963, no 17, pp. 288–314

— 'Byzantine circus factions and Islamic *futuwwa* organizations (Neaniai, Fityan, Ahdath)', *Byzantinische Zeitschrift* 58, 1965, pp. 46–59.

Weber, Max, *The City*, Glencoe, IL, Free Press, 1958.

Notes on Chapter 9

1   The following complete editions of this work have been printed: *Kitab Ikhwan al-Safa'*, ed. Wilayat Husayn, Bombay, 1888; *Rasa'il Ikhwan al-Safa'*, 4 vols, ed. Khayr al-Din al-Zarkali, Cairo, 1928 with two separate introductions by Taha Husayn and Ahmad Zaki Pasha; *Rasa'il Ikhwan al-Safa'*, 4 vols, ed. Butrus Bustani, Beirut, Dar Sadir, 1957 (page numbers in the present work refer to the latter edition, abbr. Beirut/Bustani); *Rasa'il Ikhwan al-Safa'*, 5 vols, ed. 'Arif Tamir, Beirut and Paris, Manshurat Uwaydat, 1415/1995 (abbr. Beirut/Tamir).

2   The following editions of the concluding sections of the *Rasa'il* have been printed: *al-Risalat al-Jami'a*, 2 vols, ed. Jamil Saliba, Damascus, 1969 (the editor considers the attribution of this work to al-Majriti as valid); *al-Risalat al-Jami'a*, ed. Mustafa Ghalib, Beirut, Dar Sadir, 1974; and the same work included in the fifth volume of Beirut/Tamir, mentioned above.

3   See particularly Marquet, 1986 and the bibliography contained in it; also Hamdani, 1976; Ali, 1948; Tibawi, 1955; Nasr, 1978; Stern, 1946, 1947 and 1964; also the studies in note 4 below.

4   Hamdani 1978, 1979, 1983 and 1984 (among other studies on the subject).

5   Abu Hayyan al-Tawhidi, the celebrated man of letters, was reading the *Encyclopaedia* between 373/983 and 375/985 as mentioned in his *Kitab al-imta' wa'l-mu'anasa*, which was composed in those years.

6   Lewis, 1943.

7   Lewis, 1937–8.

8   Massignon, 1920, 1987a, 1987b.

9   Marquet, 1961.

10 Lewis, 1943, p. 143. The description that follows is summarised from this article which has the best analysis of this eighth epistle.

11 Bustani, 1957, vol. 4, p. 165.

12 *Ibid.*, p. 188.

13 *Ibid.*, p. 151.

14 Massignon and Lewis, in their works cited in the Bibliography, maintained that there was such a link. In his article on 'Futuwwa' in the *Encyclopedia of Islam*, Claude Cahen says that 'there have probably always been guilds (*sinf*, pl. *asnaf*, Turkish *esnaf*) in the towns of the Islamic Orient' but that he doubts their link with the *futuwwa* of earlier centuries. He does admit, a few lines further on, that the guild documents of the sixteenth century were known as Futuvvet-namehs. On these documents, see Breebaart, 1972. For earlier *futuwwa*, see Massignon, 1952.

15 Bustani, 1957, vol. 4, pp. 51–2. The English translation is that of Lewis, 1940, pp. 94–5.

16 Bustani, 1957, vol. 3, p. 501.

17 *Ibid.*, vol. 4, p. 187.

18 See Hamdani, 1976.

19 Bustani, 1957, vol. 4, p. 186.

20 Massignon, 1920, 1987a, 1987b.

21 Lewis, 1937–1938.

22 Ashtor-Strauss, 1956, 1958.

23 Elisséeff, 1956.

24 Labib, 1965.

25 Semenova, 1966, p. 166.

26 Stern, 1970.

27 *Ibid.*, p. 37.

28 *Ibid.*, p. 40.

29 *Ibid.*, p. 39.

30 See Boak, 1937.

31 *Ibid.*, p. 45. For a view contrary to that of Stern's: Vryonis, 1963, 1965.

32 This view is indirectly stated, buttressed by Max Weber's view that the absence of municipal institutions in Islam is due to tribal traditions of the Arabs: Weber, 1958, p. 100; Stern, 1970, pp. 30, 49.

33 Stern, 1970, p. 42. However, Claude Cahen, in a postscript to his article, 'Y a-t-il eu des corporations professionelles dans la monde musulmane classique?' (Cahen, 1970, p. 63), writes about Stern's and his contributions as follows: 'Il est évident que ces deux efforts se recouvrent partiellement, et chacun de nous par consequent dois renvoyer à l'autre. Cependant, bien entendu, chacun de nous a sa maniere propre, et les deux communications ne sont pas identiques. Leur convergence n'en a que plus de poids.'

34 Cahen, 1958, 1959a, 1959b.

35 Goitein, 1966, pp. 267–70; Goitein, 1967.

36 Lapidus, 1967, pp. 96, 98, 101.

37 Baer, 1970.

38 Stern, 1970, pp. 30–1.
39 *Ibid.*, p. 43.
40 *Ibid.*, p. 48.
41 *Ibid.*, pp. 33–4.
42 *Ibid.*, p. 45.
43 Shayzari, n.d., p. 12.
44 Ibn Mi'mar, 1958, sixth and seventh chapters on *futuwwa* organisation and rules of behaviour, pp. 190–296.
45 *Ibid.*, 'Addendum', pp. 297–301.
46 *Ibid.*, 'Introduction', pp. 13, 53.
47 These details are given in Mustafa Jawad's introduction, *Ibid.*, pp. 5–99, particularly pp. 49–51.
48 Hourani, 1970, pp. 13–4.
49 Stern, 1970, p. 35.
50 Cahen, 1959a, pp. 54–5. Cahen acknowledges that later (seventh century) *futuwwa* groups, as described by Evliya Celebi, did have professional guild structure, but doubts that there has been a convergence between the *futuwwa* and professional organisations in earlier times.
51 Stern, 1970, p. 37.
52 Cahen, 1959a, pp. 55–6.
53 '... et d'abord, une image vivante d'une cite islamique du Moyen age, où grouille une foule de commercants, artisans, courtiers, caravaniers. Tout semble bien organisé; le commerce est fractionné.' Fahd, 1965.
54 I am grateful to John B. Thornberry, professor of Management at the American University in Cairo (AUC) for pointing out this work to me and for his critique of my paper. I am also grateful to David Blanks of the AUC's English department for going through my paper and making useful criticisms.
55 Olson, 1965, p. 35.
56 *Ibid.*
57 *Ibid.*, p. 47.

Part Three:
MONEY

CHAPTER 10

Interaction Between the Monetary Regimes of Istanbul, Cairo and Tunis, 1700–1875

Şevket Pamuk

Until the sixteenth century, the Ottoman state, which covered most of Anatolia and the Balkans, had a unified monetary system based on the gold sultani and the silver akçe. As the Ottoman state territorially expanded to become a fully fledged empire, however, this simple system could not be continued. Across the large empire, the Ottomans pursued a two-tiered approach to money and currency. With a single gold coin, the ultimate symbol of sovereignty, the empire was unified from the Balkans to Egypt and the Maghreb. Whether Ottoman gold coinage was issued in a territory depended upon its status – whether it was part of the empire proper or whether it was considered a province with some degree of autonomy. The standards of the sultani (or sherif, as it was also called), that is its weight and fineness, were kept identical to those of the Venetian ducat, which had become the accepted standard of payment in long-distance trade across the Mediterranean and beyond.

In the silver coinage used in daily transactions and, to some extent in long-distance trade, the central government chose to retain most of the local currencies in the newly conquered territories. The most important reason for this preference was the wish to avoid economic disruption and possible popular unrest. It is also not clear whether the central government had the fiscal, administrative and economic resources to unify the silver coinage of the empire.

This study examines the recovery of the Ottoman monetary system during the eighteenth century and the monetary linkages between Istanbul, Cairo and Tunis, as well as Algiers and Tripoli, until late in the nineteenth century.[1]

The New Ottoman Kurush in the Eighteenth Century

The decline and disappearance of the akçe during the seventeenth century had posed serious challenges to the Ottoman administration. Without control over the currency, its control over the economy diminished considerably. In addition, in the absence of a currency, the government could not use debasements as a means of obtaining fiscal revenue in times of difficulty. Perhaps most important of all, the disintegration of the monetary system and the increasing reliance on foreign coins had serious political implications. During the second half of the seventeenth century, the government made numerous attempts to establish a new currency but these were unsuccessful due to the continuation of wars and fiscal difficulties. After a long interval of inactivity, the mint in Istanbul resumed operation in 1685, producing akçes and copper mangirs. Large volumes of copper coinage issued from 1689 to 1691 provided the hard-pressed treasury with the much-needed fiscal support; the government then renewed its efforts to establish a new currency system around a large silver unit modelled after the European coins circulating in the Ottoman markets since the middle of the sixteenth century.[2]

The first large silver coins were minted in 1690, after the popular Polish isolette or zolota which was imported in large quantities by Dutch merchants during the seventeenth century.[3] These coins were about one-third smaller than the Dutch thalers. The new monetary scale was not clearly established, however, until the early decades of the eighteenth century, when the new Ottoman kurush or piastre was fixed at 120 akçes or 40 paras. The early kurush weighed six and a quarter dirhams (20g) and contained close to 60 per cent silver. The zolotas were valued at three-quarters of the kurush or 90 akçes. Their fractions were then minted accordingly. By the 1720s, a full spectrum of silver coinage had thus emerged, from the kurush down to the para and the tiny akçe. While the kurush, zolota and 20-para piece were used for medium and larger transactions, the para became the basic unit of account for small transactions.[4] In order to provide some perspective of the monetary magnitudes here, it might help to mention that the daily wage of an unskilled construction worker in Istanbul was approximately 8 paras or 24 akçes during the early decades of the eighteenth century.[5]

Until the end of the 1760s, the eighteenth century was a period of relative peace, stability and economic expansion for the Ottoman Empire. Available evidence on production is limited, but it does point to an increasing trend for agriculture and artisanal activity, as well as investment in manufacturing in many parts of the Balkans and Anatolia.[6] There also occurred a considerable expansion in the trade with Ottoman Central and Western Europe during this period, especially through the Mediterranean and, to a lesser extent, across land in the Balkans. French merchants based in Marseilles controlled the maritime trade until the French revolution.[7] This was a period of stability for state finances as well. Archival evidence shows that from the 1720s until the end of the 1760s the trend was towards balanced budgets, and surpluses were enjoyed in many years. The improvement in financial conditions was especially apparent during the extended period of peace in the mid-century, from 1747 to 1768.[8]

The Ottoman kurush was relatively stable during this period. In addition to favourable state finances, the new currency was supported by rising levels of mint output. This trend was, in part, due to the operation of new silver mines in Anatolia, Gümüşhhane, Keban and Ergani, whose combined annual output reached 35–40 tonnes during the 1730s. The older silver mines in the Balkans, in Sidrekapsi and Kratova, also continued to contribute. Economic expansion, coupled with fiscal stability and rising levels of mint output, thus helped the kurush to establish itself as both the leading unit of account and the leading means of exchange – first in areas close to Istanbul and later on in the century in the provinces. In addition, the fact that global monetary conditions were more stable during the eighteenth century in comparison to the seventeenth certainly helped the new currency.

Silver thus regained a position of prominence within the Ottoman monetary system. The silver content of the kurush declined at a moderate pace, by a total of 40 per cent from the 1720s until the end of the 1760s (see end of chapter). The exchange rate of the Ottoman currency against the ducat declined at a similar pace, from 3 kurush to 4 kurush during these four decades. This overall rate of debasement is certainly not insignificant. Nonetheless, the stability of the kurush during this period stands in sharp contrast to both the seventeenth century, when the akçe had disappeared from circulation, and the early nineteenth century, when the silver content of the kurush declined very rapidly.

At the same time, however, periodic scarcity of coinage continued in the provinces. Moreover, the silver content of the new coins fluctuated frequently, especially in the earlier period, causing a considerable amount of confusion and eroding confidence towards Ottoman coins. As a result, the popularity of European coins persisted, especially in the distant provinces. In many provinces, the kurush did not become the leading currency until the second half of the eighteenth century. Nonetheless, in most of the Balkans and Anatolia, and later on in Syria and elsewhere, prices, government payments and obligations and, more generally, larger monetary magnitudes began to be expressed in terms of this new unit. The eastern Mediterranean began to be drawn increasingly to European circuits of finance and multilateral payments during the eighteenth century. As a result, bills of exchange, which had circulated for centuries in this region, began to be used much more frequently not only between Ottoman and European ports but also within the empire.

Another important trend in the eighteenth century was the increasing centralisation of mint activity in the former akçe region stretching from the Balkans to eastern Anatolia. Continuing a pattern which began in the seventeenth century, the number of active mints in this region remained sharply reduced. In the second half of the century, the kurush and its fractions were minted almost exclusively in Istanbul. The provincial mints in the Balkans, Anatolia and Syria struck a limited amount of copper coinage.[9]

As for gold coins, the Ottoman sultani, which had remained close to the standards of the Venetian ducat since the fifteenth century, was discontinued late in the seventeenth century. In the early part of the eighteenth century, however, as gold made a comeback in Europe and elsewhere, Ottoman minting activity also resumed. In the place of the sultani, a number of new gold coins called tughrali, jedid Istanbul, zincirli, findik and zeri-mahbub were initiated between 1697 and 1728. Eventually, the findik became the most widely used gold coin across the empire.

The relative success of the kurush diminished the role of European currencies, especially in regions close to Istanbul. European silver units such as the Dutch thaler, Spanish eight-real piece and their German and Austrian counterparts continued to be used in international trade and domestic payments, but not as widely as in the seventeenth century. The Venetian ducat reasserted itself in the eighteenth century as the leading European coin and the leading unit of account in international payments around the eastern Mediterranean. Gold coins were used for large transactions and for store of value purposes, but they played a limited role in daily transactions. The exchange rates of all gold and foreign coins continued to be determined in local markets, although during extraordinary periods such as wars the government attempted to control all monetary rates.

Linkages with Other Currencies of the Empire

Another important development of the eighteenth century was the strengthening of ties between Istanbul and other currencies of the empire. The disappearance of the akçe and the fiscal, political and administrative difficulties of the central government during the seventeenth century had made it impossible for Istanbul to control or direct monetary practices in the provinces. In the areas bordering Iran, the shahi was discontinued in the early part of the century and the silver nasri of Tunis also had difficulties. By comparison, the para of Egypt did reasonably well in the seventeenth century, expanding at the expense of the akçe in Syria and other bordering areas, such as the island of Crete. Even in the *para* region, however, European coins had gained ground against Ottoman currencies.

In contrast, ties between Istanbul and currencies in different parts of the empire – such as Egypt, Tripoli, Tunis and Algiers – recovered, and even strengthened during the eighteenth century. The following survey, based on numismatic and other sources, examines this important trend for the first time. The new evidence from monetary history thus suggests that linkages between the centre and periphery of the empire were stronger during the eighteenth century than has been assumed until now.

The Para in Egypt

The historiography of Egypt has long emphasised that the provinces gained considerable autonomy from the central government during the eighteenth century.[10] However, recent research has shown that Istanbul continued to exert a good deal of control, and that political and administrative ties to the capital were considerable.[11] Examination of the monetary linkages between Istanbul and Cairo during this period has revealed a good deal of evidence supporting the latter thesis.

Despite the minting of large silver coins and the creation of a new monetary unit in Istanbul, the para continued as the basic silver coin and leading unit of account in Egypt until late in the eighteenth century. Even though the government in Istanbul demanded the minting of larger silver coins in Egypt, local authorities resisted this request. Officials from Istanbul were periodically sent to Cairo to inspect the mint to ensure that the standards established for the para of Cairo would be followed.[12]

One issue of almost permanent concern for Istanbul was the lower standards or lower silver content of the Egyptian para vis-à-vis the para and kurush of Istanbul. Since the exchange rate between the two units remained fixed, the divergence in the respective silver contents led to an outflow of silver from the Istanbul region to Egypt. Another reason for the government's concern was the annual remittance sent from Cairo to Istanbul, which had been fixed at 600,000 gold sultanis per annum – not an insignificant amount in terms of both budgetary receipts in Istanbul and Cairo and inter-regional payments flows within the empire. The amounts reaching Istanbul were far below that amount, however, and the actual payments were often made in Cairo paras. During the first half of the eighteenth century, these varied between 8 and 30 million paras, averaging 18 million paras or 135,000 gold pieces per year.[13] In addition, the annual remittances sent from the account of the sultan in Egypt to the holy cities in Arabia in the eighteenth century rose from about 500,000 paras to 10 million paras.[14] The decline in the standards of the para thus meant lower actual receipts for the treasury in Istanbul.

Despite Istanbul's efforts, however, the gap between the silver content of the coins minted in Istanbul and Cairo persisted. The size of this difference fluctuated and occasionally reached 20 or even 30 per cent.[15] Nonetheless, despite the short-term fluctuations and an almost permanent gap between the actual silver content of the two units, the para of Cairo remained linked to the kurush and the para of Istanbul on a long-term basis. As the latter lost about 40 per cent of their silver content from the 1720s to the 1760s, the Egyptian unit followed it downwards. The exchange rates of the two units against the benchmark ducat also show that the two were well linked.[16] This broad linkage between the two units was severed in the 1760s, however, as the economic and fiscal crises in Egypt led to a sharp decline in the silver content of the para to about the half of that of corresponding coins minted in Istanbul.[17]

The large silver kurush, together with its multiples and fractions, finally began to be minted in Cairo in 1769–70 during the rule of 'Ali Bey. This practice was continued until the end of the century by his successors.[18] The first kurush of Cairo weighed about 15 grams and its fineness varied between 31 and 48 per cent. It thus contained 40–60 per cent less silver than the contemporary kurush of Istanbul.[19] On the eve of the occupation of Egypt by Napoleon in 1798, the silver content of the kurush of Cairo was still comparable to but lower than the kurush being minted at Istanbul. The gap between the two units had closed because of the major debasement in Istanbul in 1789.

The absence of a large domestic silver coin in Egypt until late in the eighteenth century created additional demand for and put pressure on the domestic and European gold coins as the medium of circulation, especially for larger transactions.[20] In the last decade of the seventeenth century, following the lead of Istanbul, a series of new gold coins were minted in Egypt. The Istanbul or tughrali began to be minted in 1696–7 as the replacement for the sherifi, which had been issued since the early part of the sixteenth century; the zincirli replaced it in 1707. The last addition to the list was the findik, which began to be minted in 1725.[21]

In the second half of the eighteenth century, the most frequently used gold piece in both Egypt and Istanbul was the zeri-mahbub. The findik, zeri-mahbub and other gold coins of Egypt contained less gold, and so exchanged at a discount against their Istanbul counterparts. For example, in 1731, the official rate in Istanbul for the tughrali of Istanbul was 3 kurush and for the zincirli of Istanbul was 3 kurush and 40 akçes. During the same year, the official rates in Istanbul for the tughrali of Egypt was 2 kurush and 75 akçes, while the zincirli of Egypt was at 2 kurush and 90 akçes, indicating that the value of the Egyptian coins was 15–20 per cent less than the value of the Istanbul coins.

The government in Egypt encouraged the trade and inflows of gold from the south across the Sahara. These flows – closely related to the arrival of Muslim pilgrims from sub-Saharan Africa – continued in the early part of the eighteenth century, but apparently declined after the 1730s. It is also estimated that by this period their volume was not large in comparison to the mint activity in Cairo.[22] Because of this connection and possibly for other reasons, Egypt generally experienced a relative abundance of gold, but had shortages of silver in relation to the Istanbul region. In its bilateral payments with Istanbul, Egypt often experienced outflows of gold but inflows of silver.[23]

In Istanbul, copper coinage remained exceptional in the eighteenth century, whereas varieties of copper coins called fels and jedid were minted in Egypt. Most of these coins weighed about 40–50 per cent of a dirham (1.2 to 1.6 grams). Their nominal values varied from 8 to 18 jedid for one para. Copper coinage was discontinued towards the end of the century, however, when debasements and inflation made it unnecessary to issue fractions of the para.[24]

Of the European coins in Egypt, the Dutch thaler (esedi gurush) and the Spanish eight-real piece (riyal kurush) declined in importance during the first half of the eighteenth century, as elsewhere in the eastern Mediterranean. They were replaced by the Venetian ducat – called bunduqi or naturalised as sherifi bunduqi, which made a comeback in the eighteenth century, and by the Hungarian gold piece (sherifi magar), the German thaler and the Austrian (Maria Theresa) thaler, which was especially popular in Yemen and the Arabian peninsula.[25]

Syria continued to play the role of a zone of transition between the currencies of Anatolia and Egypt during the eighteenth century, as had been the case earlier. The akçe of Istanbul had disappeared in Syria with the decline of mint activity in Istanbul and Anatolia after the 1640s. As a result, the para of Egypt had become the leading unit of account for small magnitudes in most of Syria during the seventeenth century.[26] For larger magnitudes, the Dutch thaler remained the leading unit of account, as well as being the basic medium of exchange in Syria until the early part of the eighteenth century.

Along with the emergence and modest success of the kurush, the new unit began to establish itself as the basic silver currency and leading unit of account in many parts of Syria. As the century progressed, the kurush of Istanbul gained in importance, replacing not only the para of Egypt – which was having its own difficulties, especially after mid-century – but also some of the European coinage. There existed considerable regional variations within Greater Syria, however.[27] In Aleppo, in the north, for example, the kurush, together with its fractions and multiples, became the unit of account as well as the leading means of exchange.[28] Similarly, along the Syrian coast, the Dutch thaler, the Spanish riyal kurush and the Venetian ducat were the leading currencies in the early part of the century. After mid-century, the Ottoman kurush became increasingly prominent, both in long-distance trade and domestic transactions.[29] In Damascus, the kurush became the leading unit of account and means of payment in medium and large transactions, but the Egyptian para (misriyya) survived at least as a unit of account for small magnitudes until the end of the eighteenth century.[30]

Linkages between the money markets of Anatolia, Syria and Egypt grew stronger during this period. Recently compiled evidence from the court records shows that the exchange rates in Damascus between the leading gold and large silver coins of Europe, such as the ducat, esedi gurush and riyal kurush closely followed those in Istanbul and Cairo.[31] One might speculate here that, given the re-establishment of the Istanbul-based currency in many parts of Syria – especially in the north – as well as the general economic expansion of the eighteenth century, economic linkages between Anatolia and Syria must have increased during the eighteenth century.

The kurush was less successful in Iraq. While it gradually emerged as the leading unit of account during the eighteenth century, its availability remained limited until it began to be minted in Baghdad in 1814 (1229 AH).[32] There is, however, evidence of increasing popularity of the kurush even amongst the tribal population of Iraq during the latter part of the eighteenth century.[33]

The early decades of the nineteenth century, that is from the occupation of Egypt by Napoleon in 1798 until the monetary reforms of Muhammad 'Ali in 1834, were a turbulent period for currency in Egypt. In the absence of detailed information about the silver content of the Egyptian coinage during this interval, the deterioration of the Egyptian para can be followed from its exchange rates. Between 1798 and 1834, the para lost more than 80 per cent of its value against the Maria Theresa thaler, a stable silver coin – declining from 150 paras per thaler to 800. This is a little less than but quite close to the total decline of the kurush of Istanbul during the same period. In addition, the timing of the overall decline was remarkably similar to that in Istanbul.[34] It thus appears that, despite considerable political tensions and even military confrontation between the centres, the para and kurush of Cairo followed the Istanbul unit downwards.[35] Regarding gold coins, the administration of Muhammad 'Ali continued to mint the zeri-mahbub of the eighteenth century, but these were of limited significance.

It is interesting that, even during the 1820s and 1830s, when the reformist governor Muhammad 'Ali successfully fought the Ottoman armies for the independence of Egypt and threatened to replace the Ottoman dynasty with his own, he chose to keep the two currencies linked. The strength of the commercial linkages between the two regions must have played an important role in the persistence of the monetary linkage.[36] It is also likely that, in the rapid depreciation of the kurush in Istanbul, Muhammad 'Ali saw an opportunity for his own government to generate additional fiscal revenue and thus went along with the debasements.[37] As Muhammad 'Ali was a number of steps ahead of Istanbul in the reform process, he was also the first to invite European monetary specialists. Following their advice, Egypt adopted the bi-metallic standard in 1834.

With these monetary reforms, Egypt had embraced the bi-metallic system 10 years ahead of the Ottomans in Istanbul.[38] Gold and silver standards adopted for Egyptian coinage were then retained until the First World War. All coins minted in Egypt during the era of Muhammad 'Ali and his successors continued to bear the names of the Ottoman sultans.[39]

The Riyal of Tunis

Following two decades of civil war, Husayn ibn 'Ali – a leader of the Turkish Janissaries who had settled in Tunisia – obtained the title *beylerbeyi pasha* from the Ottoman sultan and established a new hereditary dynasty in 1705, which was to rule Tunis for more than two centuries. After a failed attempt to re-establish its authority in 1715, the Ottoman government contented itself with demonstrations of submission from this distant province without contesting the autonomy which its rulers enjoyed. While Egypt was expected to send an annual remittance to Istanbul, the same did not apply to the Maghreb, Tripoli, Tunis or Algiers. Aside from occasional gifts to the sultan and other influential people, regular payments to the state treasury were not expected from these provinces.[40]

The most important economic developments in Tunisia during the eighteenth century were growing trade with Europe based on the exportation of agricultural products and the decline in corsairing under pressure from the European powers. Since Tunis did not possess mines, external trade balances determined the changes in its specie stocks. The Mediterranean trade was the most important, but the regency also had access – albeit to a lesser extent than Algiers – to sub-Saharan gold, through trade with that region. The volume of mint activity increased during periods of trade surpluses and declined with trade deficits as the specie stock declined.[41]

Tunis had experienced a good deal of monetary instability during the seventeenth century, as was the case in many parts of the Mediterranean. The small, square nasri and the larger harruba, which began to be minted towards the end of the century, could not meet the economy's demand for a stable medium of exchange. Attempts at monetary reform had began in the early part of the eighteenth century after the devaluation in 1703. The reform of coinage operations by Husayn ibn 'Ali in 1714 severed the official one-to-one link between the debased local currency and the Spanish real; it prohibited the use of the latter in domestic transactions and established a new unit called the riyal.[42] The mint in Tunis began to issue larger silver coins with the denomination of a one-quarter riyal in the same year. Other fractions began to be minted later and the one-riyal coin arrived in 1766.[43]

With these large silver coins, the mint in Tunis re-established monetary links with Istanbul that had been severed in the seventeenth century. The Tunisian riyal included inscriptions such as 'sultan of the two lands and lord of the two seas; sultan, son of the sultan' and 'may his victory be glorious'; these were identical to those used in the large kurush coinage minted in Istanbul, beginning with Mustafa II (1695–1703) and Ahmed III (1703–30). The designs of these coins, including the tughra of the sultan, may have been sent from Istanbul. The Tunisian mint continued with the same design until the early part of the nineteenth century, even though Istanbul had adopted a variety of other designs later in the eighteenth century.[44]

While the designs of the coinage were closely related, if not identical, the silver content of the riyal and the kurush followed independent courses in the short and medium terms. Between 1700 and 1850, however, the overall rate of debasements in Tunis, Istanbul and Cairo were roughly comparable. The riyal experienced a sharp debasement and depreciation in the early part of the century, especially during the first decade after it had been issued. Between 1725 and the 1760s, it lost about 60 per cent of its initial silver content, while the kurush of Istanbul was more stable, losing less than 30 per cent of its silver content. When the first full riyal or piastre coin of Tunis was minted during the reign of Mustafa III (1757–74), it weighed 15.2 grams and contained 39 per cent fine silver – 5.9 grams of pure silver. At that time, the kurush of Istanbul contained approximately 12.9 grams of pure silver. The riyal remained little changed during the half century until the 1810s, and then experienced another round after rapid depreciation. It lost about one-third of its silver content from 1800 to 1830, by which time its silver content stood at 22 per cent of its 1725 level.

Unlike the case of the mint in Cairo, no evidence has so far been located, either at the Ottoman archives in Istanbul or at the mint archives in Tunis, to suggest that the central government in Istanbul tried to control the course of the currency in Tunis. The circumstances behind the depreciation of the riyal are not yet well understood. If the experience of the kurush in Istanbul is any guide, fiscal causes probably played an important role, but additional research on the monetary and fiscal conditions in Tunis are needed before that question can be answered more satisfactorily.[45]

The gold coins issued by the Tunis mint during the first half of the eighteenth century continued to follow the design and the standards of the sultanis even though the latter were discontinued in Istanbul and Cairo in the 1690s.[46] However, the sultanis and half-sultanis (as they were called) that were minted in Tunis had lower gold content than their seventeenth-century counterparts in the eastern Mediterranean. The standards of the sultanis of Tunis may have been following the zeri-mahbub gold pieces minted in Istanbul and Cairo at that time. In any case, after mid-century, the gold pieces of Tunis also began to be referred to as zeri-mahbub.[47] The volume of these issues were limited, especially in relation to the gold coins minted in Algiers.[48] They were carried to the eastern Mediterranean by European merchants and used in Mediterranean trade.[49]

In Tunis, the nasris or aspres were minted irregularly until at least the end of the eighteenth century. In addition, copper coinage called bourbe, fels and qafsi were issued throughout the century. European coinage, especially the Spanish eight-real piece, the Dutch thaler and the Venetian ducat, continued to play an important role in trade and payments. Of the two leading European silver coins, the Spanish piastre was used more widely in the western Mediterranean, Algiers and Tunis, whereas the Dutch thaler was more prominent in Tripoli and the eastern Mediterranean.[50] Moroccan coinage also circulated in Tunis during the eighteenth century.

With the coinage reform of 1847, 13 years after a similar move had been undertaken by Muhammad 'Ali in Egypt and three years after a similar shift in Istanbul, the Tunisian currency moved to the bi-metallic system at the gold–silver ratio of 14.85. To some extent, Istanbul and Tunis were both influenced by the example of Muhammad 'Ali. More importantly, however, international pressure – institutional, political and economic – played a key role in the transition of these monetary systems to bi-metalism at about the same time. The new standards of Tunisian coinage remained unchanged for the rest of the nineteenth century.[51]

The monetary policies of the Tunisian government soon lost all independence: no reform could be undertaken without the foreign consulates first being informed. In 1847, the *bey* of Tunis decided to open a bank, issue paper notes and mint new coinage, and the announcement of these measures provoked a meeting of foreign merchants and a protest by the French. Inevitably, Tunisian finances headed for a cycle of external borrowing, rising debt and eventually a moratorium, which culminated in the French occupation of Tunisia in 1881.[52]

Algeria

The evolution of monetary conditions and practices in Algeria differed from those in Tunis in a number of important areas. Most importantly, there occurred a distinct improvement in monetary conditions in Algeria during the eighteenth century after the turbulence and instabilities of the seventeenth century. Moreover, even though the political ties between Istanbul and Algeria remained limited, the linkages between the coinages of Algiers and those of Istanbul grew stronger. Gold coinage minted in Algiers continued to adhere to the empire-wide standards in one way or another. In silver, there was a shift in the early part of the century towards larger coins, as was the case in Tunis, and the designs of the coins increasingly resembled those minted in Istanbul and elsewhere in the empire.[53]

Thanks to the steady supplies of gold from the sub-Saharan regions, large volumes of gold coins were issued in Algiers during the eighteenth century and early part of the nineteenth century. Even though new types of gold coinage – especially the zeri-mahbub – began to be minted elsewhere in the empire, including Tunis, in the second half of the eighteenth century, the larger sultani, locally referred to as the dinar, continued to dominate in Algiers.[54]

Moroccan, Portuguese, Spanish, Italian and other European coins circulated extensively in Algeria during the seventeenth and early eighteenth centuries. The Spanish eight-real piece was by far the most prominent of these. Just as a reform of coinage operation was undertaken in Tunis in 1714, European sources indicate that local authorities began to issue large silver coins issued in the second decade of the eighteenth century.[55] Thanks to the growth of exports and increasing availability of specie, Algeria enjoyed considerable monetary stability during the rest of the century. Of the local coins circulating in the 1820s, one budju or riyal budju, a large silver coin weighing more than 10 grams and containing 85 per cent fine silver equalled 3 batlakas, which weighed about 3.4 grams, and 24 billon mazunas. Multiples of the budju were also issued. In addition, smaller silver coins called harrubas and two- and five-aspre pieces were minted for small daily transactions.[56] A comparison of the exchange rates of Algerian coins in the 1820s with those in the 1730s suggests that Algerian currency lost about half of its silver content during these hundred years. In other words, the budju and batlaka were considerably more stable during this period than the kurush of Istanbul, the para of Cairo and the riyal of Tunis. Following a trend that had been initiated in Tunis, Algierian silver coins began to be styled more closely after the contemporary Ottoman issues – especially in the 1820s.[57] French occupation of Algeria that began in 1830 was not completed until 1848 (and was never completed in some regions) due to local resistance struggles. During this period, new mints were opened at Constantine and Medea, and mints at al-Taqidemt and al-Mascara produced Ottoman-style coins in the name of the resistance fighter, 'Abd al-Qadir (1834–7).[58]

Tripoli

In Tripolitania in 1711, a kuloglu (the son of a Turkish soldier and a Maghrebi woman) established the Karamanli dynasty which, with the exception of 1793–5, ruled the province until 1835. Trade with Europe and corsairing remained the leading economic activities. Beginning in the 1780s, the Istanbul government exerted increasing pressure to augment its influence over the region. In 1835, these efforts culminated in the dissolution of the Karamanli dynasty rule: direct Ottoman rule under a governor appointed from Istanbul was established.[59]

The Karamanlis continued to issue sultanis and later zerimahbubs with the name of the Ottoman sultans on them. They also issued a variety of silver coins in the first half of the eighteenth century under influence from Tunis, Istanbul and Cairo. This included fractions of riyals, harrubas and multiples of paras. After mid-century, the Istanbul-based kurush system began to exert greater weight, even though other coins, including fractions of the riyal budju of Algiers, continued to be issued. After the first full riyal or piastre was issued in Tunis in 1766 with the design of the Ottoman kurush, the kurush and its fractions, from 5 to 30 paras, were issued in Tripoli under the name of Abdulhamid I (1774–89). The debasement of the kurush during the first year of Selim III's reign, and of the new and larger denominations of coins that were initiated in Istanbul, followed in Tripoli. Although archival evidence is not available, it is possible that instructions and samples were sent from Istanbul regarding the design of these coins.[60]

During the rapid debasement of the Istanbul kurush under Mahmud II (1808–39), five series of kurush and its fractions were issued in Tripoli again under the influence of Istanbul, Tunis and Cairo. In fact, the greatest variety of coins from the Mahmud II era anywhere in the empire were issued by the Tripoli mint. These also included large volumes of copper coinage. Although the weight of the Tripoli kurush declined only moderately in the 1830s, from about 16 to 10 grams, its silver content followed the deteriorating standards in Istanbul and Cairo rather than that of the riyal or piastre of Tunis, which remained relatively stable during this period.[61] It is not clear whether this debasement was due to financial difficulties of the Tripoli government arising from the decline of corsairing under pressure from European governments, or whether the ongoing debasements and deterioration of the currency in Istanbul had had an impact on Tripoli coinage.[62] In 1835, after direct Ottoman rule was established, the Tripoli mint was closed down and Libya returned to using coins from Egypt, Tunis and Istanbul as well as the usual variety of European coinage; this situation lasted until the end of Ottoman rule in 1911.

Conclusion: Convergence of Currencies

One important conclusion to be drawn from this survey is that the eighteenth century was a period of economic recovery, with stronger linkages between the centre and the periphery. With the establishment of the new kurush and the centralisation of mint activity in the core regions of the empire, the imperial mint in Istanbul was reasonably successful in supplying silver coinage to a large geographical area from the Balkans to Anatolia, as well as to Syria and Iraq. Growing interaction also occurred between the silver currencies of Egypt, Tripoli, Tunis, Crimea and Algiers with that of Istanbul during this period. These linkages were strong for Cairo and Tripoli and weaker for Tunis, Crimea and Algiers. This picture, based on money and currencies, may appear paradoxical, because the eighteenth century is generally regarded by historians as a period of increasing decentralisation of the empire.

Another important similarity between Istanbul and these distant provinces took place in the early decades of the nineteenth century when Cairo (1834), Istanbul (1844) and Tunis (1847) all undertook virtually identical monetary reforms, adopting the bi-metallic system with fixed exchange rates between gold and silver coinage and, at the same time, abandoning the debasement of silver currencies as a means of raising fiscal revenue. It was not the interaction between these governments that brought about this shift, it was the rapid increase in trade with Europe, the growing interaction with European merchants and governments in addition to their advice and pressure that led governments in Cairo, Tunis and Istanbul to embrace those monetary institutions which conformed to the requirements of international trade.[63]

The decision to abandon debasements as a means of raising fiscal revenue without the elimination of budget deficits, however, had very serious long-term consequences for all three governments. During the 1850s, all three began to borrow in the European financial markets in order to meet their short-term budgetary needs. By the middle of the 1870s, with their annual debt payments far in excess of their ability to pay, all were forced to declare moratoriums on their outstanding debt. The establishment of the European Public Debt Administration in Istanbul

(1881) and, even more dramatically, the occupation of Tunis (1881) and Egypt (1882) by the European powers were directly linked to these moratoriums.

Table 10.1: Silver Content of Coins

	(Grams) x 10			(Grams)		
	Silver content of kurush	Silver content of Egyptian para	Silver content of Tunisian riyal	Silver content of kurush	Silver content of Egyptian para	Silver content of Tunisian riyal
1700	79	82	–	–	–	–
1701	79	82	–	–	–	–
1702	79	82	–	–	–	–
1703	79	82	–	–	–	–
1704	79	82	–	–	–	–
1705	79	76	–	–	–	–
1706	79	76	–	–	–	–
1707	79	76	–	–	–	–
1708	77	76	–	–	–	–
1709	77	76	–	–	–	–
1710	77	76	–	–	–	–
1711	77	76	–	–	–	–
1712	77	76	–	–	–	–
1713	77	76	–	–	–	–
1714	77	76	–	–	–	–
1715	77	76	–	–	–	–
1716	79.5	76	–	–	–	–
1717	79.5	76	–	–	–	–
1718	79.5	76	–	–	–	–
1719	79.5	76	–	–	–	–
1720	79	76	–	–	–	–
1721	79	76	–	–	–	–
1722	79	76	–	15.8	16.4	–
1723	79	76	–	15.8	16.4	–
1724	79	76	–	15.8	16.4	–
1725	79	76	72	15.8	16.4	–
1726	79	76	72	15.8	16.4	–
1727	79	76	72	15.8	15.2	–

| | (Grams) x 10 | | | (Grams) | | |
	Silver content of kurush	Silver content of Egyptian para	Silver content of Tunisian riyal	Silver content of kurush	Silver content of Egyptian para	Silver content of Tunisian riyal
1728	79.0	76	72	15.8	15.2	–
1729	79.0	76	72	15.8	15.2	–
1730	74.5	76	72	15.4	15.2	–
1731	74.5	76	72	15.4	15.2	–
1732	74.5	76	72	15.4	15.2	–
1733	74.5	76	72	15.4	15.2	–
1734	74.5	76	72	15.4	15.2	–
1735	74.5	68	46.5	15.4	15.2	–
1736	74.5	68	46.5	15.4	15.2	–
1737	74.5	68	46.5	15.4	15.2	–
1738	74.5	68	46.5	15.9	15.2	–
1739	74.5	68	46.5	15.9	15.2	–
1740	72.5	68	46.5	15.9	15.2	–
1741	72.5	68	46.5	15.9	15.2	–
1742	72.5	68	46.5	15.8	15.2	–
1743	72.5	68	46.5	15.8	15.2	–
1744	72.5	68	46.5	15.8	15.2	–
1745	72.5	68	46.5	15.8	15.2	–
1746	72.5	68	46.5	15.8	15.2	–
1747	72.5	68	46.5	15.8	15.2	14.4
1748	72.5	68	46.5	15.8	15.2	14.4
1749	72.5	68	46.5	15.8	15.2	14.4
1750	72.5	68	46.5	15.8	15.2	14.4
1751	72.5	68	46.5	15.8	15.2	14.4
1752	72.5	68	46.5	14.9	15.2	14.4
1753	72.5	68	46.5	14.9	15.2	14.4
1754	71.0	68	46.5	14.9	15.2	14.4
1755	71.0	68	46.5	14.9	15.2	14.4
1756	71.0	68	46.5	14.9	15.2	14.4
1757	57.0	68	46.5	14.9	13.6	9.3
1758	57.0	68	46.5	14.9	13.6	9.3
1759	57.0	68	46.5	14.9	13.6	9.3
1760	57.0	36	46.5	14.9	13.6	9.3
1761	57.0	36	46.5	14.9	13.6	9.3

	(Grams) x 10				(Grams)		
	Silver content of kurush	Silver content of Egyptian para	Silver content of Tunisian riyal	Silver content of kurush	Silver content of Egyptian para	Silver content of Tunisian riyal
1762	57	36	46.5	14.5	13.6	9.3
1763	57	36	46.5	14.5	13.6	9.3
1764	57	36	46.5	14.5	13.6	9.3
1765	57	36	46.5	14.5	13.6	9.3
1766	57.5	36	29	14.5	13.6	9.3
1767	57.5	36	29	14.5	13.6	9.3
1768	57.5	36	29	14.5	13.6	9.3
1769	57.5	36	29	14.5	13.6	9.3
1770	57.5	36	29	14.5	13.6	9.3
1771	57.5	36	29	14.5	13.6	9.3
1772	57.5	36	29	14.5	13.6	9.3
1773	57.5	36	29	14.5	13.6	9.3
1774	54.5	36	29	14.5	13.6	9.3
1775	54.5	36	29	14.5	13.6	9.3
1776	54.5	36	29	14.2	13.6	9.3
1777	54.5	36	29	14.2	13.6	9.3
1778	54.5	36	29	11.4	13.6	9.3
1779	50	36	29	11.4	13.6	9.3
1780	50	36	29	11.4	13.6	9.3
1781	50	36	29	11.4	13.6	9.3
1782	50	36	29	11.4	7.2	9.3
1783	50	36	29	11.4	7.2	9.3
1784	50	36	29	11.4	7.2	9.3
1785	50	36	29	11.4	7.2	9.3
1786	50	36	29	11.4	7.2	9.3
1787	50	36	29	11.4	7.2	9.3
1788	47	36	29	11.5	7.2	5.8
1789	34.5	28	26	11.5	7.2	5.8
1790	34.5	28	26	11.5	7.2	5.8
1791	34.5	28	26	11.5	7.2	5.8
1792	34.5	28	26	11.5	7.2	5.8
1793	34.5	28	26	11.5	7.2	5.8
1794	29.5	28	26	11.5	7.2	5.8
1795	29.5	28	26	11.5	7.2	5.8

	(Grams) x 10				(Grams)		
	Silver content of kurush	Silver content of Egyptian para	Silver content of Tunisian riyal	Silver content of kurush	Silver content of Egyptian para	Silver content of Tunisian riyal
1796	29.5	28	26	10.9	7.2	5.8
1797	29.5	28	26	10.9	7.2	5.8
1798	29.5	16	26	10.9	7.2	5.8
1799	29.5	–	26	10.9	7.2	5.8
1800	29.5	–	26	10.9	7.2	5.8
1801	29.5	–	26	10.9	7.2	5.8
1802	29.5	–	26	10	7.2	5.8
1803	29.5	–	26	10	7.2	5.8
1804	29.5	–	26	10	7.2	5.8
1805	29.5	–	26	10	7.2	5.8
1806	29.5	–	26	10	7.2	5.8
1807	29.5	–	26	10	7.2	5.8
1808	29.5	–	25.5	10	7.2	5.8
1809	22.1	–	25.5	10	7.2	5.8
1810	18.7	–	25.5	9.4	7.2	5.8
1811	18.7	–	25.5	6.9	5.6	5.2
1812	18.7	–	25.5	6.9	5.6	5.2
1813	18.7	–	23	6.9	5.6	5.2
1814	18.7	–	23	6.9	5.6	5.2
1815	18.7	–	23	6.9	5.6	5.2
1816	18.7	–	23	5.9	5.6	5.2
1817	18.7	–	23	5.9	5.6	5.2
1818	22.1	–	23	5.9	5.6	5.2
1819	22.1	–	23	5.9	5.6	5.2
1820	14.75	–	23	5.9	3.2	5.2
1821	14.75	–	23	5.9	–	5.2
1822	11.6	–	23	5.9	–	5.2
1823	11.6	–	23	5.9	–	5.2
1824	11.6	–	23	5.9	–	5.2
1825	11.6	–	16.5	5.9	–	5.2
1826	11.6	–	16.5	5.9	–	5.2
1827	11.6	–	16.5	5.9	–	5.2
1828	7.35	–	16.5	5.9	–	5.2
1829	3.6	–	16.5	5.9	–	5.2

| | (Grams) x 10 | | | (Grams) | | |
	Silver content of kurush	Silver content of Egyptian para	Silver content of Tunisian riyal	Silver content of kurush	Silver content of Egyptian para	Silver content of Tunisian riyal
1830	3.6	–	16.5	5.9	–	5.1
1831	2.65	–	16.5	4.42	–	5.1
1832	4.7	–	16.5	3.74	–	5.1
1833	4.7	–	16.5	3.74	–	5.1
1834	4.7	–	16.5	3.74	–	5.1
1835	4.7	–	16.5	3.74	–	4.6
1836	4.7	–	16.5	3.74	–	4.6
1837	4.7	–	16.5	3.74	–	4.6
1838	4.7	–	16.5	3.74	–	4.6
1839	4.7	–	16.5	3.74	–	4.6
1840	4.7	–	16.5	4.42	–	4.6
1841	4.7	–	16.5	4.42	–	4.6
1842	4.7	–	16.5	2.95	–	4.6
1843	4.7	–	16.5	2.95	–	4.6
1844	5	–	16.5	2.32	–	4.6
1845	5	–	16.5	2.32	–	4.6
1846	5	–	16.5	2.32	–	4.6
1847	5	–	13	2.32	–	3.3
1848	5	–	13	2.32	–	3.3
1849	5	–	13	2.32	–	3.3
1850	5	–	13	1.47	–	3.3

Bibliography

Abun-Nasr, Jamil M., *A History of the Maghrib in the Islamic Period*, Cambridge/New York, Cambridge University Press, 1987.

Adel, Ismail, *Documents diplomatiques et consulaires rélatifs à l'histoire du Liban*, Beirut, Editions des Oeuvres Politiques et Historiques, 1983.

Alleaume, Ghislaine, 'La politique monétaire de Muhammed 'Ali: nouvelles données, nouvelles hypothèses', paper presented to the Conference on Money and Currencies in the Ottoman Empire 1690–1850, Istanbul, November 1997.

Bernard, Samuel, *Déscription d'Égypte*, vol. 16, 'Les Monnaies d'Égypte', 2nd ed., Paris, 1825.

Boubaker, Sadok, 'Le transfer des capitaux entre l'Empire Ottoman et l'Europe: utilisation de la lettre d'éhange à Smryne (1760–1772)', *Revue d'Histoire Maghrébine*, vols 21/75–6, 1994, pp. 199–218.

Broome, M.R., 'The 1780 restrike talers of Maria Theresia', *The Numismatic Chronicle*, seventh series, vol. 12, 1972, pp. 221–45.

Carrière, Charles, 'Refléxions sur le problème des monnaies et des métaux précieux en Méditerranée orientale au XVIIIe siècle', *Cahiers de la Méditerranée, Commerce de gros, Commerce de détail dans les pays Méditerranéens, XVIe–XIXe siècle*, Université de Nice, 1976.

Cohen, Amnon, *Palestine in the Eighteenth Century*, Magnes Press, Jerusalem University, Jerusalem, 1973.

Cuno, Kenneth, *The Pasha's Peasants, Land, Society and Economy in Lower Egypt, 1740–1858*, Cambridge/New York, Cambridge University Press, 1992.

Establet, Colette and Jean-Paul Pascual, 'Damascene probate inventories of the 17th and 18th centuries: Some preliminary approaches and results', *International Journal of Middle East Studies* 24, 1992, pp. 376–83.

— *Familles et Fortunes à Damas, 450 Foyers damascains en 1700*, Damascus, Institut Français d'Études Arabes de Damas, 1994.

Farrugia de Candia, J., 'Monnaies Husseinites, 1705 à 1782', *Revue Tunisienne* 21, 1935, pp. 15–36.

Fattah, Hala, *The Politics of Regional Trade in Iraq, Arabia and the Gulf, 1745–1900*, Albany, NY, State University of New York Press, 1997.

Fenina, Abdelhamid, *Les Monnaies de la Régence de Tunis sous les Husaynides, Études de Numismatiques et d'Histoire Monétaire (1705–1891)*, thèse de doctorat, Paris, Université de Paris-Sorbonne, 1993.

— 'Fausse Monnaie et Faux-Monnayeurs dans la Régence de Tunis sous les Husaynides' in Abdeljelil Temimi (ed.), *Actes de 1er Congrès International sur le Corpus d'Archéologie Ottomane*, Zaghouan, FTERSI, 1997, pp. 31–56.

Frangakis-Syrett, Elena, *The Commerce of Smyrna in the Eighteenth Century (1700–1820)*, Athens, Centre for Asia Minor Studies, 1992.

Genç, Mehmet, 'XVIII. Yüzyilda Osmanli Ekonomisi ve Savap', *Yapit* 4, 1984, pp. 52–61.

Greene, Molly, 'Commerce and the Ottoman conquest of Kandiyye', *New Perspectives on Turkey* 10, 1993, pp. 95–118.

Hallaq, Ahmad al-Budayri al-, *Hawadith Dimasq al-Yawmiyya, 1154–1175 AH 1741–1762*, ed. Ahmad Izzat 'Abd al-Karim, Cairo, 1959.

Hathaway, Jane, *The Politics of Households in Ottoman Egypt, the Rise of the Qazdaglis*, Cambridge/New York, Cambridge University Press, 1997.

Holt, P.M., *Egypt and the Fertile Crescent, 1516–1922: A Political History*, Ithaca, NY/London, Cornell University Press, 1966.

Jem Sultan, *Coins of the Ottoman Empire and the Turkish Republic, A Detailed Catalogue of the Jem Sultan Collection*, 2 vols., Thousand Oaks, CA, B. and R. Publishers, 1977.

Kocaer, Remzi, *Osmanli Altin Paralari*, Istanbul, Güzel Sanatlar Matbaasi, 1967.

Krause, Chester L. and Clifford Mishler with Colin R. Bruce II, *Standard Catalog of World Coins*, 21st ed., Iola, WI, Krause Publications, 1994.

Lachman, Samuel, 'The coins struck by Ali Bey in Egypt', *The Numismatic Circular* 83, 1975, pp. 199–201 and pp. 336–8.

— 'The eighteenth-century Egyptian copper coinage', *The Numismatic Circular* 86, 1978, pp. 238–9.

— 'The silver coins of Trablus Gharb towards the end of the Qaramanli Rule', *The Numismatic Circular* 87, 1979, pp. 240–1.

MacKenzie, Kenneth M., 'Coins struck in the name of Sultan Selim III at the Tripoli Mint, 1789–1795', *Journal of Turkish Studies* 13, 1989, pp. 107–14.

— 'Coins of Tripoli: Fertile field of study', *World Coins*, 7 September 1983, pp. 104–7.

Mantran, Robert, *L'Empire Ottoman du XVIe au XVIIIe siècle: Administration, Économie, Société*, London, Variorum Reprints, 1984.

Marcus, Abraham, *The Middle East on the Eve of Modernity, Aleppo in the Eighteenth Century*, New York, Columbia University Press, 1989.

Marino, Brigitte, 'Monnaies d'or et d'argent à Damas, 1750–1830', paper presented to the Conference on Money and Currencies in the Ottoman Empire 1690–1850, Istanbul, November 1997.

Merouche, Lemnouar, 'Les Fluctuations de la monnaie dans l'Algérie Ottomane' in Abdeljelil Temimi (ed.), *Mélanges Charles-Robert Ageron*, Zaghouan, FTERSI, 1996, pp. 609–30.

Ölçer, Cüneyt, *Sultan II: Mahmud Döneminde Darp Edilen Osmanli Madeni Paralari*, Istanbul Yenelik Basımevı, 1970.

Pamuk, Sevket, 'In the absence of domestic currency: Debased European coinage in the seventeenth-century Ottoman Empire', *The Journal of Economic History* 57, 1997, pp. 345–66.

— *A Monetary History of the Ottoman Empire*, London/New York, Cambridge University Press, 2000.

Panzac, Daniel, 'International trade and domestic maritime trade in the Ottoman Empire during the 18th century', *International Journal of Middle East Studies* 24, 1992, pp. 189–206.

— 'Négociants ottomans et activité maritime au Maghreb (1686-1707)' in Daniel Panzac (ed.), *Les Villes dans l'Empire Ottoman: Activités et Sociétés*, Paris, Editions du CNRS, 1994, pp. 221–41.

— 'L'Économie-monde ottomane en question: les clauses monétaires dans les contrats d'affrètement maritime au XVIIIe siècle', *The Journal of the Economic and Social History of the Orient*, vol. 39, 1996, pp. 368–78.

— 'La Piastre et le Cyclotron: essai sur les monnaies ottomanes, 1687–1844', paper presented to the Conference on Money and Currencies in the Ottoman Empire 1690–1850, Istanbul, November 1997.

Paris, Robert, *Histoire du Commerce de Marseille, Tome V: de 1660 a 1789*, Le Levant, Paris, Librairie Plon, 1957.

Raymond, André, *Artisans et Commerçants au Caire au XVIIIe siècle*, 2 vols, Damascus, Institut Français d'Etudes Arabes de Damas, 1973–4.

— 'Les provinces arabes (XVIe siècle–XVIIIe siècle)' in Robert Mantran (ed.), *Histoire de L'Empire Ottoman*, Paris, Fayard, 1989, pp. 340–420.

Sahillioglu, Halil, *Bir Asirlik Osmanli Para Tarihi*, unpublished thesis for associate professorship, Istanbul Üniversitesi Iktisat Fakültesi, 1965.

Schaendlinger, Anton C., *Osmanische Numismatik*, Braunschweig, Klinkhardt and Biermann, 1973.

Sebag, Paul, 'Les monnaies tunisiennes au XVIIe siècle', *Revue des Mondes Musulmans et de la Méditerranée*, nos 55–6, Villes au Levant, Hommages à André Raymond, 1990, pp. 257–65.

Shaw, Stanford, *The Financial and Administrative Development of Ottoman Egypt, 1517–1798*, Princeton, NJ, Princeton University Press, 1962.

Sultan, Fouad, *La Monnaie Égyptienne*, Paris, Librairie Nouvelle de Droit et de Jurisprudence, 1914.

Tabakoglu, Ahmet, *Gerileme Dönemine Girerken Osmanli Maliyesi*, Istanbul, Dergah Yayinlari, 1985.

Valensi, Lucette, *Tunisian Peasants in the Eighteenth and Nineteenth Centuries*, London/New York, Cambridge University Press, 1985.

Walz, Terence, 'Gold and silver exchanges between Egypt and Sudan, 16th–18th centuries' in J.F. Richards (ed.), *Precious Metals in the Later Medieval and Early Modern Worlds*, North Carolina, Carolina Academic Press, 1983, pp. 305–28.

Notes on Chapter 10

1   The evolution of the Ottoman monetary system from the fourteenth through the seventeenth centuries is examined in Pamuk, 2000.

2   Pamuk, 1997.

3   Sahillioglu, 1965, p. 91.

4   Schaendlinger, 1973, pp. 112–33.

5   Wage observations are taken from the account books of various *vakif* (pious foundations) available from the Ottoman state archives as part of a long-term study of the history of wages in Istanbul.

6   Genç, 1984, pp. 52–61.

7   For example, Panzac, 1992, pp. 189–206; Frangakis-Syrett, 1992; Paris, 1957.

8   Tabakoglu, 1985, pp. 13–39, 74–113.

9   Schaendlinger, 1973, pp. 112–35.

10   For example, Holt, 1966.

11   Hathaway, 1997.

12   See, for example, the documents in Istanbul, Prime Ministry, Ottoman Archives, Cevdet, Darphane Collection.

13   Tabakoglu, 1985, pp. 61–3.

14   *Ibid.*, pp. 59–63 provides a detailed list of net annual inflows to the treasury from Cairo for the first half of the century; also Shaw, 1962, pp. 283–312.

15   Since one kurush equalled 40 paras, identical standards between Istanbul and Cairo would have meant that the silver content of the para of Cairo equalled one-fortieth of that of the kurush of Istanbul. For example, in Istanbul, in 1762, Hatibzade Ahmet Aga fixed the weight of 1000 paras at 125 dirhams of 58 per cent fine silver. This meant that one para of Cairo contained 0.23 grams of silver: Bernard, 1825, pp. 47–8, cited in Lachman, 1975, p. 200. Around the same time, one Istanbul kurush weighed six dirhams and contained about 60 per cent pure silver. One-fortieth of this piece contained 2.7 grams of pure silver.

16   Raymond, 1973–4, vol. 1, pp. 34–6.

17   *Ibid.*, pp. 17–52. In contrast, the para of Cairo had been more stable than the akçe in the seventeenth century.

18   Twice during the eighteenth century, Ottoman control of Egypt was threatened and, on both occasions, small changes were made to the coin designs to reflect the changed circumstances. In 1769 Ali Bey, the governor of Egypt, revolted and declared Egypt to be independent, but he was defeated three years later. During his

rebellion, coins were issued in the name of the Ottoman sultan, Mustafa III (1757–74), but with the name of Ali added. Similarly, during the French invasion of Egypt, coins with an Arabic B (for Bonaparte) were issued: Lachman, 1975, pp. 198–201.

19 Raymond, 1973–4, pp. 33–4; Lachman, 1975, pp. 198–201; Krause and Mishler, 1994. See also table 10.1 above, also in S. Pamuk, *A Monetary History of the Ottoman Empire*, Cambridge University Press, 2000, p. 163.

20 For example, because of the debasement of the para and the absence of a large silver coin, an imaginary unit of account called the riyal, equal to 90 paras, was widely used in the last quarter of the eighteenth century: Raymond, 1973–4, vol. 1, pp. 39–40; Cuno, 1992, p. 211.

21 Raymond, 1973–4, pp. 29–31.

22 Walz, 1983, pp. 311–25.

23 Sahillioglu, 1965, pp. 112–14.

24 Lachman, 1978, pp. 238–9; Raymond, 1973–4, vol. 1, pp. 34–6.

25 Raymond, 1973–4, vol. 1, pp. 20–5. The Austrian thalers continued to be re-issued and exported to the Arabian peninsula and other destinations in the Near East until the middle of the twentieth century: Broome, 1972; Carrière, 1976.

26 Similarly, with the growth of trade between Crete and Egypt, and in the absence of the akçe itself, the para of Egypt became the leading unit of account in Crete late in the seventeenth century: Greene, 1993.

27 For the coinage in circulation in eighteenth-century Palestine: Cohen, 1973, pp. 179–269.

28 Marcus, 1989, pp. 121–35.

29 Adel, 1983, *passim.*

30 Establet and Pascual, 1992; *ibid.*, 1994, pp. 59–112; Hallaq, 1959, pp. 4–10 – I am indebted to Abdul-Karim Rafeq for detailed excerpts from this book; Marino, 1997.

31 Establet and Pascual, 1992, pp. 381–3.

32 Schaendlinger, 1973, pp. 135–42.

33 Fattah, 1997, pp. 31–3, 223.

34 Cuno, 1992, p. 212.

35 For the rapid decline in the silver content of the para of Egypt during the early part of the nineteenth century: Cuno, 1992, Appendix 2, pp. 211–15.

36 From the numismatic catalogues and collections available in Egypt, it is clear that Istanbul coinage circulated widely in Egypt during this period: Sultan, 1914, pp. 34–45.

37 For a detailed examination of Muhammad 'Ali's policies of taxation and extraction of the agricultural surplus from the peasant producers: Cuno, 1992, pp. 121–46.
38 Alleaume, 1997.
39 The new standard for the Egyptian pound was 8.54 grams of 0.875 per cent fine gold, which equalled 100 silver kurush. The pound also contained 140 grams of 0.833 per cent fine silver. The gold–silver ratio was thus fixed at 15.87: Sultan, 1914, pp. 34–45; Krause and Mishler, 1994.
40 Abun-Nasr, 1987, pp. 285–91.
41 Judging from the volume of gold issues, access to sub-Saharan gold was limited in Tunis during the eighteenth century. Mint activity was mostly in silver, bullion and copper coinage: Fenina, 1993.
42 An important reason for this de-linking was the growing scarcity of the Spanish real around the Mediterranean: Boubaker, 1994, pp. 57–8.
43 Fenina, 1993; Sebag, 1990; Farrugia de Candia, 1935.
44 Fenina, 1993; compare with Jem Sultan, 1977.
45 See Fenina, 1997.
46 Fenina, 1993; Kocaer, 1967, pp. 112–44.
47 Kocaer, 1967.
48 Lucette Valensi suggests that the volume gold as well as silver coin output of Tunis increased after the mid-eighteenth century: Valensi, 1985, p. 213.
49 For trade and payments flows between the Maghreb and Ottoman ports in the early part of the eighteenth century: Panzac, 1994.
50 Panzac, 1996, p. 233 has recently emphasised this geographical division.
51 Fenina, 1993.
52 Valensi, 1985, p. 219.
53 Abun-Nasr, 1987, pp. 158–61; Raymond, 1989, pp. 407–12.
54 Walz, 1983, pp. 305–28; also Schaendlinger, 1973, pp. 120–40; Merouche, 1996; Kocaer, 1967.
55 Merouche, 1996; compare with Schaendlinger, 1973, pp. 114–20.
56 Schaendlinger, 1973, pp. 120–40; Krause and Mishler, 1994.
57 Ölçer, 1970, pp. 64–76; Krause and Mishler, 1994.
58 Ölçer, 1970, pp. 64–76.
59 Abun-Nasr, 1987, pp. 193–205; Mantran, 1984.
60 It is not clear whether the weight and silver content of these coins followed the changing standards of coinage at Istanbul during this difficult period.

61 MacKenzie, 1983, 1989; Ölçer, 1970, pp. 92–110; Krause and Mishler, 1994.
62 Lachman, 1979, pp. 240–1, argued for the first cause and Ölçer, 1970, pp. 92–110, proposed the second.
63 The Ottoman transition to bi-metalism is discussed in Pamuk, 2000, pp. 206–11. For the pressures on the government of Egypt to shift to bi-metalism, see Alleaume, 1997.

CHAPTER 11

Monetary Causes of the Financial Crisis and Bankruptcy of Egypt, 1875–8

Ghislaine Alleaume

The bankruptcy of the khediviate in 1876–7 represents one of the most decisive events in Egypt's history in the nineteenth century. The establishment of the dual-control in relation to the country's finances marked the real beginning of colonial intervention and put an end to a 75-year-long process of independent national development. The explanation that is usually given for these events is the mismanagement of finances by the last two khedives. Isma'il (1863–79), in particular, has gone down in history as a spendthrift who loved luxury and who built numerous palaces as the debts of Egypt were increasing. This explanation of a major phenomenon in the history of modern Egypt is based upon an individual's behaviour. The present study challenges this explanation, exploring some long-term factors that go beyond the decisions or policies of a particular ruler in order to explain what happened at the end of the nineteenth century. The spectacular bankruptcy of 1876–7 occurred at a seemingly odd time, since it followed a long phase of economic growth. This phase, although difficult to measure with accuracy, can be observed through a single indicator in a country where the state's resources were still largely dependent, through fiscality, on the expansion of agriculture: between 1820 and 1840, the total surface of cultivated surface area doubled, and it did so again between 1840 and 1880.

The pattern which led to the state's increasing indebtedness in the decade prior to the beginning of the financial crisis is well-known.[1] But the reasons put forward to explain it – the carelessness of spendthrift khedives and the impact of unscrupulous business circles[2] – remain unconvincing in light of the agricultural situation. Egypt's bankruptcy came at the same time as that of the Central Ottoman treasury and of the regency of Tunis: the whole Ottoman economy collapsed. In Tunis, as in Istanbul, the reasons usually given for this financial catastrophe are the same as in Cairo, and they always relate to two factors. The first is the inability of the Ottoman rulers to manage public affairs, while the second relates to the despotic nature of a political order which had no economic aim but to loot the lands placed under its authority.[3] Individual rulers are thus blamed for bringing about this major economic phenomenon.

The present research aims at moving away from the individualistic explanation for the end of the nineteenth-century crisis. It argues that Egypt's bankruptcy stemmed from a double transformation. The first was endogenous and was linked to the long-term evolution of the Egyptian monetary system and its integration into the Ottoman economy. The second transformation was exogenous and was tied to the conversion of the European monetary system following the signing of free-trade agreements from 1860 onwards. Although this study undertakes a re-examination of the 1875 financial crisis by focusing solely on its monetary aspects, they alone cannot explain this event, nor do they play a central role in it. The scope of this study is narrowed to this aspect for purely practical reasons. Although much has been written on the history of Egypt's public debt, no work has yet been done on the history of money and prices, despite the fact that such an endeavour must precede any serious attempt at studying economic trends. This surprising gap reflects the bias towards a strictly political reading of the processes of indebtedness and bankruptcy. A return to monetary history also allows one to avoid falling into Egyptocentric analyses of a crisis which all consider to have had a significant impact on international relations.

A Long-term Monetary Crisis

Throughout the rule of Muhammad 'Ali (1805–48), Egypt witnessed monetary crises, the severity and recurrence of which seem surprising since the country's economic performance was improving at a steady pace at the time. These crises had historical causes and are in line with the long-term crisis which had plagued the economies of all the Ottoman territories since the middle of the seventeenth century.[4] Indeed, generally speaking, the monetary situation in Egypt in the first half of the nineteenth century corresponded to the account that Samuel Bernard gave of it at the time of the French expedition.[5] As was the case in the entire Ottoman Empire, Egypt fell into a double monetary system in which foreign and local currencies were in simultaneous use; regarding the regulation of international exchanges, the country was dominated by European currencies. This unfavourable situation played against the local currency which, from the middle of the eighteenth century onwards, entered a long phase of devaluation that the reforms of neither 'Ali bey al-Kabir (1769) nor Muhammad 'Ali (1836) could stop. The para changed from the 100 index in 1681–8 to the 32 index in 1795.[6] This steady decline was to continue – even accelerate – during the first half of the nineteenth century.[7]

A crisis so long and so deep necessarily has many causes, both technical and economic. The first problem for Egypt and the Ottoman Empire lay in a chronic lack of precious metals. With regard to the Ottoman Empire, this lack is usually thought of as a result of a deficit in the balance of trade: while it was positive with Europe, Ottoman trade showed a negative balance with the Far East. In view of the asymmetrical pattern of its trade, the Ottoman government was unable to hoard the large monetary flows which circulated in the empire. In Egypt, the argument may be less convincing, except if one accepts as a fact that, on this particular point, the country was totally constrained by its integration into the Ottoman trade system. Whatever the real reason, the fact is that the Cairo mint always had difficulty finding the required volume of precious metals necessary to carry on its activities. This scarcity partly explains the small amounts of monetary issuing and the resulting lack of metal coinage in circulation, a situation which impelled the authorities to make foreign currencies legal tender.

The situation was worsened by technical problems, most of them well-known, but which must not nonetheless be underestimated. First, coins were bad quality, a problem which made their alteration by holders easier and encouraged their counterfeiting. This consequently raised the value of the finest coins, whether they were new Egyptian or Ottoman coin mints (those by which the authorities strove to keep the situation under control) or coins imported from Europe. In any case, there was great speculation over these coins and they quickly disappeared from circulation, thus contributing to the reduction of monetary circulation. The poor quality of coin production also brought extra costs, which made the Cairo mint particularly non-competitive compared to the European mints. Therefore, merchants of precious metals tended to reserve their stock for customers abroad, where costs were lower and benefits greater. Finally, the ratio of gold to silver, slightly higher in Egypt than Europe, led to the export of gold coins, which were disadvantaged by the overvalued silver estimated on the local market at a lower rate than that obtained from the value of their weight in fine metal in Europe.[8]

These various factors combined to increasingly dissociate the three values of a coin: the intrinsic value of the precious metals from which it was made when the coin itself was a trading commodity, the legal value set by the state through a tariff, as was the case in Egypt, and the market value stemming from trade exchanges. During the period covered by this study, the gap between the legal and market values was on average between 10 and 15 per cent. But it could reach much higher percentages in times of monetary scarcity or heavy speculation: over 100 per cent in 1806, over 55 per cent in 1820 etc. These strong pushes were obviously short-term, but they reflected the unstable nature of the Egyptian monetary system.[9]

Under the rule of Muhammad 'Ali, the increasing pace of exchanges and the increase in their total volume raised the tensions bearing upon the monetary system, making the Egyptian economy even more dependent on monetary imports from Europe. By an apparent paradox, monetary shortage was greater as growth became stronger. To settle his purchases in Europe, Muhammad 'Ali could only pay in kind by exporting increasing quantities of foodstuffs.[10] The highly extroverted nature of the Egyptian economy and the policy on monopolies[11] can both be explained by this pressing need for hard currencies: they may have had less to do with a will to control Egypt's trade than with an urgent need to keep all the benefits of monetary imports for the treasury. Moreover, the only periods of respite in the steady devaluation of the Egyptian currency were those brought about by European wars. This was notably the case during the Crimean War which caused a sharp price increase for foodstuffs on the Mediterranean market. Since Egypt was supplying foodstuffs to the British fleet in Malta at a high price at that time, the country was able to enjoy a few years of economic prosperity.

The unequal development of the different Ottoman provinces created an additional obstacle for the financial policy of Egypt. Despite the growing autonomy given to Egypt in this domain – the right to mint coins and to promulgate tariffs different from those of Istanbul – the Egyptian government was compelled to integrate the Ottoman monetary system, to use the same currencies and the same customs regulations etc. The difference in value between the Cairo piastre and those of Damascus or Istanbul caused speculation and stimulated capital flows detrimental to the Egyptian economy. Exchanges with Syria seemed the most unfavourable. For example, in 1816 a strong speculative rush on currencies led to the massive export of paras to Syria, where they were used to purchase riyals: since the rate in Damascus was 300 nisfs (compared to 360 in Cairo), the exchange brought a net benefit of 60 nisfs per riyal. Muhammad 'Ali himself indulged in this triangular trade at a rate of 1000 purses (*kis*) of silver per month: the imported riyals were then re-melted down in Cairo for a lower value.[12] Although in the short term this activity may have seemed beneficial to the state treasury for the profits that it yielded, the drawback was that it thereby also affected the reforms implemented by the mint. By allowing the outward flow of paras, it made the shortage of small coins more acute, coins which were badly needed for the most common transactions; it also strengthened the domination of European currencies on the international market.

Attempts at Monetary Reform

During the first three decades of his rule, Muhammad 'Ali strove to do away with the deficiencies of the monetary system through the same means as those used by all of the previous Ottoman regimes, that is the minting of silver coins of better quality and the promulgation of tariffs setting the exchange rates for all the currencies that were allowed to circulate. He stumbled upon the same obstacles and met with the same failures as previous rulers. The first important reform was held in 1836, a time when the debasement of the Ottoman currencies reached a peak, and in the aftermath of the first Egyptian–Ottoman war.[13] A decree of the Majlis-i Mülkiyye issued on 27 Dhu 'l-Hijja 1251/14 April 1836[14] was implemented as the first step toward a national currency policy.

The reform instituted by law the bi-metalism on which the Egyptian monetary system was actually already based in practice, introducing two units of currency: a silver 20-piastre coin and its five fractionals and a gold coin of the same value whose weight was set at a ratio of 1 to 15.5 compared to the silver coins. The Egyptian legislature thus sought to adjust the relative value of both metals to rates that were in use in Europe. The text of the statute indeed states that 'there must be a similarity of value between gold and silver coins',[15] and that this similarity must also 'link foreign currencies and those of Egypt'. And since 'the circulation of the latter at higher or lower rates must be forbidden', the reform came with the promulgation of a new tariff which set the exchange rates of the various currencies (see Appendix I).

Furthermore, the reform established the free thalari as the monetary standard. This coin, also known as abu taqa (the Austrian thaler), weighed 120 qirats and was available in smaller coins of 60 (nisf), 30 (rub'), 6 (piastre), 3 (20 paras) and 1.5 qirats (10 paras). In a trial essay at the Cairo mint, the new standard was set at 833 thousandths, 120 qirats of fine metal per 144 qirats. One may be surprised to see that a government which was apparently anxious to have its own monetary system had chosen a foreign currency as its standard. However, the US did just the same in 1792 when it based its monetary system on the Spanish piastre (abu madfa' riyal) with a ratio of 15 to 1 between the dollar-gold and the dollar-silver.[16] When they opted for trade currencies renowned for the quality of their minting and that were, at that time, the major currencies used in world trade, the two countries were making the same choice for basically quite similar reasons.[17]

Egypt's choice of the Austrian thaler stemmed from the fact that it was already in high favour throughout the Ottoman Empire, where it bore the stamp of the Ottoman government.

For various reasons, the new system did not meet its expectations and bi-metalism did not really function. Since it relied too heavily on raw materials provided by the government, the mint was unable to meet the needs of the market. 'The quantity of coins produced was insufficient to meet the requirements of trade', except for the piastres, which were plentiful but in such bad condition that 'counterfeiting became a real trade for some'.[18] The lack of coins of smaller value also hindered common transactions and incurred heavy losses for the least privileged classes.[19] Once more, the failings of local currency left the field clear for foreign currencies in the regulation of exchanges. The mere existence of a tariff that made them legal tender encouraged these foreign currencies gradually to replace the local one.

In 1841, an even more severe financial crisis led to the creation of a committee for monetary reform. This committee was assigned five specific tasks: to prevent foreign currencies from hindering the circulation of the local one, to increase the available quantity of local currency, to increase the share of ingots in the total amount of metal currency and, to that end, to bear or reduce the excess in production costs and to create a new currency system.[20] In November 1841, an English expert metallurgist named Harris submitted a report stressing the need to devaluate the Egyptian currency once again by promulgating a new tariff which would bring the Egyptian para down to its real value.[21] Hardly convinced by the arguments brought forward, the Egyptian government decided to create a committee for currencies in 1842, headed by Charles Lambert, a Saint-Simonian who had just been named head of the mint and who was already director of the École polytechnique and the Observatoire. The structure of this committee was decided by Sharif pacha, director of the Diwan al-maliyya (Office of Finance). It had five members, all selected for their technical skills. In addition to the chemists Thibaudier and Figari (who was the director of the Pharmacie centrale des armées), the committee included three Saint-Simonians: Dr Perron (director of the École de médecine), Charles Lambert and 'Abd al-Rahman

Rushdi, a mechanical engineer trained in France who, after having been Lambert's assistant at the École polytechnique for a long time, had just been named head of the khedivial steamships and of the Overland Road Transit Organisation (Maslahat al-Murur).

The committee's work went on for more than two years. It resulted in a number of proposals, the most urgent of which dealt with the reform of coining and the promulgation of a new tariff.[22] Initially, in order to meet the five objectives of the government, the committee made a detailed study of the Egyptian monetary system and its deficiencies. The report begins with a gripping summary of the problems mentioned above. The problems with regard to supplying the mint and the consequent paucity of monetary supply both stemmed from 'the considerable costs linked to coin production'. This, in turn, induced 'gold and silver traders not to supply the Mint with the raw materials needed, preferring to send them to other countries where the costs are lower; thus the price of gold and silver is higher'. The chronic monetary scarcities resulted from the fact that 'the coins minted in the country disappear almost immediately after their issuing'. The reasons for this disappearance were mentioned many times and by different people: gold was mixed with silver instead of copper in the gold coins, there was gold in the silver coins, the actual value of silver coins was often higher than their face value, gold and silver coins were often too heavy. Consequently, the committee 'has undertaken to keep a record of the costs of each stage of production' and gathered 'every day to discuss ways to improve production'. They focused on eight main issues: setting the tariff calculated on the internal costs of coinage; choosing the most economical and assured way of separating gold from silver; using the most accurate processes in the testing of materials; improving the weights and weighing equipment or methods; making alloys at the required value without silver being found in gold coins and without gold being found in silver coins; coining economically and accurately, retaining control over issuing and the benefits of the process of re-melting and the advantages of undertaking it in order to get rid of coins which were in bad condition.

Since all of these measures required time, the committee suggested the creation of a standing committee for the improvement of coinage, and asked for the building of a laboratory for control operations which would be headed by d'Arnaud, a French metallurgist who had just returned from a mineralogical expedition on the White Nile.[23]

Once translated into Turkish by 'Abd al-Rahman Rushdi, the report was submitted to Muhammad 'Ali a few weeks later. The Pasha found that the translation was unclear, and thought that the analysis did not correspond to his initial request. Therefore, his secretary, Artin Bey, an Armenian close to the Saint-Simonians, wrote back to Lambert:

> His Highness has taken note that the committee focused mainly on production processes. His Highness is far from opposing the measures proposed by the committee on this matter, but he would have liked you to devote your attention to the question of the value and the title of Egyptian coins in their relation to foreign currencies so that a new system may be adopted which would lead to a perfect balance between these different currencies. His Highness thinks that up until today, no satisfactory solution to this important issue has been found.

The letter ends with a new request being made, but this time stated in very clear terms:

> Please give me your opinion concerning the title and the relative value of currencies. As you know, the problem at hand is that of reaching a balance between the coinage of the country and the value of metal abroad so that the export of money ceases to be a form of speculation beneficial to trade.[24]

In a written reply, Lambert said that the committee 'tackled that which was most pressing and which influences the mathematical balance of currencies', but that the committee was aware of the problem as a whole and had provided a partial answer: what prevented a fair balance between Egyptian and foreign coins was the fact that Egyptian coins were too rich (richer than set by the tariff), hence, the technical reforms which were suggested. Lambert also asked whether there was really enough coinage being minted for its sudden disappearance to seem to stem from serious and important reasons. The low level of coin minting, combined with the increase in the proportional production costs which had created and was still creating another evil, the rise of foreign currency rates or, more generally speaking, the lack of a stable monetary standard.[25]

Since the Pasha insisted, Lambert also sent him a more personal reply, including a more economical analysis of the Egyptian monetary system which was identified with the system of exclusion of the European colonies.

> With regard to its monetary system, Egypt finds itself in a very peculiar situation. As the main locus of transit between Europe and India and being rich in agricultural products, it is the place where the transactions of all nations are made ... it is now able to enjoy a political life of its own, but it still comes under the strong influence of both its suzerain and the protective powers of Europe. All currencies flow to it, but since it only has little itself, it was compelled to use the method of the great colonies, namely the tariff. The tariff at par which, for the other nations, serves as a means of control, a commercial gauge regarding foreign currencies and a guide for their exchange is, for Egypt, the genuine monetary system.[26]

As a true follower of Adam Smith, Lambert thus proposed to do away with the tariff system. But since it was as yet impossible to do without imported currencies, and the double monetary circulation could not be abolished in the short term, he suggested the transformation of the tariff into a simple means of control over the title and weight of imported currencies; applying a customs duty to the latter would make them less attractive for speculation.

In a country which operated under a tariff system, as Egypt does today, the principle of protection can be linked to currency by applying a tariff set below par to all foreign currencies circulating in the country which means imposing a customs duty on them. Harris's suggestion that the national currency be changed can usefully be transformed into the idea of protection until the abundance and accuracy of this currency make it possible to forbid others as currencies and accept them only as goods. At that point, the application of a tariff at par that would no longer be mandatory in monetary transactions would serve as a gauge and guide to call to order these goods by indicating the quantity of pure gold and silver that they hold.[27]

Finally and foremost, he suggested the use of paper money in order to do away with the scarcity of precious metals. To resolve the immediate crisis, he went so far as to propose making a loan, offering the services of the Saint-Simonian banks, which were prospering and seeking external markets.[28] This time, the offer was perceived by Muhammad 'Ali as being too bold; he did not even give it a reply. In any case, his room for manoeuvre on this issue was restrained by the conditions of the 1841 treaty and by his dependence on the sultan as regards foreign affairs and international treaties.

However, the monetary committee's report and Lambert's remarks may have had an indirect impact. Indeed, they came slightly before the founding of the first Egyptian bank in 1844, a kind of joint stock bank established by Muhammad 'Ali and two European merchants, who were also his two main trade partners: Jules Pastré, a merchant and ship owner from Marseilles who was Muhammad 'Ali's principal partner for exchanges in the western Mediterranean and Tossitza, a Greek merchant who was Muhammad 'Ali's principal partner for trade in the eastern Mediterranean.[29] The history and activities of this bank, the first in Egypt and probably one of the oldest in the region, are unfortunately still only very little known. Judging from the documents of the Diwan al-Tijara wa'l-mabi'at (Office of External Trade and Sales), it seems to have had mainly commercial functions.

Conclusion: Transformation of the World Monetary System

Despite its failure, the Saint-Simonian project is interesting in that it had planned, at a relatively early stage, to solve the problem of monetary scarcity by developing fiduciary money. Paper money, bank money and credit devices could indeed have been the means to solve, at least partly, the country's monetary problems. On this issue, Lambert's suggestions could have allowed Egypt to be part of the transformation of the world monetary system that began precisely around the middle of the nineteenth century and ended with Europe's adoption of a free trade system dominated by Britain.

Indeed, with the coming of the industrial revolution in Europe and the development of financial capitalism, the intrinsic value of money gradually decreased, while its commercial value followed the opposite trend, becoming increasingly determined by the total value of exchanges. Britain, which at the time was the first industrial and trading power, also had the first modern banking organisation. It was also the first to abandon bi-metalism. From 1860 onwards, the signing of free trade treaties hastened the pace of evolution on the continent and favoured the dropping of bi-metalism and the gradual adoption everywhere in Europe of the gold sterling standard. However, this change brought problems for Europe itself. It particularly affected the countries tied to bi-metalism, whose monetary reserves were consequently based on a double hoarding of gold and silver. It was the case first and foremost for the countries linked in some way or other to the 'silver network' that regulated monetary exchanges between Europe and the orient since the beginning of the seventeenth century. Spain, which boasted the richest mines, was the prime producer and exporter of metal silver. At that time, it was converting part of its production into coins earmarked for export: the 'piastre from Spain' or 'colonnate' (known in Egypt as the *abu madfa'* riyal). Its outlets were found mostly in the colonial market of the Americas, but also in the Ottoman Empire and in the Far East. Spain was also exporting part of its production to Germany, where the best monetary workshops in Europe were found. In turn, these workshops would export their production to these same distant markets.

These old monetary powers were also threatened by the global overproduction of silver that followed the discovery of new mines which turned out to be among the richest in the world. In December 1865, France, Belgium, Switzerland and Italy created the Latin Union, a co-ordinating body set up to develop a common strategy to avoid the sudden collapse of the prices for silver. The first measures taken by the Latin Union aimed at setting a policy to restrict exports of silver coinage. This alliance did not succeed in preventing a triple speculation against silver which led, among other things, to silver–gold conversions towards third countries, causing significant gold outflows. Gold mono-metalism was officially established by the 1874 and 1876 agreements, which imposed gold as the sole means of payment in relations with the outside.[30] Moreover, the clause soon applied to the liquidation of the Egyptian and the Ottoman public debts.

In the end, one may wonder if the cover of Ottoman state loans was not the means for conversion, in the literal sense of the word, of the old monetary exchanges which had prevailed over centuries in the world economy. The crisis at the end of the nineteenth century, often attributed to Khedive Isma'il, can be understood instead from a broad perspective of economic conditions that affected a wide region, each country reacting to the transformations according to its conditions.

Appendix I: Tariff of 5 July 1798/1st Muharram 1213

Currency	Value (paras)
Gold	
Quadruple from Spain	2352
Half quadruple from Spain	1176
Quarter quadruple from Spain	588
Eighth quadruple from Spain	294
Sixteenth quadruple from Spain	147
Double-louis from France (40 franc coin)	1344
Louis from France (20 franc coin)	672
Sequin from Venice	340
Zeri-mahbub sequin from Cairo	180
Half sequin	90
Constantinople sequin	200
Fondoukli (non-tariffed)	300
Sequin from Hungary and Holland	300
Silver	
6-franc crown from France	168
5-franc crown from France	142
3-franc crown from France	84
1.5-franc coin	42
0.75-franc coin	21
Crown from Rome	140
Single crown from Malta	84
Double crown from Malta	134
2.5 crown from Malta	168
Piastre from Spain	150
Talari	150

Currency	Value (paras)
8-pound crown from Genoa	186
6-pound crown from Milan	130
Turkish piastres* (four different kinds)	
1	100
2	80
3	60
4	40

*At the time of the French Expedition, four different kinds of Turkish piastres were used in Egypt, bearing the same name, but with different weights and values. This abnormal situation was due to the continual depreciation of Ottoman currency during the seventeenth and eighteenth centuries

Source: Vaucher, 1949.

Appendix II: Tariff of 1834

Currency	Value (paras)
Abu taqa talari	800
5-franc coin	770
Colonnate	828
Talari from America	760
English pound	3900
Louis d'or (20-franc coin)	3086
Sequin	1826
Bondouki	1857
Dabloun	12549

Source: Arminjon, 1921.

Bibliography

Primary Sources
Archives de l'Arsenal, Paris, Papiers de Charles Lambert.
Compte-rendus des travaux de la Commission de la dette publique, published annually from 1876.
National Archives in Cairo (Dar al-Watha'iq al-Qawmiyya), Sijillat Diwan Khidiwi.

Published Studies

Alleaume, G., 'Les sources de l'histoire économique de l'Égypte moderne aux Archives Nationales du Caire I. Les registres de la Direction du Commerce et des Ventes (Diwan al-tigara wa'l-mabi'at)', *Annales islamologiques* 27, 1993, pp. 269–90.

Arminjon, P., 'Le tarif monétaire égyptien et ses effets', *L'Égypte contemporaine* 12, 1921, pp. 406–25.

Bernard, Samuel, 'Mémoire sur les monnaies d'Égypte' in *Déscription de l'Égypte, État moderne*, Paris, 1812.

Clay, C., 'The financial collapse of the Ottoman State, 1863–1875' in D. Panzac (dir.), *Histoire économique et sociale de l'Empire ottoman et de la Turquie*, Leuven, Peeters, 1995, Collection Turcica VIII, pp. 119–31.

Crouchley, A.E., *The Economic Development of Modern Egypt*, London, 1938.

Cuno, K., *The Pasha's Peasants: Land, Society, and Economy in Lower Egypt 1740–1858*, Cambridge, Cambridge University Press, 1992 and Cairo, American University in Cairo Press, 1994.

Hitta, A.M. al-, *Tarikh Misr fi 'l-qarn al-tasi' 'ashar*, Cairo, Maktabat al-Nahda, 1958.

Jabarti, 'Abd al-Rahman al-, *'Aja'ib al-athar fi 'l-tarajim wa'l-akhbar*, Bulaq, Bulaq National Press, 1306/1889.

Landes, D., *Bankers and Pashas. International Finance and Economic Imperialism in Egypt*, London, Heinemann, 1958.

Lelart, M., 'Le thaler allemand et la piastre mexicaine: deux monnaies internationales', paper presented to the Conference on Money and Currencies in the Ottoman Empire 1690–1850, Istanbul, November 1997.

Raymond, A., *Artisans et commerçants au Caire au XVIIIe siècle*, Damascus, Institut Français d'Études Arabes de Damas, 1973–4.

Régnier, P., *Les saint-simoniens en Égypte*, Cairo, Amin F. Abdel-Nour, 1989.

Rowley, A., *L'évolution économique de la France du milieu du XIXe siècle à 1914*, Paris, SEDES (Société d'Édition et de Diffusion de l'Enseignement Supérieur), 1981.

Sami, Amin Pacha, *Taqwim al-Nil*, Cairo, Dar al-Kutub al-Misriyya, 1936.

Sultan, Fouad, *La monnaie égyptienne*, Paris, Arthur Rousseau, 1914.

Vaucher, G., 'La livre égyptienne de sa création par Mohamed Aly à ses récentes modifications', *L'Égypte contemporaine* 41, 1949, pp. 115–46.

Notes on Chapter 11

1   For a history of the Egyptian public debt, see the *Compte-rendus des travaux de la Commission de la dette publique*. On the economic history

of Egypt in the nineteenth century, the best accounts remain those of Crouchley, 1938 and Hitta, 1958.

2 On the activities of the business community and the influence of international finance: Landes, 1958.

3 See, for example, Clay, 1995.

4 On the monetary history of Ottoman Egypt: Raymond, 1973–4, vol. 1, pp. 17–52.

5 Bernard, 1812.

6 Figures taken from the conversion table of the para prepared by Raymond, 1973–4, vol. 1, p. 42.

7 For an estimate of this devaluation, see Cuno, 1992, Appendix 2, pp. 211–13, which gives an account of the values of the thaler and the Spanish piastre from 1798 to 1846.

8 Bonaparte benefited from this situation at the time of the promulgation of the tariff in 1798. Vaucher, 1949: 'Since, in Egypt, silver was slightly more expensive than gold, Egyptian gold coins, especially the zeri-mahbub, were put to a disadvantage by the 1798 tariffing. On the basis of the weight of the fine gold which it held, the value of the sequin should have been set at 202 paras instead of 180 which was its trade price in Cairo. The end result was that, for the traders who had to make payments abroad or the soldiers who were returning to France, it was more beneficial to export zeri-mahbubs instead of louis d'or since the quantity of fine gold in the former was proportionately larger than in the latter.'

9 These values are taken from a databank that is presently being built up which gathers both information stemming from the official documents concerning the price for coins and notes taken from various historical sources. For the years cited here, the numbers correspond mainly to different decrees which modify tariffs and to real prices given by Jabarti, 1306.

10 On this aspect of Muhammad 'Ali's trade policy: Alleaume, 1993.

11 Contrary to what is understood from consular correspondence, the policy on monopolies does not concern all sectors of trade but only those related to export.

12 Sami, 1936, vol. 2, p. 259; according to Jabarti, 1306, vol. 4, p. 258 (end of year 1231).

13 Vaucher, 1949, wrongly dates this reform to 1834 while giving an exact hegirian date for the statute that institutes it.

14 A French translation can be found in Sultan, 1914, pp. 48–51.

15 Cited by Arminjon, 1921.

16 The comparison, which seems relevant, is from Vaucher, 1949, pp. 120–1.

17　On the similarities which can be drawn between these two trade currencies: Lelart, 1997.

18　Sultan, 1914, p. 57.

19　Arminjon, 1921, p. 410.

20　See Papiers de Charles Lambert no 7750/3, note entitled 'But du gouvernement' 1842, *Archives de l'Arsenal*, the content of which is actually taken from the Harris Report.

21　See Papiers de Charles Lambert no 7749/4, the Harris Report of 24 November 1841, *Archives de l'Arsenal*. The original document is written in Italian. There is also a French translation annotated by Lambert.

22　See Papiers de Charles Lambert no 7750/3, 'Note sur la monnaie égyptienne', *Archives de l'Arsenal*.

23　See Papiers de Charles Lambert no 7749/3, draft of a report dated 12 July 1842, *Archives de l'Arsenal*.

24　*Ibid.*, letter of Artin to Lambert dated 9 September 1842.

25　*Ibid.*, letter of Lambert to Artin dated 14 September 1842.

26　See Papiers de Charles Lambert no 7750/3, 'Considérations générales sur les monnaies', *Archives de l'Arsenal*.

27　*Ibid.*, rough copy of the 'Note sur la monnaie égyptienne'.

28　On the influence of the Saint-Simonians, see Régnier, 1989, whom I thank for having referred me to the documents concerning the offers of credit made by the Saint-Simonians to Muhammad 'Ali.

29　The statutes of this bank are kept in the archives of the Diwan Khidiwi, record no 2/8/11 of the year 1259. I thank Khalid Fahmy for having given me the reference for this document of which I did not know the original draft, but that I had found mentioned in the archives of the Diwan al-Tijara.

30　Rowley, 1981, pp. 133ff.

CHAPTER 12

The Financial Resources of Coptic Priests in Nineteenth-century Egypt

Magdi Girgis

This research is based on the judicial records of the Coptic patriarchate in Cairo (1853–83) which recorded all cases brought before the patriarch or his judicial agent. These records included many cases relating to priests. This study deals with the incomes of Coptic priests, who constitute one element of the religious structure of the Coptic church. It will not deal with other groups such as patriarchs, bishops or monks.

The sources of priests' incomes in the nineteenth century followed rules and provisions that had been set up at a much earlier date: some of them in the thirteenth century, others long before – sometimes even before the Arab conquests. They developed as a result of a long historical process.

Despite the religious character of this position, a number of non-religious factors played a role in the way that the incomes of priests was determined. In the course of its long history, the church acquired functions and dimensions that were not strictly religious and which distinguished it from other churches. The Council of Chalcedon of 451, for instance, resulted in the separation of the Coptic church from the Roman Empire and its development of an identity which was separate both in doctrine and culture and in the way that priesthood, rituals and religious celebrations developed.

A new element was introduced following the Arab conquest: the Arab administration began Islamising life in Egypt, pushing Copts to seek out the church for their social activities, including entertainment. Thus, the competence of the priests came to include functions that were not strictly religious but which brought them a good income. Moreover, the church's sources of income were brought under administrative and *shari'a* laws limiting the patriarchs' power vis-à-vis Coptic notables whose activities were not always in conformity with church teachings. This was the case with priests as well, since they accommodated the wishes of notables to assure themselves extra sources of income.

These dynamics remained in place until the Fatimid period (circa late tenth century AD),[1] when changing circumstances forced the church to face the deteriorating state of priesthood and the Coptic community. The patriarchs then moved to reform these conditions, a movement which continued for three centuries until the end of the thirteenth century, and under which all the structures and functions of the church, including the priesthood, were reformed. The church had to accept certain excesses that had become entrenched as part of its system over a long period of time and were difficult to overthrow. That is particularly true because priests were not ready to give up the extra income which these excesses allowed them. The system of priesthood remained intact from the thirteenth century until the 1970s. It was Pope Shinuda III (1971–) who restructured the priesthood – especially priests' incomes – and put them under the control of the church's administration.

The Priest and Society

The Coptic priest, like other members of the population, had social and financial obligations. He had a family to provide for and needed to appear presentable before society in terms of his clothes and housing. The priest's job put him in a prominent position on most religious and social occasions. His house was open to visitors, whether they were from his parish or not. Therefore it was important for him to make sure that he had an acceptable income and to try to increase it if possible.

However, the priest was in an uncomfortable position: part of his livelihood was from preaching Christian teachings, which call for disregarding material things and concentrating on spirituality, of giving without asking for something in return. Yet a priest received – even asked for – material returns for his spiritual services. In addition, the system by which a priest earned his living partly depended on his relationship with his parishioners, since they were his only source of income. The church, in fact, did not force anyone to provide for the priest but only encouraged them to do so.

The Work of a Priest and its Organisation

The church gave a priest the authority 'to teach, to baptise and to bless the faithful'.[2] Most church sacraments and religious rituals needed a priest. Thus, six of the seven sacraments of the church – baptism, confirmation, the Eucharist, matrimony, penance and extreme unction – had to be performed by a priest. Even though a priest did not have the authority to enforce punishments on those who transgressed church or religious laws, these duties were enough to keep him busy much of the time.[3]

The regional bishop fixed the geographical limits of each church within which a priest's activities were undertaken and which, to a large extent, determined his income. Overstepping these limits was consequently closely monitored by neighbouring churches. Encroachment by any priest was strictly dealt with by the regional bishop. For example, in 1862, when one of the priests of Uskur in Jiza performed a marriage in al-Mu'arqab which was under the jurisdiction of the Church of Naj' Abu Far in Jiza, he was punished. The matter caused enough concern to be taken to the patriarch for his consideration. He reaffirmed the geographical limits of the church of Abu Far to include Naj' Abu Far, al-Mu'arqab, al-Matanya, Bimha, Tahma, Baht, Jaraza, al-Qatura, al-Riqa Sharq and Gharb, Saft Midum and Atwab.[4]

So much for the organisation among churches of the same region. As for the organisation within each church, it followed two principles. The first was a geographical division for each priest or family of priests within the same church. Each priest was in charge of providing spiritual and religious services to the people of the area defined for him. He alone was responsible for performing rituals of baptism, matrimony, praying for the dead, *al-tula'* (visits to the cemeteries) and extreme unction. Thus, for example, in 1856 Anba Athanasiyus, the bishop of Manfalut, divided the village of Shu among three priests: al-Qummus Habashi and al-Qummus Falta'us, the sons of Madun, were in charge of Darb Awlad Dawud, Darb Sa'id Habashi, Darb 'Uwayl, Darb al-Sawalim and Nazlit Awlad Abu 'l-Khayr. Al-Qummus Qam was in charge of only seven houses in Darb Awlad Dawud which were listed by name.[5] These very specific definitions of each area were presumably set up and recorded in writing to avoid conflict.

The second principle was that of the prayers within the church especially in ones with many priests. The church of Sharuna in Minya, for example, had 10 priests who belonged to four different families. The feast prayers were divided among them as such: Qummus Yusuf 'Ayita: Palm Sunday, Pentecost, feast of the apostles, Transfiguration, feast of the Virgin (3 Kiyahk/29 November), third Sunday of Kiyahk, fourth Sunday of the Holy Fast; Qummus Hanna Atnasiyus: Epiphany, Maundy Thursday, Ascension Day, week of the Great Feast, marriage feast at Cana, feast of the Virgin (21 Kiyahk/17 December), fourth Sunday of Kiyahk, third Sunday of the Holy Fast; Qummus Hanna Yusef, his brother and cousin (total of five priests): feast of Michael the Archangel (12 Hatur/8 November), Holy Saturday, *Ahad al-tanasir*, the last Friday of the Fast, feast of the cross (17 Tut/14 September), feast of the Virgin (16 Misra/9 August), second Sunday of Kihayk, first Sunday of the Fast, Second Sunday of the Fast, circumcision; Qummus 'Abd al-Masih and his nephews (total of three priests): Christmas, Easter Sunday, Commemoration of Archangel Michael (12 Ba'una/6 June), entry of the Holy Family into Egypt, *nawruz* (Coptic new year), feast of the Virgin (21 Ba'una/15 June), first Sunday of Kiyahk, fifth Sunday of the Holy Fast.

The prayers for the remaining days of the year and for minor feasts rotated among them.[6]

This division of religious duties among these 10 priests was not meant to prevent crowding the sanctuary of the church but to ensure a fair distribution of income. The priest who performed the mass received two-thirds of the money that the faithful donated.

Priesthood tended to be concentrated in a few families and was passed down within these families, generation after generation. It was not unusual to have three or four priests within a single family. It was a social disgrace when a family lost the profession of priesthood, and families of priests were consequently careful not to lose that blessing. This principle became entrenched despite the attempts of the patriarchs to resist it.[7] A priest who did not belong to a family of priests did not have the same social status as one who did. We have specific references in documents which identify them as 'not belonging to a house of priests'.[8]

A Priest's Sources of Income

Legal Basis

According to Canon law, a priest was expected to receive all his needs from the church.[9] Even though African laws did not prohibit a priest from seeking other professions,[10] this was considered unacceptable. Any person who decided to embark on priesthood had to forgo his former profession.[11] The church specified the sources of income for priests. These were *al-'ushur* (tithes), *al-bukur* (first fruits) and *al-nudhur* (votive offerings). *Al-'ushur* were for distribution between priests and the poor, *al-bukur* were exclusively for priests and *al-nudhur* were for priests, the poor, widows and strangers.[12] Since the twelfth century, the church had legitimised other sources of income for the priests, such as money that they received directly from the faithful on special occasions like baptisms, marriages and funerary prayers. The church, however, was careful to specify that such payments were entirely voluntary and that under no condition could a priest consider them to be his rightful payment.[13]

Types of Income

Even though the priest's sources of income were clearly defined, the actual proportions which each priest received varied greatly. The terms used to denote the sources of income were also frequently changed. For the first part of the nineteenth century, the terms used for the financial commitments of the church were *'ushur, bukur* and *nudhur*; subsequently these were replaced by terms like *rusum, ma'alim* (sing. *ma'lum*) and *'awayid*.[14] The priests' income came from two sources, firstly through the church. The Coptic church appointed an overseer for every parish church in charge of financial and administrative matters. Among priests, it was customary for the *nizara* to be an inheritable right in families, a position that a priest held as long as he lived 'and his offspring after him, generation after generation, as long as God wills'.[15] The *nazir* was sometimes one of the church's priests or one of the notables of the community. The *nazir*'s work was monitored by the priests who recorded income and expenditure in two copies, one of which was kept with the *nazir* and the other with them. Each party signed the other's copy to avoid disputes.[16] In addition, it was customary for the priests to receive two-thirds of the church's income, leaving one-third for the church.[17]

Church income was made up of a number of items.

Plates of Offerings *(Atbaq Al-'ata')*

Every Sunday, during mass, the faithful made payments in plates which were passed around in church. In an attempt to avoid the disruption that this caused during prayers, Pope Murqus VIII (1796–1809) tried to have this custom performed after mass, but to no avail – presumably because the amounts collected were small once people had dispersed after a service.[18] Even though the poor were theoretically supposed to have a share of one third of the *'ushur*, it was in fact divided into one-third for the church and two-thirds for the priests. The *nazir* divided the priests' share amongst them. In some regions, where the prayers for feast days were undertaken by different priests, the one who performed the prayers directly received two-thirds of the offerings; the offerings which were collected during the weekly service were divided among priests according to set portions.[19]

Unfortunately, the information which survives deals with the shares of income of these offerings but not with the actual amounts of money. It is known for example, that, in the church of Ibsikhiriun al-Jindi, Bihiyu, near Samalut, in the province of Asiyut, 'the sixteen *qirats* which constitute two-thirds of the offerings, are divided into five shares: Qummus Sulayman has two shares and the other three priests each receives one share'.[20]

In the church of Abu Yahnas al-Qasir al-Sharq, in the province of Mallawi, Anba Tumas, the bishop of Minya, divided the income of the church as follows: 'the church's share is eight *qirats*, Qummus Mikha'il has 12 *qirats* and the priest, Jirjis, receives four *qirats*. The church's share remains in the hands of Qummus Mikha'il since he is the *nazir al-kanisa*.'[21]

Al-Nudhur

The laws for *nudhur* (votive offerings) predate Christianity (Leviticus 22:18–23). *Nudhur* have been the most important source of church income, part of which was directed towards priests. In most areas of Egypt, both Copts and Muslims had a custom of slaughtering animals in the names of saints. In addition to the share of meat which a priest received as a donation, people were also obliged to give them the heads and skin of votive animals. The *nazir* sold these and divided the income amongst the priests of the church according to the regular division of one-third to the church and two-thirds to the priests.

In the church of al-Amir Tadrus al-Shatbi, in Disya, in the province of Fayum, for instance, since there was no *nazir* for the church, the '*urafa*', *qawma* (janitors) and porters monopolised the skins of slaughtered animals and left only the heads to the priests, a matter which was brought to the attention of the patriarch, who promptly intervened to put matters right.[22] However, the implementation of *nudhur* differed markedly from one place to another. In regions where *mulids* (saints' days) were celebrated, income was abundant and included, in addition to slaughtered animals, money and jewellery which people gave as gifts to the saint that they were celebrating. Priests received their shares from all that. Therefore, when Anba Isaac, the bishop of Fayum and Bahnasa, forbade the celebration of the *mulid* of Mari Jirjis in Biba because of the folly that accompanied it, the priests of the monastery of Mari Jirjis in Biba, Bani Suwayf, complained to Pope Dimitriyus II (1862–70). The Pope gave in to the priests and their material concerns, and broke a church law by overruling the bishop's order.[23] He issued a letter to all Copts in Egypt, urging them to celebrate the *mulid*, saying: 'It is not permissible to stop a tradition that has been practised since early times, and our intent is to maintain everything as it was'.[24]

The second type of income is that which the priest received directly from parishioners. This includes the *ma'lum* and income from religious and social occasions.

The Ma'lum *(Al-Bukur)*

The *ma'lum* was a specified share of grain, fruits, dairy products, honey or *kishk* (an Egyptian dish made of yoghurt and wheat) which the priest received seasonally from families in his region. The term *ma'lum* is itself Islamic and came into use in the second half of the eighth century/fourteenth century. It originated in Sufi institutions, referring to the salaries of Sufis who lived there. As Sufism spread, Sufis interpreted the Qu'ranic verse, 'But the sincere (and devoted) Servants of God, For them is a Sustenance Determined [*rizq ma'lum*]' as referring to themselves.[25] Hence, what was paid to Sufis was referred to as *ma'lum*. The first mention of that term is in the *waqf* of the Mamluk *amir*, Sarghatmash (757/1356) and then in the *waqf* of Sultan Hasan (760/1358). It came to be used for all salaries of employees in religious institutions and students. Historians prior to Maqrizi did not use this term. Therefore, for example, when referring to the salaries of Sufis and religious employees, Ibn 'Abd al-Zahir (692/1292) used the term '*nuwalat*', while Ibn Mamati (606/1209), Ibn Wasil (697/1297), Abu al-Fida' (732/1331), Ibn Kathir (774/1372) and Ibn al-Furat (807/1404) used the terms '*al-jiraya*' and '*al-jamkiyya*'. Maqrizi (845/1441) was the first to use the term *ma'lum* at several points. In his narration of Salah al-Din al-Ayyubi's establishment of the Sufi *khanqa* of Sa'id al-Su'ada', he referred to Salah al-Din's arrangement of *ma'alim* for the Sufis who lived there. This term became very common in historical writing following Maqrizi, and was such an integral part of Egyptian discourse that a popular saying in the seventeenth century was 'al-rizq 'ala Allah ma'lum' ('God knows where the blessings will come from').

Whatever gifts or offerings priests received fell under the general rubric of *sadaqa*, charity, Copts borrowed the term *ma'lum* and used it to refer to that which priests received directly from the faithful. It is difficult to ascertain when the term was first used in Coptic discourse; the earliest text which the author has come across dates back to 1208/1793.[26]

The priest received his *ma'lum* according to the division followed by his particular church. Usually a member of the community volunteered to collect the priest's *ma'lum* and give it to him. If the priest's home was in the same village, his *ma'lum* was sent there directly. Problems and disputes between priests and parishioners often led them to withhold payment of or decrease the *ma'lum*. In that case, priests complained to the patriarch, who in turn wrote to those who withheld payment urging them to pay.[27] In other instances, parishioners withheld payment of *ma'lum* in order to support the *nazir* of a church if he was in conflict with the priest, so as to force the priest to give in to the *nazir*'s wishes.[28] Pope Kirulus IV (1853–61) wanted to restructure the system in such a way that priests would have salaries paid directly by the patriarchate instead of the *ma'lum* that they received from parishioners.[29] This would have radically changed the situation insofar as priests' incomes were concerned. This reform, however, was abandoned under his successor, Dimitriyus II, along with many other of his reforms. Interestingly enough, the term *ma'lum* was still in use until the 1970s, when Pope Shinuda III succeeded in abolishing it, thus restoring the reforms of Dimitriyus II.

Religious and Social Occasions

The Coptic church organised a system of rituals which followed a human being through from birth to death. The church had a role in all important steps in a person's life. In addition, social secular occasions were introduced into the church and given religious overtones and rituals which required priests. These provided another source of income for priests. These social celebrations are as follows:

Baptism

The first of the seven sacraments of the church, baptism was performed 40 days after a boy's birth and 80 days after a girl's birth. It had to be performed by a priest in church and was one of the happiest occasions for a Coptic family. A priest received sums of money from the family of the child, especially at the performance of '*hall al-zinna*' (literally 'the suspension of the girdle'), which is the last rite of baptism.[30]

Male Circumcision

This celebration is not essentially religious. It was a religious celebration in Jewish rituals of the Old Testament, and many Copts customarily performed circumcisions on happy occasions. A child might be circumcised on the morning after a family wedding or during a saint's *mulid* at the monastery where it was held. Only boys were circumcised; the celebration was accompanied by banquets and *nuqut* (presents of money).[31] When the celebration was performed in a monastery, both the priests and the barber who performed the circumcision received a portion of the presents. Thus, the priest of the monastery of Abu Ishaq al-Dafrawi at al-Hammam, complained that the barber had monopolised all the *nuqut* received during circumcisions held at their monastery during the *mulid*. On this occasion, the patriarch personally intervened to prevent the barber from competing with the priests.[32]

Betrothal/Engagement

Until the age of Kirulus IV, an engagement was considered '*aqd al-imlak*, a suspended marriage contract similar to the Muslim *katb al-kitab*.[33] The marriage would only be consummated after the actual *iklil* (wedding). This was one of the happy occasions on which priests received many gifts. In fact, priests of other regions were invited to attend ceremonies and shared in the rewards: it was a matter of social pride and prestige to have as many priests as possible attending. Thus, at the engagement of a notable's son in Mit Ghamr, the priests of the regions of Zifta, Daqadus, Sahrgat and Kafr al-Shahid, and the priests of Mit Ghamr itself, all attended the ceremony.[34]

Marriage

Akalil[35] was the ritual finalising a marriage and making it public. It was the most important and happiest occasion for a Coptic family. In the Egyptian countryside, marriage festivities customarily lasted a long time, sometimes up to two months, reaching a peak on the actual wedding day. The *akalil* consisted not only of prayers, but lasted all of the wedding day. After the official prayer rituals, the couple remained seated, wearing wreaths or crowns. The groom wore a silk girdle. The *'arif*, or priest, chanted certain happy hymns while a relative of the groom moved around with a scarf collecting *nuqut* from the guests. All this money was given to the priest who performed the marriage. If an *'arif* was involved in the ceremony, he would also be given a portion of the *nuqut*. The ceremony ended when the priest untied the groom's girdle, which he did only when he was satisfied with the gifts that he received from the groom and his family. The other priests who attended the wedding received presents only from the groom's family.[36]

Death

Egyptians have long been fascinated by death rituals, and have taken pains to perform them properly. Even though Christianity forbids grieving over death (1 Thessalonians 4:13), the Pharaonic influence predominated. Egyptians continued to perform their funerary rituals with care and concern, whether the deceased was a Copt or a Muslim. The efforts of some *walis* (governors)[37] and some patriarchs[38] to repress these customs ended in failure. Funerals were also occasions to show off, and hence cost families a lot of money.[39]

The fact that priests took part in these rituals meant two things. Firstly, it meant that people abided by the rituals set out by the church.[40] Secondly, it meant that priests had to turn a blind eye to behaviour which did not conform to religious teachings, so as not to lose a main source of their income. Patriarchs could not condemn such customs, so as not to antagonise the priests. In fact, some patriarchs went so far as to recommend performing such customary rituals in order to ensure that priests receive the incomes to which they were accustomed on such occasions.[41]

Priests received different kinds of incomes from funerary rituals.

Praying for the Dead (Al-Kharja)

When a notable died, the patriarch might be asked to lead the prayer, or the bishop himself might perform it, along with the priests of the region.[42] The number of priests present in a funeral mass – especially if the bishop or patriarch was present – was something to boast about. Those priests who took part in the prayers received sums of money which varied according to the deceased's social standing. When the deceased was a rich man, the priest received significant amounts of money. Our sources provide some examples: 195 piastres for Father Jirjis, the family priest, 38 piastres for Father Yusuf of Babilun, Misr al-Qadima, 38 piastres for Father Jirjis of Harat al-Saqa'iyyin and 152 piastres for four priests from the churches of Cairo.[43] At the funeral of a notable from Bardis in Upper Egypt, the priests of Jirja, Bardis and Baliana who took part in the prayers received a total of 17,000 piastres.[44]

When the deceased were not so rich, the amounts that priest received were limited, and were sometimes paid after the inheritance was divided.[45]

Salat Al-Thalith *(The Prayer on the Third Day after Death)*

These were prayers held on the third day after the death of a person. The priest also received a sum of money for performing these rites. The amount was less than that which was paid at the funeral. Thus, for example, the inheritance of Milika Antun, who died in 1876, listed '16 piastres for Father Matta for the *salat al-thalith*'.[46]

Al-Tarhim

This was a mass held for the soul of the deceased. The deceased's family paid for the incense, candles and offerings, in addition to sums which were paid to the priests who held the mass. The amounts differed radically according to the social status of the deceased. Thus, priests received 154 piastres for holding a mass for a deceased woman;[47] for the mass of a notable man, however, they received 4018 piastres.[48]

Tarahim were sometimes held in several churches simultaneously. Hence, the *tarahim* of a notable from Bardis in Upper Egypt were held at the churches of Jirja, Bardis and Baliana.[49] For one Cairene notable 10 *tarahim* were held at the church of Anba Ruways and five at the church of al-'Adhra' (the Virgin Mary) at Harat Zuwayla.[50]

The Sabi' *(Seventh Day after Death)*, Khamis 'ashar *(Fifteenth Day) and* Arbi'in *(Fortieth Day)*

These were all occasions following a death for mass to be held, followed by banquets for family and friends. The priests received money for those prayers as well.[51]

Tula' *(Visitations to Cemeteries)*

These were visitations to cemeteries on feasts and other special occasions, an ancient Egyptian tradition. The word '*tal'a*' (pl. *tula'*) – literally 'outing' – is the translation for the hieroglyphic *brt*. Priests were accustomed to accompanying families and relatives to cemeteries to burn incense on each grave, in return for a fee paid by the families. *Tula'* were held on the major feasts, those related to Jesus Christ, such as Christmas, Epiphany and Easter, as well as other feasts and occasions like *nawruz* (Coptic new year), the feast of the cross, mid-fasting and *Shamm al-Nasim* (the Monday after Easter Sunday). This was an important and recurrent source of income for priests, since the families of the deceased regularly visited the cemeteries even years after their loved ones had died. Hence, the number of prayers was in constant increase. Huge banquets called *mawajib* were arranged at the cemeteries during the *tula'*.[52]

It was not possible to calculate how much money a priest received during *tula'*. However, there is data concerning the total expenses of a *tal'a*. A *tal'a* on *nawruz* cost 146.3 piastres for one deceased man[53] and 1000 piastres for another.[54] Here, again, the range was wide between people of modest social standing and the rich.

Waqf *and a Priest's Income*

Despite the large number of *waqfs* founded for most churches and monasteries in Egypt, priests did not benefit from them. Coptic *waqfs* differed in their administration from Islamic *waqfs*.[55] However, some priests benefited from *al-rizaq al-ahbasiyya*, which were set up by the state to finance monasteries.[56] There is an exceptional case of the priests of the monastery of al-'Adhra' in Jabal al-Tayr, in Samalut, who benefited from a *rizqa* that had been set up for their monastery: since it had no monks, the *rizqa* was divided among the priests.[57]

The survey of the various sources indicate the sources of income available to Coptic priest in the nineteenth century. However, it is still not possible to reach a general conclusion as to whether a priest's income covered his needs, since that involved various factors.

The Region where a Priest Served

A priest's income varied according to where he served. A priest whose church was in a rich region enjoyed a larger income compared to the one whose church was in a poor region. For example, two priests, who were also cousins, complained about their shared life in Balut, in the province of Asiyut, because they were responsible for too many estates and cattle; they asked to divide their properties.[58] On the other hand, the priest of the church of Mari Mina, at Tahna, in the province of Minya, did not find a way to support himself except through begging. Dimitriyus II allowed him to beg 'to earn a living for himself and his children'.[59] A priest's income was also determined by the number of priests in any church with whom he would have to share receipts.

Establishing *Waqfs* for a Monastery

Patriarchs customarily set up certain areas whose income from *nudhur*, *rusum* and *ma'alim* would be used to establish *waqfs* to fund particular monasteries. Manfalut and Bani Kalb, for instance, were set up as *waqf* for the monastery of al-Mahriq.[60] Al-Mahalla al-Kubra, Mit Ghamr, al-Mansura, Salamun al-Qammash and al-Raydaniyya were set up as *waqfs* for the monastery of Anba Bishoy at Tarana,[61] and the incomes of the priests in these *waqf* regions were consequently sharply reduced. Sometimes bishops interfered to nullify certain *waqfs* in order to allow priests to have a source of income, which of course caused complaint from the monasteries.[62]

A Priest's Relationship with his Parishioners

A priest's income was also affected by his relationship with his parishioners. Disputes erupted with some notables and *nazirs*, leading to some people withholding their *ma'lum* or even going as far as to ignore the priest on most social occasions. These disputes were either due to objections concerning a priest's behaviour,[63] or because a priest let those close to him read more *tafasir* (interpretations of the Bible) to the congregation on social occasions.[64]

Conclusion

In conclusion, although priests' sources of income were essentially linked to church regulations, these were often adapted and modified under the influence of Egyptian customs and traditions. Moreover, because these incomes were dependent, to a large extent, on the generosity of churchgoers, the priests' performance of their religious duties could be influenced by their material concerns. Thus, through the study of the sources of incomes of these priests, one can get a deeper understanding of the complex relations between religious structures and material conditions, and of the way that one particular group in nineteenth-century Egyptian society earned a living.

Bibliography

Primary Sources

Library of the Patriarchate of Cairo: Official Correspondence of Pope Murqus VIII; Official Correspondence of Pope Butrus al-Jawli

Al-Sijillat al-qada'iyya li-batriarqiyat al-Qabat al-urthuduks bi'l-Qahira (official correspondence of Pope Dimitriyus II, 111th patriarch).

Sijill al-Turk.

Published Sources

'Abd al-Rahman, *'Abd al-Rahim, al-Rif al-misri fi 'l-qarn al-thamin 'ashar*, Cairo, Madbuli, 1986.

Amin, Muhammad Muhammad, *al-Awqaf wa'l-haya al-ijtima'iyya fi Misr*, Cairo, Dar al-Nahda al-Arabiyya, 1980.

'Awwad, Jirjis Filtha'us, *Dhikra muslih 'azim*, Cairo, Matba'at al-Tawfiq, 1911.

Fuwwa, Yusab Usquf, *Tarikh al-aba' al-batariqa*, Cairo, Mimeographed, n.d.

Girgis, Magdi, *Al- Qada' al-Qibti fi Misrirasa Tarikhiyya*, Dar Mirit lil-Nashr, Cairo, 1999

Ibn 'Abd al-Zahir, *Tashrif al-ayyam wa'l-'usur fi sirat al-malik al-mansur*, ed. Murad Kamil, Cairo, Ministry of Culture, 1961.

Ibn al-'Assal, Safiy al-Din ibn, (died around 1260), *al-Majmu' al-safawi*, Cairo, Jirjis Filuna'us, n.d.

Ibn al-Furat, *Tarikh al-duwwal wa'l-muluk*, ed. Hassan Muhammad, Basra, 1967.

Ibn Iyas al-Hanafi, Muhammad b. Ahmad, *Bada'i' al-zuhur fi waqa' al-duhur*, Cairo, al-Hay'a al-'amma li-qusur al-thaqafa, n.d.

Ibn Wasil, *Mufarrij al-qulub fi akhbar bani Ayyub*, Cairo, Ministry of Culture, 1972.

Ibn Taghribirdi, *al-Nujum al-zahira fi muluk Misr wa'l-Qahira*, Cairo, Ministry of Culture, n.d.

Iskarus, Tawfikq, *Nawabigh al-aqbat wa-mashahiruhum fi 'l-qarn al-tasi' 'ashar*, Cairo, Matba'at al-Tawfiq, 1910.

Jabarti, al-, *Tarikh 'aja'ib al-athar*, Beirut, Dar al-Jil, n.d.

Jirgjis, Majdi, *al-Qada' al-qibti fi Misr*, Cairo, Mirette, 1999.

Kassab, Hananiya Ilyas, *Majmu' al-shar' al-kanasi*, Beirut, Manshurat al-Nur, 1975.

Maghrabi, Yusuf al-, *Daf al- isr 'an kalam ahl Misr*, ed. with an introduction by 'Abd al-Salam Ahmad 'Awwad, Moscow, Akadamiyat al-'Ulum Lil Ittihad al-Sufyiti, 1968.

Qilada, Wilyam Sulayman, *Kitab al-dusquliyya: ta'alim al-rusul*, 2nd ed., Cairo, Dar al-Thaqafa, 1989.

Shaw, Stanford J., *The Financial Organization and Development of Ottoman Egypt, 1517–1798*, Princeton, NJ, Princeton University Press, 1962.

Suryal, Riyad, *al-Mujtama' al-qibti fi 'l-qarn al-tasi' 'ashar*, M.A. thesis, Cairo University, Faculty of Arts, Cairo, 1969.

Tawil, Tawfil al-, *al-Tasawwuf fi Misr ibban al-'asr al-'uthmani*, Cairo, Al-hay al-Misriyya Lil-Kitab, 1988.

Yuhana, Mansi, *Tarikh al-kanisa al-qibtiyya*, Cairo, Maktabit al-Mahaba, n.d.

Yusuf (the bishop of Fuh), *Tarikh al-aba' al-batariqa*, Cairo, Samu'il al-Siryani and Nabih Kamil, n.d.

Yusuf Ali, Abdullah, *The Holy Quran: Text, Translation and Commentary*, New York, Hafner, 1946.

Acknowledgement

This chapter translated by Amina Elbendary.

Notes on Chapter 12

1 For more on the circumstances which allowed the Church to restructure itself see Girgis, 1999, pp. 49–52.

2 Ibn al-'Assal, n.d., vol. 1, p. 65.

3 *Ibid.*, vol. 1, p. 66.

4 Al-Sijillat al-qada'iyya, no 2, p. 22 dated 13 Sha'ban 1279/1862.

5 *Ibid.*, p. 11 (Official Correspondence of Anba Athanasiyus, the Bishop of Manfalut), dated 19 Misra 1572/1856.

6 *Ibid.*, no 5, pp. 2, 3, 9 (dated 1879).

7 Correspondence and sermons of Pope Yuanas 107 (1769–96).

8 Al-Sijillat al-qada'iyya, no 2, p. 28.

9 Qilada, 1989, p. 465.

10 Kassab, 1975, p. 408.

11 Al-Sijillat al-qad'iyya, no 5, pp. 125–6.

12 Ibn al-'Assal, n.d., vol. 1, pp. 189–90. This is a continuation of old testament laws which determined that priests were to receive one-tenth of the *'ushur* paid by the people (Deuteronomy 18:26–8 and Numbers 18:14–9) as well as the first fruits of various crops (Deuteronomy 26:1–10) as well as votive offerings (Leviticus: 27).

13 A law issued by Pope Kirulus 67 (1078–92): Yusuf, n.d., p. 127.

14 The change in terminology can be traced by examining the official correspondence of the Patriarchs who headed the Church between 1796 to 1870. The correspondence of Patriarch Murqus

VIII mentions '*al-'ushur* and *al-nudhur* and the first fruits (*al-bukur*) of everything, even the first offspring of a donkey has to be made up for by another offering': official correspondence of Pope Murqus VIII, ms 345 Lahut/470, Library of the Patriarchate of Cairo, folio 8: recto; Butrus al-Jawli (1809–52): '*al-'ushur* and *al-bukur* and *al-nudhur* are a duty to God Almighty from each believer by his name': official correspondence of Pope Butrus al-Jawli, ms 259 Lahut/447, Library of the Patriarchate of Cairo, folio 117: verso; Kirulus IV urged the people of Tima to pay their *nudhur* to Mariqassam al-Usimi al-Jundi and mentioned the rights of the bishop of Esna as being *al-rusumat* and *al-'awayid*: al-Sijillat al-qada'iyya, no 1, pp. 11–12; Dimitriyus II, in more than 10 instances, mentioned financial obligations as being '*al-nudhur, al-rusum* and *al-ma'alim*' or '*al-nudhur, al-rusum,* al-*'awayid al-diyariyya*': al-Sijillat al-qada'iyya, no 2, pp. 19, 25, 40, 41, 46, 47, 51, 60, 62, 91, 93 and 111. Pope Kirulus V (1874–1927) mentioned the same: al-Sijillat al-qada'iyya, no. 5, pp. 9, 31.

15 The Church gave the bishop the authority to deal with Church property (law 15 for the Council of Ankara 314 AD). The Council of Ghanfar (325–381 AD) passed a law that gave authority to the bishops to appoint deputies to collect Church dues and redistribute them. Pope Na'ufilus al-Sakandari (384–412 AD) was the first to refer to the appointment of a manager to oversee Church finances. This office was later called *nazir al-kanisa*; the person holding the office was in charge of '*al-nudhur, al-wuqufat, al-maqbud* and *al-masruf*... and oversaw the priests' performance of prayers at their specified times': the 94th decree of Pope Yuanas (1484–1524), appointing the *nazir* of the church of Marjirjis in Sadanfa in the province of Mahalla: ms 291 Lahut/301, Library of the Patriarchate of Cairo, folio 13: verso, folio 14: recto; al-Sijillat al-qada'iyya, no 1, p.11, no 2, pp. 11, 27, 51.

16 Disputes developed between priests because one of them (or his family) monopolised the *nizara* of a particular church. Dimitriyus II appointed *nazirs* from among the community to prevent disputes among priests. However, this did not pre-empt disputes between priests and nazirs: for example, al-Sijillat al-qada'iyya, no 2, p. 20.

17 This division seems to have been in place for centuries. None of the manuscripts and documents consulted for the period before the nineteenth century mentioned an official statement which included the share of the poor (one-third) as part of the priests' share.

18 Official correspondence of Pope Murqus VIII, ms 345 Lahut/470, Library of the Patriarchate of Cairo, folio 15: recto.

19 Al-Sijillat al-qada'iyya, no 5, p. 9.

20 Al-Sijillat al-qada'iyya, no 2, p. 28.

21 *Ibid.*, p. 20.

22 *Ibid.*, p. 32.

23 Church laws sustained the rights of each bishop over his bishopric and forbade any bishop from interfering in the affairs of another. Laws nos 9 and 3, Council of Antioch 341 AD and law no 6, council of Afsas 431 AD. In fact, in the tenth century, one bishop considered the Pope's praying in his bishopric without his permission to be a violation of the bishop's rights and forbade the Pope from leading prayers: Yuhana, n.d., p. 36.

24 Al-Sijillat al-qada'iyya, no 2, p. 111.

25 *The Qu'ran*, al-Saffat (37: 40–41), English wording from Yusuf Ali, 1946, p. 1196.

26 Ibn Iyas, n.d., vol. 1, pp. 521, 757, 758, vol. 3, p. 280; Ibn 'Abd al-Zahir, 1961, vol. 1, pp. 127, 235; Ibn al-Furat, 1967, vol. 4, pp. 3, 5, 78; Ibn Wasil, 1972, vol. 5, pp. 158, 160, 303; Iskarus, 1910, vol. 1, p. 270; Tawil, 1988, vol. 1, p. 44; Jabarti, n.d., vol. 1, p. 495; Amin, 1980, pp. 191, 192, 212, 217, 237, 251, 253, 268, 274; Maghrabi, 1968, p. 40.

27 Al-Sijillat al-qada'iyya, no 2, pp. 25, 41, 51, 62, 93, 111.

28 Al-Sijillat al-qada'iyya, no 2, pp. 23, 53, 56.

29 'Awwad, 1911, p. 187.

30 Al-Sijillat al-qada'iyya, no 2, p. 62.

31 Jabarti, vol. 3, p. 614.

32 Al-Sijillat al-qada'iyya, no 2, p. 52.

33 The term '*nisf iklil*' or 'half marriage' is still used today to describe the rituals of the engagement in reference to the meaning of engagement in that period.

34 Al-Sijillat al-qada'iyya, no 5, pp. 36–7.

35 An *iklil* is literally the wreath or crown worn by the bride and groom during an Orthodox wedding ceremony.

36 Al-Sijillat al-qada'iyya, no 2, pp. 22, 62.

37 For example, Muzahim ibn Khaqan, governor of Egypt in 253/867, issued a decree prohibiting lamentations accompanying funerals: Ibn Taghribirdi, n.d., vol. 2, p. 338.

38 For example, Pope Kirulus 67 and Pope Kirulus V tried to quell these customs: Suryal, 1969, pp. 325–326; Fuwwa, n.d., p. 127.

39 'Abd al-Rahman, 1986, p. 266.

40 The *dusquliyya* arranged for funerals. Ibn al-'Assal completed these processes and copied from the laws of the prophets the days on

which the deceased was to be remembered with prayers. These are the third day, the seventh day, one month and one year after the funeral. The poor should be paid from the deceased's money. Ibn al-'Assal commented that, in his time (the thirteenth century AD), offerings were made on the day of the funeral, on the tenth day, after one month, six months and one year, and that most who could afford it made forty offerings from the time of death: Qilada, 1989, pp. 755–6; Ibn al-'Assal, n.d., vol. 1, pp. 206–7.

41 It is not necessary to mark the emphasis of Dimitriyus II on the importance of such rituals. It suffices to quote from his letter to the people of Nahiyat al-Zarabi in Asiyut: 'You are obliged to visit the dead on the major feasts and the customary days every year on time since this is designated for the priests of the monastery of Anba Athanasiyus.' Al-Sijillat al-qada'iyya, no 2, pp. 91, 93.

42 The file of the inheritance of Yusuf Nasralla, Archives of the Patriarchate, folio 9.

43 *Ibid.*, folio 11.

44 Sijill al-Turk, 'The inheritance of Shinuda Lawindi', Archives of the Patriarchate, p. 106.

45 'The inheritance of Shunuda Suwaiha', Archives of the Patriarchate, folio 3.

46 Sijill al-turk, p. 112.

47 *Ibid.*, p. 84.

48 *Ibid.*, p. 41.

49 *Ibid.*, p. 104.

50 *Ibid.*, p. 70.

51 *Ibid.*, for example, pp. 57, 94.

52 *Mawagib* are banquets which accompanied funerals and *tula'*: al-Sijillat al-qada'iyya, no 2, p. 6; Sijill al-Turk, pp. 42, 98.

53 Sijill al-Turk, p. 84.

54 'The Inheritance of Yusuf Nasrallah', The Archives of the Patriarchate, folio 21.

55 The author is currently working on a comprehensive research on Coptic *waqfs*.

56 Translator's note: a *rizqa ihbasiyya* was a portion of the revenue imposed by the ruler on *multazims* who administered agricultural land to be paid to a pious or charitable institution: Shaw, 1962, p. 46.

57 Documents of the Patriarchate, Rizqat Jabal al-Tayr, unnumbered, dated 1284/1867. The two terms, *dayr* (monastery) and *kanisa* (church) are used interchangeably in the documents, since all schools of *fiqh* did not allow *waqfs* to be established for a *kanis*, while *waqfs* were allowed to be established for a *dayr*. Therefore,

the founders of *waqfs* resorted to using the term dayr for a church so that the Muslim judge would legitimise their *waqf*. Therefore, the *rizqa* was for a Dayr Jabal al-Tayr, even though it is not believed to have actually been a monastery. My colleague Ramiz Wadi' Butrus is preparing his doctoral dissertation at the University of Strasbourg, France, on the history of that *dayr*.

58 Al-Sijillat al-qada'iyya, no 3, p. 2.
59 Al-Sijillat al-qada'iyya, no 2, p. 12.
60 *Ibid.*, p. 38.
61 *Ibid.*, p. 47.
62 *Ibid.*, p. 91.
63 Al-Sijillat al-qada'iyya, no 5, pp. 39, 103.
64 *Ibid.*, pp. 36–7.

CHAPTER 13

Perceptions of the Greek Money-lender in Egyptian Collective Memory at the Turn of the Twentieth Century

Sayyid 'Ashmawi

Introduction

The present study attempts to clarify one of the forms of Western capitalist expansion and penetration into Egyptian society during the end of the nineteenth and the beginning of the twentieth century, a period of great transformation in this society. The spread of European financial capitalism in rural areas coincided with imperial expansion; thus, it took a particularly crude and brutal form. The role of bankers and money-lenders increased as they provided loans, not only to the state apparatus, but also to small agriculturists. As relations with the West developed between the eras of Muhammad 'Ali (1805–48) and Isma'il (1863–79), these groups saw their networks and channels of influence and activity assume wider proportions, spreading throughout Egypt. Because of the capitulations, the state was no longer capable of controlling domestic developments. The combination of all these factors affected peasants, bringing about significant transformations in their lives.

Through literary sources, this study analyses the role of one particular group, the Greeks, in the development of this process of expansion into rural Egypt. It explores two levels of this reality. First, it analyses the input of Greeks in the spread of capitalism in rural areas. Secondly, it analyses the way in which these Greeks were perceived by Egyptians through different forms of expression, such as literature, film and song.

There was a significant Greek presence in Egypt at the turn of the twentieth century. Members of the Greek community lived in many different parts of the country, not only in Cairo and Alexandria but also in the provincial towns of upper and lower Egypt. Although they carried out varied commercial and professional activities, the present work will study only those individuals involved in one particular activity, money-lending, whose activities, in fact, were linked in the collective mind to all Greeks in Egypt.

The sources for the historiography of this period include published archival material, diplomatic reports, private papers and letters, decrees, memoranda, memoirs, urban planning maps, dictionaries and academic theses. Contemporary literary and artistic works have also been used: the slogans and poetry of Hafiz Ibrahim, Bayram al-Tunsi and 'Abd Allah al-Nadim; the novels of Muhammad Hafiz Ibrahim, Yahya Haqqi and Jamil 'Atiya Ibrahim; the biographies of 'Abd Allah al-Nadim and Sayyid Darwish; the literary critiques of Muhammad Muhammad Husayn and 'Abd al-Muhsin Taha Badr. The study of contemporary European literature further clarified the picture, especially the works of E.W. Lane, Lucy Duff Gordon, Edmond About, Clot Bey, Edward Gouin, Emile Ludwig and Lawrence Durrell; these sources are being used here in a relatively new way for the study of contemporary Egyptian history.

The Greek phenomenon is unique in modern Egyptian history as a prototype of the penetration of foreign capital into the Egyptian countryside. The literary sources of the time confirm this. Around the middle of the nineteenth century, Duff Gordon put it trenchantly in a letter to her mother, to whom she wrote that Greek money-lenders followed Coptic treasury officials as the eagle followed the cow. Lord Cromer's comments on Greek money-lenders and the presence of Greeks in every corner of Egypt, made at the beginning of the twentieth century, were characteristically expressive: turn over any rock in Egypt, he remarked, and you will find a Greek. The image of the Greek was multifaceted, but perhaps most prominent image was the Greek as merchant or money-lender, both of whom attempted to realise ever-greater profits through the purchase and sale of commodities and loans made to the peasants at very high rates of interest. There was also the image of the middleman (*comprador*), who resold commodities and purchased primary products for export, providing links between the local and European markets. These images were reinforced when some of the Greeks – the most numerous of the non-indigenous communities in Egypt and the closest to the Egyptians – began to trade in grain, flour, onions, cotton, tobacco, alcohol and even drugs. They invested their money in numerous financial, industrial and agricultural activities. The growing numbers of Greeks who opened postal savings accounts, and the increase in the amounts of money that they placed there, are indications of their capital accumulation between 1903 and 1910, as Muhammad Tal'at Harb indicates in *'Ilaj Misr al-iqtisadi wa-mashru' Bank al-Misriyyin aw-Bank al-Umma*. Further indications are provided by the spread of Greek banks: between the period of Muhammad 'Ali's rule and the early twentieth century, a number of new Greek banks opened, such as the Athens Bank, the Ionian Bank, the Eastern Ionian Bank, the Greek Community Bank and the Athens Greek Community Bank. New enterprises dealing in chromium, alcohol, land reclamation, tobacco, cotton export, ginning and contracting were also established.

Although Greeks in Egypt pursued numerous activities, one particular image of the Greek dominated the popular Egyptian collective memory: that of the middleman. This memory developed around the more negative aspects of Greek economic activity, especially in rural areas. The image was of the Greek who often tried to defraud peasants of their land and their crops, after they became unable to pay their debts due to the exorbitant rates demanded by money-lenders. The spread of capitalism in this particular form was to the direct detriment of small producers – peasants, merchants and artisans. These money-lenders sometimes hoarded crops, which were then resold on the black market; they also sometimes purchased small peasant holdings from bankrupt peasants. Some of these capitalists thus became the owners of large estates in al-Buhayra and Alexandria.

At times, the response to the presence of foreigners in general, and to Greeks in particular, was violent. When the oppression of deprived groups reached its peak, resistance in all its forms inevitably intensified. This resistance became an important characteristic of the national liberation movement in Egypt at the time. In other words, this resistance to capitalist penetration was linked to the struggle against colonialism. At times, resistance took an active shape in attacks on money-lenders, murders of money-lenders and the display of their corpses and attacks on their shops, stalls or taverns. At other times, it took the form of passive resistance through literary or artistic expression.

The Image of the Greek Money-lender in Collective Memory: Late Nineteenth/Early Twentieth-century Egypt

The elaboration of a negative image of Greeks, in this context, needs to be seen in relation to a number of factors. First of all, one must consider the relative weight of the Greek presence in Egypt in relation to the other foreign communities as well as the role of this community in the local economy; these are significant elements for understanding how the image of the Greek was created in the collective popular memory. The existing literature and statistical findings – sometimes exaggerated[1] – confirm that this community was among the largest, most influential and widespread in Egypt at the end of the eighteenth century, when its population reached approximately 4000. By the end of the following century, this number had reached 40,000. The community continued to multiply throughout the first quarter of the twentieth century, after which there were 70,000 Greeks in Egypt. The magnitude of this increase may be better apprehended in table 13.1.[2]

It is essential to place this marked increase in the number of Greeks in Egypt within the context of population growth in the country during this period, a growth which affected both Egyptians and foreigners even if this growth slowed or was reversed during certain periods, especially after the abrogation of the capitulations. The large number of Greeks explains Cromer's remark, referred to earlier, that under every stone in Egypt, one could find a Greek.[3] Cromer seems to have been quite fond of this phrase – which he had coined – since he repeated it on another occasion, speaking of a Greek and the 'hole in a rock in which he had set up a temporary shop'.[4]

Writing about the Egyptianisation of some communities, the Jesuit priest Henri 'Ayrut mentions the Greeks as being the 'most numerous and closest to the people'.[5] This view is shared

Table 13.1: The Greek Population in Egypt

Year	Number of Greeks
1827	5900
1871	3400
1882	27,301
1886	37,301
1898	38,208
1907	62,973
1917	56,731
1927	76,264
1937	68,559
1947	57,427

by numerous scholars, who consider that the Greeks were the most closely integrated with the Egyptians.[6] Yunan Labib Rizq's study of *al-Ahram* newspaper noted that the Syrians and Greeks shared a characteristic unique to them among the other foreign communities in Egypt: they were present in all parts of Egypt, even in the smallest villages.[7]

The Greek presence gradually became an integral part of the fabric of Egyptians' daily lives. This fact is reflected in art – particularly in literature. Through such sources, one may glimpse the lives of individuals, their reactions to larger historical trends and the active part that they played in shaping trends. In such early films as *'Antar wa-Lublub* or *Salama fi 'l-Khayr*, Greeks are shown residing in the popular quarters of the city, rather than in the Europeanised parts. Colloquial and classical poetry (for instance, the works of 'Abd Allah al-Nadim, Bayram al-Tunsi and Hafiz Ibrahim), novels and short stories are full of images of the Greeks of Egypt. In the 22 December 1926 issue of *al-Jarida al-Siyasiyya*, Yahya Haqqi published a story entitled 'Qahwat Dimitri' ('Dimitri's Café'), beginning with the words:

> It is not the specific characteristic of only one place. It is, if you like, the trademark of many cafés spread throughout the Egyptian countryside, north and south, in every small town and every large village. They all resemble each other in that the manager is a man who could be called Dimitri in one town or Mikhali in another. His name would have to be one of those names or one resembling them: Tudri, Christo, Yanni, Kharalambo... These cafés

occupy their place in peace and quiet. They continue to expand because they maintain the traditions which brought about their inception, depending on one environment from which they do not deviate. Eventually, they become one of the characteristics of this environment, a phenomenon which profoundly affects the various aspects of people's lives just as important as any other phenomenon.[8]

In the multinational throng of characters in Durrell's *The Alexandria Quartet* – especially *Justine*[9] – Greeks appear more frequently than other foreigners living in Alexandria. In the recently published *Awraq Sakandariyya*, Jamil 'Atiya Ibrahim deftly sketches the Greek Mikhali. One of the characters in the novel remarks, 'Among the European peoples, the Greeks are closest to the Egyptians'.

As concerns social organisation, the Greek presence in Egypt had long-standing historical antecedents. Until the 1830s, they were an integral part of the Ottoman Empire and could move unimpeded between the different provinces. Some writers, however, distinguished between 'Greek subjects' and 'Greek foreigners'. Subhi Wahida, discussing the presence of foreigners in Egypt, notes that they were divided into two groups. One was made up of 'real Westerners', who entered different countries with the intention of investing their money and, ultimately, either departed or settled there, retaining links with their own countries; the other was composed of immigrants who came to Egypt in the last century from the Mediterranean and Ottoman lands. These acquired citizenship but kept their foreign passports in order to enjoy the advantages which this afforded them. They lived on the fringes of Western life as they had known it in their homelands. The first group was mainly made up of a few businessman who expanded their activity outside Europe and who, at the beginning of the twentieth century, eventually lost the political influence which they had exercised. As for the second group, more numerous than the first, they can neither be described as Egyptian nor European in composition. Rather, they were the result of an aberrant political, social and economic condition, determined by the specific relations obtained between the subjects of the Ottoman sultanate and those under the protection of the 'Christian nations' in the Islamic East during the eighteenth and nineteenth centuries. Indeed, individuals enjoying the protection of one of the European powers were neither completely nor directly subject to the authority of a European government nor to the sultan's jurisdiction. For this reason, the protected communities were able to act as they saw fit, pursuing their own material interests and remaining detached from the national crises which could befall the countries in which they lived.[10]

The increase in the number of Greeks in Egypt gave rise to the creation of community organisations in Alexandria (1843), Cairo (1856) and, subsequently, in other parts of Egypt. Each community's executive council had a head and several counsellors. The councils themselves were divided into several committees. When the committees reached a decision, they displayed a solidarity which astonished the commercial and financial communities, often acting collectively – especially in times of recession. The committees worked together in order to realise maximum profit on the deals made by each individual. They bought and sold together as a group. They replenished their accounts by way of letters of credit exchanged among themselves and, in times of crisis, they considered that each individual enterprise belonged to the collectivity. In such cases, they exerted every effort to extricate their respective commercial establishments from any rough spots.[11] Thus, in times of crisis, the individual became more immersed within the community.

Wherever they settled, they founded religious and educational establishments, the Greek Orthodox patriarchate and Greek associations. A few individuals funded schools which spread throughout Egypt, especially in the larger cities of Cairo, Alexandria, Mansura, Tanta, Port Said, Zaqaziq, Shibin al-Kum, Isma'iliyya and Suez.[12]

Numerous factors contributed to the Greek migration to Egypt. Some were related to the capitulations and the benefits they afforded in terms of security, tax and tariff exemptions, freedom of movement and investment, and judicial protection. Others were linked to the Ottoman state's relative tolerance of minorities, especially members of the Greek Orthodox community.[13] At specific times in history, migration also resulted from oppression in the Greek homeland – in particular at the end of the eighteenth and the beginning of the nineteenth centuries, especially during the 1821 revolution. Muhammad

'Ali was sympathetic toward these victims of oppression perhaps, in part, because he came from Kavala himself. He employed Greeks in the reconstruction of the Egyptian state, in such sectors as industry, the army, hospitals, translation and commerce. Many prisoners of war brought to Egypt from Greece by Muhammad 'Ali did not return to their homes – according to E. Gouin[14] – even after the signing of the peace treaty.

This process of migration, however, was not continuous, and underwent phases of expansion and contraction. Under Khedive 'Abbas, for instance, an end was put 'to the spread of Greek influence throughout the country as well as to their departure from Cairo and Alexandria for the countryside where they had traded with the peasants'.[15]

Reading the letters and decrees of 'Abbas, gathered and printed by Muhammad 'Ali, one discovers further dimensions to this forced withdrawal of the Greeks.[16] The matter, indeed, prompted the intervention of France's consuls to protect Greek families throughout the country:

> ... among these Greeks are upright people who have nothing to do with corruption or treason. Therefore, those of them who present strong guarantees of their good conduct and accept our protection must be allowed to remain; [they should not be] not forced to depart. Those who are ill and incapable of travelling must also be allowed to stay. As for the poor, they must be given money for their tickets and sufficient provisions for the duration of their voyage.[17]

These conditions were, however, an exception in modern Egyptian history. Immigration and the establishment of Greek communities was the rule for over a century. This fact prompted Milner, writing at the turn of the twentieth century, to say that resident foreigners – particularly Greeks – increased in number; they were prone to causing an uproar, especially since the capitulations had given them despotic powers.[18]

In the first years of the twentieth century, Jean Vallet noted that the majority of the newly arrived Greek immigrants had no source of income. For this reason, they accepted any work offered to them. The workers offered their employers many advantages, such as flexibility, perseverance, energy and strength. Moreover, they were exceptionally frugal and thrifty. Thus, these immigrants were able to perfect many trades in a short time, after which they moved into commerce and finance.[19]

The Greeks were able to benefit from laws allowing foreigners to own land. In 1888, the Mixed Court of Appeals[20] ruled that foreigners had absolute freedom in owning property in Egypt. Ownership was facilitated by the fact that they could appropriate land by obtaining rulings on the basis of contracts drawn up at their consulates without having to provide deeds.[21] At an earlier date, Muhammad 'Ali had granted *ib'adiyyat*[22] to foreigners on the same terms that he applied to his own subjects, that is with absolute property rights over the object of the grant,[23] a matter which led some Egyptians to protest. Al-Tahtawi undertook the Pasha's defence: 'May God preserve him, he did it because of their humanity and knowledge and because they were Christians'.[24]

These immigrants were supposed to pay tax on these lands, but, as Nubar remarks, Syrians and Greeks who bought land in the villages found thousands of pretexts for avoiding payment of these taxes.[25]

Research on the development of agricultural property in Egypt, especially the writings of Girgis Hunayn,[26] Amin Sami,[27] 'Ali Barakat[28] and Ra'uf 'Abbas[29] allows one to follow the process whereby some Greeks came to own land and property, whether through gifts and grants, purchase or the seizing of property, especially after the expansion of investment opportunities for foreign capital. Foreigners settled throughout the Egyptian countryside and loaned money to peasants who were unable to pay back the amounts borrowed. This then led to the confiscation of their property and its appropriation by foreigners through the mixed courts. The years spanning the end of the nineteenth and the beginning of the twentieth centuries witnessed the return of the Syrian and Greek money-lenders who had disappeared from the scene after the 'Urabi revolution.[30] Statistical estimates mentioned by Girgis Hunayn[31] reveal an increase in the number of financiers, mostly Europeans and protected minorities, and a geographical concentration of their agricultural land. In 1898, 6494 financiers owned 565,266 *feddans* of land, while in 1904, 6139 financiers owned 582,464 *feddans*.

In his study of agricultural smallholdings and their impact on the Egyptian countryside between 1891 and 1930,[32] Yahya

Muhammad Mahmud, basing his argument on official statistics, confirms the appearance of many foreign smallholders: 4054 in 1913, 3719 in 1924 and 3501 in 1930. Since foreigners did not work the land themselves, the existence of these small properties indicates that their original owners had been forced to sell them in order to fulfil their financial obligations.

Historically, there is no doubt that some members of the Greek community controlled much of the rural retail trade. Most of them were grocers or owners of small shops and bars, activities which put them in contact with networks of social relations and acquainted them with the traditions and way of life of the Egyptian people, especially in the rural areas. They were, therefore, able to invest their money at a time when, as a contemporary observer remarked,[33] everyone was afraid to take financial risks.

Another observer, Harris, paints the portrait of a Greek grocer who, dressed in a soiled apron, slept behind the shelves of his small shop. Although he made very little profit which he used to purchase more stock, the Greek grocer lived on next to nothing and lent money to the peasants at exorbitant interest rates. He bought land, traded in cotton and built an astonishing fortune, despite being barely able to make ends meet when he first saw Egypt.[34]

The conditions outlined above form the backdrop for the development of the image of the Greek money-lender in Egypt, especially in rural areas. To a large extent, the image was negative: Greeks were often portrayed as smugglers, gamblers and tavern owners. What were the factors that contributed to the development of this image in Egypt? The context of rural Egypt in the late nineteenth and early twentieth centuries makes it easier to understand why the Egyptian popular consciousness perceived the Greeks in these negative terms. Despite the opening up of Egypt to the West and the expansion of commodity and cash relations of a capitalist nature, some traits of feudal Eastern society persisted, in one form or another, during this period of transformation. In the interior of the country, there was little differentiation between agricultural and craft workers; some markets continued to depend on barter. Many Egyptians displayed a certain aversion to money-lending because Islamic religious values prohibited usury. Money-lenders, therefore, were mainly Greeks who owned grocery shops in rural areas. They sold consumer goods to peasants on a retail basis, taking the cotton crop as security, and lending on a wide scale to rural inhabitants.[35]

According to Tal'at Harb, the number of money-lenders – most of whom were Greek – drastically increased during this period throughout upper and lower Egypt. The number of Greeks in Egypt seemed to increase day by day, leading some observers to note that, if the situation persisted, Egypt would soon be part of Greece.[36] This was an implicit reference to the Greek money-lenders' purchase of the Egyptian peasants' property.

According to the same source, money-lenders were of two types. The first lent money at exorbitant interest rates, holding promissory notes from their debtors for sums larger than the money actually owed by these debtors. The second type purchased the crop before the harvest, paying a price inferior to that recorded on the promissory note, as if this sum was the price of the crop that the peasant had pledged to deliver at harvest time. The price which was written was indeed equivalent to the current price, but the sum actually paid was far less.[37] The means to which Greek money-lenders resorted thus gave them a great measure of control over the peasants with whom they had dealings.

Tal'at Harb writes that these money-lenders came to Egypt with nothing except their sense of economy and management. Any money that they were able to accumulate in any way was immediately invested in a small village grocery shop. Their sphere of activity then widened as they began to lend money at high interest rates. When business was going well, they found it easy to borrow money from the merchants of Alexandria. Some became bankers shortly after that. Some of those who had first come to the village as modest grocers accumulated sufficient wealth to build luxurious residences there which became the administrative centres for their activities; they were the 'banks' where the peasants went to borrow money or pay back a debt to the *khawaga*.

'Most of these usurers... could neither read nor write; their greed knew no bounds nor their hearts any mercy.'[38] Such are the words of a judge who personally witnessed such scenes,[39] leading Tal'at Harb to exclaim, 'These days, so gloomy for Egyptians, were good days for others, for those who came to Egypt to drain its goodness and to trade with its inhabitants' ignorance. How many grew rich on the poverty of the Egyptians?'[40]

Another observer described the stereotypical image of the Greek money-lender who landed in Alexandria, then toured the country, getting along in Hellenised Arabic, until he settled in a village where he opened a small shop. This stereotypical money-lender was part-grocer, part-pharmacist and coffee-shop owner. He sold goods at 10 times the going price. At the same time, he lent money. For instance, he would lend 10 piastres and collect 15 at the end of the week or on market day. If circumstances were favourable, he would make whatever profit he could from the expansion of his commercial activities and loans, and would thus become a money-lender. Gradually, this Greek would become one of the most important financiers and merchants in the cotton market in Alexandria. Where he had once lent to the poorest peasants, he now lent to Khedive Isma'il.[41]

This image was further developed in different types of writings in the late nineteenth and early twentieth centuries, whether written by Egyptians or Europeans. Sharobim[42] wrote of the crushing taxes imposed upon the peasants, who had no choice but to fulfil their financial obligations. They found themselves forced to sell their livestock, their crops, their wives' jewellery and even their land. They became indebted and very frequently were compelled to leave their land. If peasants were unable to pay their debts, the tax collectors would take whatever grain or livestock they found in the peasants' possession and sell it to the money-lenders for a pittance. Sharobim noted that they did this to the people of every town and village, until the peasants' misery and torment became unbearable.

Yusuf Nahhas[43] also speaks of these money-lenders and speculators and the source of their profits: the dispossession of the peasants and the appropriation of their land through fraud and deception. He paints an eloquent portrait of the money-lenders who arrived in Egyptian villages, wearing shabby clothes but opening small shops. Having accumulated a fortune, they would return to their home country, where they would live off their gains.

These individual experiences contributed to the construction of an image which permeates the historiography of this period.

The Greek money-lender developed into a stereotype, closely associated with the illicit accumulation of astonishing fortunes. This image is deeply rooted, not only in the works of Egyptian historians, but also in those of their European counterparts. The image of the Greeks in Egypt, perhaps, was the product of their status as 'permanent immigrants'. Not entirely 'native', they were regarded with suspicion by Europeans as well.

Yahya Haqqi brilliantly describes how, during the period under consideration when the capitulations had taken root, a period immediately followed by the British occupation, taverns spread from the large cities of Egypt into small towns and large villages. Owned by foreigners, they attracted people with clean meals and good coffee, as well as the pleasant company of the owners' unveiled wives and daughters. The owners, for the most part, became money-lenders, and many peasants were ruined by loans at high interest rates.[44]

The number of money-lenders increased during Isma'il's reign, leading to the development of the image of the 'Greek usurer who followed the Coptic treasurer as the eagle follows the cow'.[45]

This image was developed through different media: in newspapers, literary works, the writings of Muhammad 'Abdu and 'Abd Allah al-Nadim, Tal'at Harb, Yusuf Nahhas, Henri 'Ayrut, Haqqi and others. European writers developed other dimensions of this image, such as the Greek innkeeper, tavern owner, middleman and pawnbroker. Milner[46] created a stereotyped image of the Greek in his attempt to explain why Isma'il created the mixed courts. Similar to other minorities, the Greeks were keen to obtain privileges through the capitulations or to make profits based on usury. Like the Jewish pawnbroker or the Syrian consumer, all of whom found it easy to obtain the protection of one of the European nations, they abused the Egyptian treasury and the Egyptian peasantry.

The *Times* of 31 March 1879 reported that the peasants sold off their livestock and the women sold their jewellery, while money-lenders filled the courts with requests for confiscation.[47] Blunt also described what he had seen with his own eyes, writing about the villages on market day when crowds of women came to sell their clothes and silver to Greek money-lenders because tax collectors with whips were in their villages. Therefore, writes

Blunt, he and his companions purchased their few trinkets, listened to their stories and joined them in cursing the government that had stripped them of everything.[48]

Another writer describes the spread of Greek money-lenders throughout the densely populated cities on the banks of the Nile, sketching a powerful picture of 'the [British] lion and the [French] tiger', savaging the '[Egyptian] bull' while the '[Greek] jackal' plundered the carcass left behind.[49]

Cromer considered that the Greeks had played an active role in building Egypt, although he hinted at the corruption of some individual members of this community who practised usury, a picture noted by many other visitors to Egypt. As Jean Vallet noted, usury caused great harm to peasants and workers in the cities. Through their commercial activities, Vallet added, Greek grocers offered usurious loans to the common people, whose debts amounted to between 50 and 100 per cent of the loan. Money-lenders would agree to the postponement of payment in exchange for more favourable terms for themselves.[50] Among the four working-class families which Vallet presented as case studies, two resorted to borrowing from money-lenders.

A number of factors, such as taxes, bribery, dependence on basic commodified cash crops like cotton, reduction in the prices of Egyptian cotton and the precipitous decline in the prices of land, forced the peasants into debt after the American Civil War. The situation was exacerbated by the fact that loans were not only made on the harvest, but also on the land itself. The debts of the peasantry rose from 1.4 million Egyptian pounds before 1882 to 15 million pounds at the end of 1892. Three million pounds of this sum were owed to the Real Estate Bank, while 12 million were owed to the foreign resident money-lenders.[51] In 1876, the mixed courts also began to lend at usurious rates and to engage in pawnbroking – especially after the promulgation of a law allowing the mortgaging of land and the right of the creditor to sell it. To allow this system to work, the creditor was permitted to appropriate the land of a debtor's who failed to fulfil his obligations.[52]

The mortgaging of land and the compulsory sale of property, a consequence of the creation of the mixed courts, led to the channelling of landed wealth into the hands of foreigners, according to Sarhank:

I know that these courts caused great damage to some Egyptians due to their ignorance of the way that legal transactions with foreigners were conducted. The foreign judges did not pursue the interests of the Egyptians nor did they know the kinds of legal tricks that some foreigners used against the peasants in order to appropriate their wealth through these courts. Yet, the Mixed Courts were far better than the consular courts.[53]

Yusuf Nahhas also mentions that speculators exploited the creation of these courts in order to benefit from the good intentions and naivety of the peasants. Some small property-holders even saw their land expropriated judicially without having been informed by these courts.[54]

'Ali Barakat refers to the registers of the *shari'a* courts which clarify the role played by foreigners – especially Greeks – in the expropriation of the peasants' land. The case of Tadrus Girgi Glano, a resident of Banha, is revealing. In 1895, he appropriated large tracts of land belonging to 13 peasants who were in his debt.[55] In one village, a Greek owned 200 *feddans*, while none of the local inhabitants owned more than a few *feddans* of land. Even the village shaykh owned only 12 *feddans*. The Greek had constituted his holdings from the land that he had expropriated from the peasants.[56]

Besides the confiscation of the peasants' crops, the seizing of their property and its transfer to the usurers continued. The surface of land appropriated by these creditors fluctuated throughout the early years of British occupation, as the following table shows.[57]

Table 13.2: Appropriations in Lieu of Debt

Year	Feddans
1883	22,470
1884	18,148
1885	17,828
1886	12,969

Schölch's important study notes that by 1879, it was said that most of the peasants did not own the land that they cultivated, while the other classes owned ninety per cent of these lands.

According to Lord Dufferin, the amounts owed between 1876 and 1882, as inscribed on the creditors' books, increased from approximately half a million pounds to seven million pounds, of which five million were owed by the peasantry. In addition to this, the peasantry owed a sum to the village usurers which Dufferin estimated to be between three and four million pounds.

Furthermore, in 1882, the mixed courts proceeded with the compulsory sale of land valued at 24 million Ottoman piastres (100 piastres equalling 1 Egyptian pound).[58] The report containing this information also reveals that, out of this sum, land worth six million piastres was located in Cairo and Alexandria, 17 million piastres worth of land was situated in the delta region and only 680,000 pounds worth of land was to be found in middle and upper Egypt since the foreign creditors were most active in the cities of the delta.

Other researchers examined the registers in which land liable for taxation was inscribed. They found that many landowners were foreign money-lenders in the Egyptian countryside: among them were Andrea Kurmadan (in Kafr al-Garayda), Hanna Stofiris, Christo Avrokhrostofides, Khruschov Toma, Yanni Khruschov (in Tanbadi), *khawaga* Jean Gregory and Yanni Ghrighori (in Minyat Mahalla Damna).[59]

Many of these names are Greek and, as Qillini Fahmi Pasha noted in his memoirs in the 1930s, much land, wealth and other possessions were handed over to Greeks, due to flagrant usury which weighed heavily upon the shoulders of the Egyptian peasantry and small landholders. He adds that a Greek, known as *khawaga* Bassili, was on very good terms with a *mudir* named Hasan Pasha Abu Nishanayn. Thanks to this friendship, Hasan Pasha would order the *ma'mur* (provincial governor) to assist Bassili in retrieving the money owed to him by the locals. Those who were found owing saw their land turned over to the *khawaga* as security.[60]

It is essential to take into consideration the close relation between the money-lenders and some members of the administration, especially the tax collectors, who made their rounds, whip in hand. The official responsible for collecting taxes on crops accompanied the money-lenders, who paid him a share of his gains. When the whip did not work on a peasant, the tax collector would admonish him: 'All this beating and you still refuse to tell us how much money you have?' When the peasant answered him in the negative, he would continue, 'Borrow', so the peasant would ask, 'And who will lend to me?' Then the tax collector would say, 'This matter can be arranged'. After a while, a Greek money-lender, who had been lurking in the background, would appear. He would examine the peasant's condition and his lack of resources and then would lend him money, no questions asked. The peasant would have to accept the situation. Then, the money-lender would give the agreed-upon part to the *mudir*, since this was a deal struck between them.[61]

Another important point is the rise in the rate of interest on usury debts and the fact that, due to the increase in interest rates, money-lenders resorted to speculation on the exchange rate. They would lend money to the peasants at 97.5 piastres as per sterling and collect their debt at 125 piastres – in other words, at an interest rate of 27.5 per cent. The peasants' ignorance benefited them in this respect. Because October was the month when peasants paid the profits to the money-lenders which were calculated for the agricultural year before it actually ended, it was known as 'the usurers' month'.[62]

Following the financial crisis of Isma'il's reign and the decline in cotton prices of 1865, al-Raf'i notes[63] the very high interest rates enforced by the usurers: 3–4 per cent for a single month, that is 36–48 per cent a year. This historian also records the oft-noted fact that money-lenders and tax collectors went hand in hand, lending money to the peasants that they needed in order to pay their taxes at very high interest rates, reaching 10–12 per cent a month – 120–144 per cent a year.

In *Modern Egypt*, Cromer also related the fact that, during the 'Urabi revolution, small money-lenders were collecting interest of 6 per cent a month on small loans to the peasants. In one of his reports, he stated that interest on these loans had reached rates of 40 per cent and more.[64]

According to Tal'at Harb,[65] the cases before the mixed courts show that, prior to the establishment of these courts, money-lenders often lent at interest rates of 5 per cent a month, but sometimes at rates as low as 4 or even 3 per cent. However, these rates could also rise to 6, 7 or even 8 per cent. Tal'at Harb himself ascertained that these rates sometimes went as high as 12.1 per cent. He adds that the first report drawn up by the

International Investigation Commission, published in 1878, stated that people who were questioned on this matter estimated that the prime reason for the crisis which had befallen Egypt was the sale of crops before the harvest and the increase in interest rates to 7 per cent a month. Dicey[66] also notes that the peasants paid interest to the usurers of between 6 and 8 per cent a month. Tal'at Harb added that, at the time when he was writing, interest rates had reached 15 per cent; the money-lenders had suggested even higher rates.

During the economic crisis of 1907, financial penury peaked as cotton prices fell from 24 to 18 riyals per *qintar*. Peasants were forced to borrow in order to pay their taxes. The newspaper *al-Ahram* of 6 April 1907 reported that the amounts which were lent were very small, but that interest rates were outrageous – as high as 150 per cent.[67] The Kitchener report of 1912 also mentioned that Egyptians' debts to foreigners had increased to such an extent because Egyptians borrowed at inordinate interest rates, reaching 30–40 per cent.[68]

Yusuf Nahhas estimated that the money-lenders' profits ranged at least between 60 and 70 per cent. Peasants often had recourse only to these money-lenders because, as 'Ayrut wrote, banks did not lend small sums; those who sought a loan had to borrow from individuals who, despite the law of 1912 which determined the ceiling on interest at 9 per cent, loaned at rates of 30 and even 50 per cent.[69]

All this implies that interest rates were not fixed: they changed over time, from one place to another, and according to the individual lending the money and, as the comments cited above indicate, were often excessive. Most studies of Egypt's socio-economic evolution from the mid-nineteenth to the mid-twentieth centuries, especially during Isma'il's reign, concur on the fact that usurers owned large expanses of land.[70] They often resorted to alliances with administrative officials such as sub-provincial governors, village shaykhs or *'umdas* to coerce poorer peasants into relinquishing their land.[71] Many merchants suffered the same fate as the peasants when they, too, incurred loans that they were unable to pay back. Forced to declare bankruptcy, they were frequently punished for crimes or misdemeanours including an inability to pay, negligence or fraud. In this way, they lost both their property and their honour; they became a burden on others and sometimes resorted to theft on a grand scale.[72] The accumulation of debts continued. In his 1912 report, Kitchener sums up the situation as follows:[73]

Table 13.3: Indebtedness, 1912

Number of indebted owners	Surface of owed land in *feddans*	Total debts owed by owners of five *feddans* or less	Total debt per *feddan*	
			Egyptian pounds	piastres
619,107	619,214	16,990,660	25	27

During the 1930s, the price of land continued to rise. Muhammad 'Ali 'Alluba records the process of property confiscation as follows:[74]

Table 13.4: Confiscations

	1937 Pounds	1938 Pounds	1939 Pounds
At the individual's request	1,152,819	689,313	641,484
At the bank's request	792,535	478,526	686,565
At the state's behest	12,434	3701	18,207
Total	**1,957,788**	**1,171,540**	**1,346,256**

Local Egyptian Reaction

The money-lender offered a loan. Failure to pay it back meant confiscation of the property which the debtor had mortgaged: land, buildings etc.

This single powerful image is repeated time and time again throughout various forms of literature, spanning over a century. Its persistence indicates that this form of economy in rural areas, controlled by a number of Greek individuals, had a profound effect on people's minds. Even if the image of the Greek money-lender tended to exaggerate his negative qualities, it played a significant role in reactions that eventually followed.

What was the Egyptian reaction to this process of appropriation in favour of money-lenders who, although well integrated in society, nevertheless remained outsiders? The reaction to the Greeks became part of a diffuse yet sometimes explosive opposition to foreign exploitation.

Popular opposition to the community of Greek money-lenders ranged from passive resistance to overt revolt. Some intellectuals and thinkers resorted to verbal attacks on money-lending as practised by the Greeks. Qasim Amin demanded:

> Has the Duke of Darcourt not heard? Most of the money that the Christians plundered in Egypt was seized criminally. Have you now understood why an Egyptian will destroy or vandalise the crops of a European? Very simply, he is taking revenge and, in his ignorance, he supposes that no Christian is worthy of respect.[75]

With the crystallisation of the 'Egypt for the Egyptians' trend, in all its various dimensions, a new kind of peasant revolt emerged. The 18 January 1879 edition of the newspaper *al-Watan* mentions the vast delegations of peasants who came to petition against the injustices of their condition, noting that this was a new development, one that Egypt had not previously witnessed.[76] The peasants were also certain that Nubar Pasha was the man responsible for the establishment of the mixed courts, an institution held in the highest regard by foreigners and loathed by the peasantry, due to their belief that these courts had accomplished what no other judicial body had previously done – placed them firmly within the grip of Greek money-lenders.[77]

'Ali Barakat also affirms that numerous factors triggered the violence which exploded during the 'Urabi revolution.[78] He explains that the Europeans who had committed the greatest number of crimes during the five years preceding the revolution were Greeks. Therefore, most of the revolutionary attacks were carried out on Greek money-lenders and merchants in both rural and urban areas. Barakat cites numerous instances recorded in the archives of the Interior Ministry (Nizarat al-Dakhiliyya) which document the confrontation between the peasantry and Greek usurers. Latifa Salim has also gathered many examples of attacks on Greek money-lenders who had appropriated land, crops and livestock of peasants who were unable to pay their debts.[79]

Eyewitness accounts corroborate these suppositions. Referring to the murder of a Greek in Banha, the British deputy consul wrote to the Foreign Secretary in June 1882 that the motive appeared to be his refusal to give papers to the peasants on which their debts were marked.[80] Another observer reported that all the peasants of the delta and middle Egypt were deeply indebted to Greek money-lenders, and it was therefore easy for this hatred to flare up against foreigners in general.[81] Emile Ludwig writes that when 'Urabi attacked the government and demanded the constitution of a large national army, the people were aware of only one fact – his determination to expel foreign money-lenders, the Greeks in particular.[82] On the basis of Salim Naqqash's work,[83] Alexander Schölch writes that when the news that the people had destroyed the mixed courts palace in Alexandria reached 'Urabi in the summer of 1882, he exclaimed: 'Thank God, Who has rid the country of them.'[84]

Other forms of resistance were employed against the money-lenders: delaying the payment of debts or denying their existence altogether, threatening creditors or promising that payment was imminent. The Greek merchants began to feel some trepidation and reduced the sphere of their activities, limiting their transactions with the Egyptians.[85] During this period, Blunt remarks that the peasants supported 'Urabi in the belief that war would free them of their debts. They, therefore, extended men and money to 'Urabi's movement.[86]

Incidents of political violence against Greeks, tinged with socio-economic overtones, multiplied in various parts of Egypt at this time: Tanta, Mahalla, Samannud, Banha, Kafr al-Zayyat, Damanhur and Alexandria all witnessed attacks in which cafés and shops were destroyed, storehouses torched, dozens of Greeks killed and some of their corpses doused with fuel and set alight.[87] Others were thrown into the Nile, while yet others were buried, especially in Mahalla al-Kubra. In the streets of Alexandria, inhabitants spat at the Greeks.

Even after the British occupation, peasants murdered many foreign property owners living in rural areas as well as money-lenders and usurers. Periodicals of the time are full of such cases, such as that of the *khawaga* Spiro Skalo, a Greek man, murdered in Damanhur on 13 September 1890, who had inspired hatred among the peasants due to his harsh treatment of them.[88] Peasants took part in the violent incidents of the 1919 revolution, and money-lenders were among their victims. This prompted Allenby to send an urgent telegram to Lord Curzon from Cairo, dated 16 May 1919.[89] Its message was brief and to the point: Greeks had 'suffered severely' and damage to Greek-owned property exceeded 600,000 pounds. Ten Greeks had been murdered and many injured.

Incidents like Red Monday,[90] which occurred on 23 May 1921 in Alexandria, during which Greeks and Italians were burned, were also triggered, at least in part, by hatred directed against the usurers. In this regard, Nubar Pasha described Egypt as a large meaty bone over which two dogs – France and Britain – were fighting. But as these two glared at each other, Greeks and Eastern Jews came in swarms, trying to get a share.[91]

Together with these violent incidents against people and property, another form of resistance emerged. It took diverse forms, such as complaints, death threats, refusal to pay debts, demonstrations, strikes and satire in speech and writing. Songs, plays and poetry of this period were part of the resistance. It must be noted, however, that forms of resistance cannot be dissociated from general conditions of the period, the calls for liberalism and the severe criticism which came from various quarters. Nor can they be viewed separately from political discourse, especially at the popular level of the national movement, strongly imbued with resentment toward foreign exploitation. The press of these years provides evidence of these trends. Furthermore, the opinion of intellectuals who sympathised with the Ottoman state in its struggle against Greece at the end of the nineteenth century reflects the grievances of the Egyptian people, especially in terms of relations with Greeks who seized the peasants' land.[92]

Many instances of this attitude appeared in literary works – articles, novels and poetry – condemning foreigners in general, and Greeks in particular. One of the most notable writers of this genre is Voltaire's grandson, Edmond About. Invited to Egypt by Nubar, he wrote a series of articles in *Revue des Deux Mondes*. The first of these, entitled 'Ahmed le Fellah', was published on 15 February 1869. In this article, he sharply criticises the arrogance of foreigners, the brutality of their oppressive practices and the contemptuous attitude of their consuls.[93]

Mahmud Fahmi Afandi's novel, *Anba' al-Zaman fi Harb al-Dawla wa'l-Yunan*, is an example of the moralistic allegories that were popular at this time, while the more pedagogical school is well represented in Muhammad al-Muwaylhi's reformist work, *Hadith 'Issa Ibn Hisham*.[94] In this work, one of the characters notes that, in this age, no-one will lend money without proper documentation. Those who take the borrower's 'fame and reputation' as guarantees, he remarks, 'must take the month on Friday' – that is a month's interest as security on a week-long loan.

The same message is expressed in *Layali Satih* by Muhammad Hafiz Ibrahim. He describes a Greek who reached the pinnacle of wealth, whereupon, having committed crimes against the Egyptians, he sought the protection of his own country. Hafiz demands sarcastically:

> In Egypt, is there a source of pride
> Other than titles and ranks?
> Heirs compete as to which of us is the richer
> With money that they have not earned.
> In the Greek, there is a lesson
> For a people serious at playing.
> He kills us, no-one retaliates,
> No-one demands retribution or intimidates him.
> He marches beneath his flag
> And it protects him from injury.

During the reign of Khedive Isma'il (1863–79), the golden age for money-lenders, dozens of pens were put to paper to attack bankers and defend peasants. Muhammad 'Abdu was perhaps among the most prolific and vehement of the polemicists. In issue no 969 of *al-Waqa'i' al-Misriyya* (the *Egyptian Official Gazette*),[95] he published an article entitled 'The Love of Poverty or the Peasant's Foolishness', in which he wrote that merchants and bankers were the greatest perpetrators and most ardent defenders of iniquity and oppression, taking interest of 200 per cent over a four-month period.

These were days of mourning for the Egyptian people and government alike, and days of joy and rebirth for Western merchants and bankers, who spread among the Egyptians like wolves among sheep, burdening the peasants and others with vast debts and forcing them to sell their property and mortgage their houses and land. They were then stripped of their property and became impoverished.[96]

The spokesman of the 'Urabi revolution, 'Abd Allah al-Nadim, wrote dozens of fiery articles and poems in *Misr*, *al-Tigara*, *al-Ta'if*, *al-Tankit wa'l-Tabkit* and *al-Ustadh* about the suffering and debts of the peasants. In his articles, 'al-Fallah wa'l-Murabin' ('The Peasant and the Usurer') and 'Muhtag Jahil fi Yad Muhtall Tami'' ('An Indigent Illiterate in the Grip of a Rapacious Occupier'), the indigent peasant was forced to borrow 100 pounds and sign a paper allowing a usurious merchant to claim that the peasant owed him 200 pounds.[97] In the first issue[98] of *al-Tankit wa'l-Tabkit* (*Jokes and Tears*), al-Nadim wrote a biting indictment, in verse, of the upward mobility of bankers and land-owners who had become 'the notables' notables' while the common people went naked, unable even to afford their tobacco.

In 1892, after the defeat of the revolution and 'Urabi's return to exile, *al-Ustadh* appeared, its pages filled with attacks on Greek usurers. Once more, al-Nadim's sarcastic writing resumed:[99]

> The foreigners have had the last laugh, religion is dead.
> No-one knows or gives a damn.
> You drink like the Europeans.
> But you don't love your country as they do theirs.
> It's truly astonishing,
> Even nonsense has reached the villages.
> They drain the bottle to the dregs.
> Before the fast begins, the *'umda* drinks cognac.
> Watch him fasting, he went to bed drunk.
> They sold the land to the Greeks for illusions
> And now the Egyptians are destitute.
> So ask Girgi and Yanni, don't ask me.
> You'll find the money – it's gone to Greece.

In one of his Friday sermons, al-Nadim exhorted his listeners not to covet the usurers' wealth, as they might be tempted to do. The usurers 'have enticed you with money', he admonished the Egyptians, then 'appropriated your real-estate and your plantations and now you must suffer ignominy in this world and torture in the next'.[100]

Al-Nadim used almost every form of the written and spoken word to influence a wide audience, from speeches and poetry to articles and even jokes. He wrote plays such as *al-Watan*, produced on the stage of the Madrasat al-Gam'iyya al-Khayriyya al-Islamiyya (the Islamic Welfare Association School), of which he was head-master. Here, he resorted to more overt literary mechanisms in his condemnation of usury and money-lenders.[101] He had a wide audience and his writing influenced many readers.

With Bayram al-Tunsi, the 'people's poet', the opposition to money-lending and foreign exploitation reached its peak. Al-Tunsi resorted to familiar themes: the Greeks who had arrived in Egypt with nothing but who accumulated vast riches by exploiting and robbing the people. However, he gave them a unique twist in his sarcastic popular poems.[102] In 'Cotton', he warned the peasants against those 'who came with suitcases':

> By January, you'll find they've become crocodiles
> And there will be court sessions, and lawyers, and summons and witnesses.

Likewise, the songs of Sayyid Darwish spread like wildfire across the various social strata. The first musical that he wrote was *Wa Law* (*Even So*) which he set to music for the Nagib al-Rihani Troupe. 'Al-Saqqa'in' ('The Water Carriers')[103] is a plaintive rendition of the daily manifestations of inequality: 'So why should Paolo and Yanni eat the best dishes and earn a salary?'

Darwish also took up one of the burning issues of the day: the appropriation of agricultural land by the banks and the foreign community of entrepreneurs.[104] The victims of this appropriation lamented, 'And when I hit rock bottom, he turned his back and said good-bye'. The theme of the Greeks' corrupting influence also surfaced here:

> We played a round of poker, had a drink of Johnnie Walker
> I played, I lost, I drank, I walked
> Until I fell into difficulties.

Conclusion

To summarise, one can consider this literary output within the context of its political dimensions. Moreover, these verses and countless others like them, as well as other literary genres adopted in the attempt to deal with perceptions and realities of foreign exploitation, reveal many aspects of life in Egypt at the turn of the twentieth century – dimensions that primary sources and traditional historiographical material do not necessarily disclose. Due to their imprecision and frequent exaggerations, they naturally cannot be used as sources of hard information, of course, but their use of metaphor and language provides unparalleled insight into the people's understanding and experience of their condition and changes taking place.

This study shows that different levels of reality did not always correspond to each other. Though the number of Greek money-lenders was significant, these individuals did not represent their community whose members occupied numerous professions, nor did they necessarily act in the interest of this community, since it was their individual personal gain which they sought. But, on another level, the image formed in the collective memory about Greek money-lenders concerned the Greeks of Egypt as a whole, probably because of many other factors prevailing at that time, some of which have been mentioned above. This image contributed to the growing resistance movement against the European presence in Egypt at the turn of the twentieth century.

Bibliography

Primary Sources

Al-Majmu'a al-Rasmiyya al-Mukhtalata, Dar al-Watha'iq, Cairo.
Rizq, Yunan Labib, 'al-Ahram, diwan al-hayat al-mu'asira', *al-Ahram* newspaper, Cairo, 3 July 1997, p. 3

Published Studies

'Abbas Hamid, Ra'uf, *al-Nizam al-ijtima' fi Misr fi zill al-milkiyyat al-zira'iyya al-kabira, 1837–1914*, Cairo, Dar al-Fikr al-Hadith, 1973.
'Abd al-Karim, Ahmad 'Izzat, *Tarikh al-ta'lim fi Misr min nihayat hukm Muhammad 'Ali ila awa'il hukm Tawfiq, 1848–1882*, vol. 2, 'Asr Isma'il', Cairo, Matba'at al-Nasr, 1945.
Adams, Francis, *The New Egypt: A Social Sketch*, London, T. Fisher Unwin, 1893.

'Afifi, Hafiz, *'Ala hamish al-siyasa: ba'd masa'ilina al-qawmiyya*, Cairo, Dar al-Kutub al-Misriyya, 1938.

'Ali, Sa'id Isma'il, *al-Mujtama' al-misri fi 'ahd al-ihtilal al-britani, 1882-1914: al-bin' al-iqtisadi wa-quwa al-tashkil al-siyasi*, Cairo, Maktabat al-Anglu al-Misriyya, 1972.

'Alluba, Muhammad 'Ali, *Mabadi' fi 'l-siyasa al-misriyya*, Cairo, Matba'at Dar al-Kutub al-Misriyya, 1942.

Amin, Qasim, *al-Misriyyun*, transl. Qasim Amin Jr, Cairo, Kitab al-Hilal, 1995.

'Ayrout, Henry S.J., *Fellahs d'Égypte*, Cairo, Editions du Sphynx, 1952, transl. Muhammad Ghallab, al-Fallahun, Cairo, Matba'at Kawthar, 1943.

Barakat, 'Ali, *Tatawwur al-milkiyya al-zira'iyya fi Misr 1813–1914 wa Atharuha 'ala al-haraka al-siyasiyya*, Cairo, Dar al-Thaqafa al-Jadida, 1977.

— 'al-Mawqif min al-ajanib fi 'l-thawra al-'urabiyya' in (collective work), *Misr li'l-Misriyyin: Mi'at 'amm 'ala al-thawra al-'urabiyya*, Cairo, Markaz al-Dirasat al-Siyasiyya wa'l-istratijiyya bi'l-Ahram, 1981, pp. 244–380.

Blunt, Wilfrid Scawen, *al-Tarikh al-sirri li-ihtilal Ingiltirra (The Secret History of the British Occupation)*, Cairo, Matba'at al-Balagh al-Usbu'i, 1928.

Cattaoui, René, *Muhammad 'Ali wa-Uruba (Muhammad 'Ali et l'Europe)*, transl. Alfred Yuluz, Cairo, Dar al-Ma'arif, 1952.

Clot Bey and Antoine Barthélemy, *Lamha 'amma ila Misr (Aperçu général sur l'Égypte)*, transl. Muhammad Mas'ud, Cairo, Matba'at Abu 'l-Hilal, n.d.

Crabites, Pierre, *Isma'il al-muftara 'alayhi (Ismail, the Maligned Khedive)*, transl. Fu'ad Sarruf, Cairo, Dar al-Nashr al-Hadith, 1937.

Cromer, *Modern Egypt*, London, Macmillan, 1911.

— *al-thawra al-'urabiyya*, transl. 'Abd al-'Aziz 'Urabi, Cairo, al-Sharika al-'Arabiyya li'l-Tiba'a, 1958.

Cuno, Kenneth M., *The Pasha's Peasants: Land, Society and Economy in Lower Egypt, 1740–1858*, Cambridge, Cambridge University Press, 1992 and Cairo, American University in Cairo Press, 1994 (this edition is cited here).

Darwish, Hasan, *Min ajl Abi, Sayyid Darwish*, Cairo, al-Hay'a al-Misriyya al-'Amma li'l-Kitab, 1990.

Dicey, Edward, *The Story of the Khedivate*, London, Rivingtons, 1902.

Durrell, Lawrence, *The Alexandria Quartet*, London, Faber and Faber, 1969.

Fahmi, Qillini, *Mudhakkarat*, Minya, Matba'at Sadiq, n.d.

— *Mudhakkarat: khulasat al-hawadith fi 'Uhud al-khidiwi Isma'il wa'l-sultan Husayn wa-jalalat mawlana al-malik Fu'ad al-awwal*, Cairo, Matba'at Misr, 1934.

Gelat, Philippe, *Qamus al-idara wa'l-qada'*, Alexandria, Matba'at Yanni Laghudaki, 1899.

Gordon, Lucy Duff, *Letters from Egypt, 1862–1869*, London, Routledge and Kegan Paul, 1969.

Gouin, Edward, *Misr fi 'l-qarn al-tasi' 'ashr*, transl. Muhammad Mas'ud, Cairo, Matba'at Abul Hul, 1931.

Hadidi, 'Ali al-, *'Abd Allah al-Nadim, khatib al-wataniyya*, Cairo, al-Mu'asasa al Misriyya lil Ta'lif wal-Tarjama wal Tiba'a, 1962.

Hamza, 'Abd al-Latif, *Adab al-maqala al-sahafiyya fi Misr*, Cairo, Dar al-Fikr al-Arabi, 1957.

Haqqi, Yahya, *Khalliha 'alallah*, Cairo, al-Hay'a al-Misriyya al-'Amma li'l-Kitab, 1987.

— *Dima' wa-tin*, Cairo, al-Hay'a al-Misriyya al-'Amma li'l-Kitab, 1997.

Harris, Murray, *Egypt under the Egyptians*, London, Champman, 1925.

Hifni, Muhammad Ahmad al-, *Sayyid Darwish*, Cairo, Maktabat Misr Cairo, 1962.

Hourani, Albert, *Arabic Thought in the Liberal Age, 1798–1939*, London, Oxford University Press, 1967.

Hunayn, Girgis, *al-Atyan wa'l-dara'ib fi 'l-qutr al-misri*, Cairo, al-Matba'a al-Amiriyya, Bulaq, 1904.

Husayn, Muhammad Muhammad, *al-Ittijahat al-wataniyya fi 'l-adab al-mu'asir*, Cairo, Maktabat al-Adab, 1954.

'Irian, Malika, *Markaz Misr al-iqtisadi*, Cairo, Matba'at Ramsis, 1923.

Kamil, Mustafa, *al-Mas'ala al-sharqiya*, Cairo, Matba'at al-Liwa', 2nd ed., January 1898.

— *Awraq al-murasalat*, Cairo, al-Hay'a al-Misriyya al-'Amma li'l-Kitab, 1982.

Khamsuna, 'aman, *'ala thawrat 1919: yawmiyat al-thawra kama waradat fi 'l-watha'iq al-britaniyya*, Cairo, Markaz al-watha'iq wa'l-buhuth al-tarikhiyya li-Misr al-mu'assira, Mua'ssasat al-Ahram, 1969.

Khanki, 'Aziz, *al-Mahakim al-mukhtalata wa'l-mahakim al-ahliyya: Madiha, hadiruha, mustaqbaluha*, Cairo, al-Matba'a al-'Asriyya, 1939.

Kitchener, Viscount, *Taqrir 'an al-maliyya wa'l-idara wa'l-hala al-'umumiyya fi Misr wa-fi 'l-Sudan li-sanat 1912 (Report on the Finances and Administration and General Situation in Egypt and the Sudan for the Year 1912)*, Cairo, Jaridat al-Muqattam, 1913.

Lahayta, Muhammad Fahmi, *Tarikh Fu'ad al-awwal al-iqtisad*, Cairo, Matba'at al-Shubuksi, 1945.

Landes, David S., *Bankers and Pashas*, London, Heinemman, 1958.

Lane, E.W., *Manners and Customs of the Modern Egyptians*, London, Dent, Everyman's Library, 1963.

Ludwig, Emile, *al-Nil: hayat nahr (Le Nil, vie d'un fleuve)*, transl. 'Adil Zu'aytar, Cairo, al-Hay'a al-Misriyya al-'Amma li'l-Kitab, 1997.

Mahmud, Yahya Muhammad, *al-Milkiyyat al-zira'iyya al-saghira wa-atharuha fi 'l-rif al-misri, 1891–1930*, MA thesis, Faculty of Arts, Cairo University, Cairo, 1989.

Milner, Viscount G.C.B., *England in Egypt*, London, Edward Arnold, 1926.

Mitwalli, Mahmud, *al-Usul al-tarikhiyya li'l-rasmaliyya al-misriyya wa-tatawwuriha*, Cairo, al-Hay'a al-Misriyya al-'Amma li'l-Kitab, 1974.

Mubarak, 'Ali Pasha, *al-Khitat al-tawfiqiyya al-jadida li-Misr wa'l-Qahira*, Cairo, al-Hay'a al-Misriyya al-'Amma li'l-Kitab, 2nd ed., 1987.

Mursi, Muhammad Kamil, *al-Milkiyya wa'l-huquq al-'ayniyya*, Cairo, al-Matba'a al-Rahmaniyya, 1923.

Mustafa, Ahmad 'Abd al-Rahim, *Misr wa'l-mas'ala al-misriyya, 1876–1882*, Cairo, Dar al-Ma'arif, 1965.

Nadim, 'Abd Allah al-, *Sulafat al-Nadim*, ed. Ibn Muntassir, Cairo, al-Matba'a al-Jam'a bi-Misr, 1897.

Nahhas, Yusuf, *al-Fallah: halatahu al-iqtisadiyya wa'l-ijtima''iyya*, Cairo, Khalil Mutran, 1926.

Naqqash, Salim Khalil al-, *Misr li'l-Misriyyin*, Alexandria, Matba'at Jaridat al-Mahrusa, 1886.

Ninet, John, *Arabi Pasha, Egypt 1800–1883*, Berne, Chez l'Auteur, 1884.

Nubar, Pasha, *Mudhakarat Nubar fi Misr*, ed. Nabil Zaki, Cairo, Akhbar al-Yawm, 1991.

Politis, Athanase G., *L'Hellénisme et l'Égypte moderne, vol. 1 : Histoire de l'Hellénisme égyptien de 1798–1927*, Paris, Librairie Felix Aleau, 1928.

Prince Muhammad 'Ali (ed.), *Majmu'at khitabat wa-awamir 'Abbas Pasha al-awwal*, Cairo, 1939.

Raf'i, 'Abd al-Rahman al-, *Niqabat al-ta'awun al-zira'iyya: nizamaha wa-tarikhaha wa-thamaratiha fi Misr wa-'Uruba*, introduction by Ahmad Bek Lutfi, Cairo Matba'at al-Nahda, 1914.

— 'Asr Isma'il, *Lajnat al-ta'lif wa'l-tarjama*, 2nd ed., Cairo, wa'l-nashr, 1948.

Rida, Muhammad Rashid, *Tarikh al-ustadh al-imam Muhammad 'Abdu*, Cairo, Matba'at al-Manar, 1906.

Rizq, Yunan Labib, *al-Ahram, diwan al-hayat al-mu'asira*, Cairo, al-Ahram, 1995.

Sabri, Muhammad, *Tarikh Misr min Muhammad 'Ali ila al-'asr al-hadith*, Cairo, Madbuli, 1991.

Sabry, M., *L'Empire égyptien sous Ismail et l'ingérence anglo-française, 1863–1879*, Paris, Librairie Orientaliste P. Geuthner, 1933.

Sacré, Amedee and L. Outrebon, *L'Égypte et Ismail Pasha*, Paris, J. Hetzel, 1865.

Salama, Girgis, *Tarikh al-ta'lim al-ajnabi fi Misr fi 'l-qarnayn al-tasi' 'ashr wa'l-ishrin*, Cairo, al-Majlis al-a'la li-ri'ayat al-funun wa'l-adab wa'l-'ulum al-ijtima'iyya, 1963.

Salim, Latifa, *al-Quwa al-ijtima'iyya fi'l-thawra al-'urabiyya*, Cairo, al-Hay'a al-Misriyya al-'Amma li'l-Kitab, 1981.

Sami, Amin Pasha, *Taqwim al-Nil*, Cairo, Dar al-Kutub al-Misriyya, 1936.

Saqr, Muhammad 'Abd al-Wahhab and Fawzi Sa'id Shahin, *'Abd Allah al-Nadim*, Cairo, Matba'at al-Adab, n.d.

Sarhank, Isma'il, *Haqa'iq al-akhbar 'an duwal al-bihar*, Cairo, al-Matba'a al-Amiriyya, Bulaq, 1964.

Schölch, Alexander, *Misr li'l-Misriyyin: azmat Misr al-ijtima'iyya wa'l-siyasiyya*, transl. Ra'uf 'Abbas Hamid, Cairo, Dar al-Thaqafa al-'Arabiyya, 1983.

Shafiq Pasha, Ahmad, *Mudhakkirati fi nisf qarn*, Cairo, al-Hay'a al-Misriyya al-'Amma li'l-Kitab, 1995.

Sha'rawi, Huda, *Mudhakkarat ra'idat al-mar'a al-'arabiyya al-haditha*, Cairo, Kitab al-Hilal, 1981.

Sharobim, Mikha'il, *al-Kafi min tarikh Misr al-qadim wa'l-hadith*, Cairo, al-Matba'a al-Amiriyya, Bulaq, 1900.

Sulayman, Mahmud Muhammad, *al-Ajanib fi Misr: Dirasa fi tarikh Misr al-ijtima'i*, Cairo, 'Ayn, 1996.

Symons, M., *Britain and Egypt: The Rise of Egyptian Nationalism*, London, Cecil Palmer, 1925.

Taha Badr, 'Abd al-Muhsin, *Tatawwur al-ruwaya al-'arabiyya al-haditha fi Misr, 1870–1938*, Cairo, Dar al-Ma'arif, 1963.

Tal'at Harb, Muhammad, *'Ilaj Misr al-iqtisadi wa-mashru' Bank al-Misriyyin aw-Bank al-Umma*, Cairo, Matba'at al-Jarida, 1911.

Tunsi, Bayram al-, *al-'Amal al-kamila*, Cairo, al-Hay'a al-Misriyya al-'Amma li'l-Kitab, 1994.

Vallet, Jean, *Contribution à l'étude de la condition des ouvriers de la Grande Industrie au Caire*, Valence, Imprimerie Valentinoise, 1911.

Wahida, Subhi, *Fi usul al-mas'ala al-misriyya*, Cairo, Matba'at Misr, 1950

Wallace, D.M., *Egypt and the Egyptian Question*, London, Macmillan and Co., 1883.

Notes on Chapter 13

1   Politis, 1928, notes that there were over 4000 Greeks in Egypt at the end of the eighteenth century; Lane, 1963, estimates their number at 5000 during Muhammad 'Ali's time; Clot Bey, n.d., repeats the latter estimate, as does 'Ali Pasha Mubarak, 1987; Gouin, 1931, believes their number to have been 10,000 in 1823: see, for instance, Politis, 1928, p. 99; Lane, 1963, p. 23; Clot Bey, n.d., p. 378; Mubarak, 1977, vol. 7, p. 145.

2 This table is based on the comments of Mitwalli, 1974, p. 238 and Sulayman, 1996, pp. 57–65.

3 'Irian, 1923, p. 146.

4 Cromer, 1911, p. 654.

5 Ayrout, 1952, p. 41.

6 Lahayta, 1945, p. 87.

7 Rizq, 1995, vol. 1, p. 15.

8 Haqqi, 1997, pp. 155–6.

9 Durrell, 1969, p. 17.

10 Wahida, 1950, pp. 276–7.

11 Landes, 1958, pp. 26–7.

12 See especially 'Abd al-Karim, 1945, vol. 2, pp. 853–6; Salama, 1963, pp. 72–3.

13 See Kamil, 1898, vol. 1, p. 72 on the policy of religious justice which led to the commercial development of the Greeks who, thanks to the Porte, became 'wealthy and led lives of ease'. Also see Cattaoui, 1952, pp. 78–9, according to whom the Greeks were 'their masters' masters thanks to their large fortunes and thriving maritime commercial interests as well as their exceptional position at the diwan in Istanbul'; Hourani, 1967, pp. 43, 273 on the influence, skill and ascendancy of the families of the Phanar.

14 Gouin, 1931, p. 724.

15 Sabry, 1933, pp. 16–7, 28–30.

16 Prince Muhammad 'Ali, 1939, pp. 90–1.

17 Sami, 1936, vol. 1, pt 3, pp. 67–9.

18 Milner, 1926, p. 318.

19 Vallet, 1911, pp. 36–7.

20 21 March 1888, al-Majmu'a al-Rasmiyya al-Mukhtalata 13, 12.

21 Mursi, 1923, pp. 16–7.

22 'Uncultivated and thus untaxed land as well as some cultivated land, 'removed' or 'set apart' from the taxed land.' Cuno, 1994, pp. 107, 149, 238, 268.

23 Gelat, 1899, voL 1, p. 136.

24 'Abbas Hamid, 1973, note 2, p. 29.

25 Nubar Pasha, 1991, p. 114.

26 Hunayn, 1904.

27 Sami, 1936, vol. 1, pt 2, p. 1928.

28 Barakat, 1977.

29 'Abbas Hamid, 1973.

30 Ludwig, 1997, p. 778.

31 Hunayn, 1904, pp. 9–11.

32 Mahmud, 1989.

33 Sacré and Outrebon, 1865, p. 214.

34 Harris, 1925, p. 173.

35 In confirmation of this point, Muhammad Tal'at Harb wrote, in November 1911, that the greatest harm to Egypt and the Egyptians is to be found in the fact that they had not grown accustomed to management, economy and investment of their money. He added that Egyptians, in every aspect of their lives, were 'the eaten, not the eaters'; that they worked to increase financial activity, but had no part in this increase; they were always debtors, never creditors, always owing, never owed and that it was to be expected that those who could gain from this activity would migrate to these areas: Tal'at Harb, 1911, pp. 6, 18. In 1938, Hafiz 'Afifi wrote (p. 209), 'in truth, the Egyptians hate commerce and this hatred is so great as to resemble loathing and repugnance'.

36 Tal'at Harb, 1911, p. 14.

37 *Ibid.*, p. 12.

38 *Ibid.*, p. 15.

39 See also Raf'i, 1948, pp. 266–7.

40 Tal'at Harb, 1911, p. 18.

41 See Salim, 1981, p. 34, citing Wallace, 1883, p. 288. In his well-known work, *The Story of the Khedivate*, 1902, p. 90, Edward Dicey also speaks of these usurers who took everything that the peasants had, then appropriated the land on which they lived and sold it for a pittance.

42 Sharobim, 1900, pt 4, p. 161.

43 Nahhas, 1926, pp. 47–8, 59–60.

44 Haqqi, 1987, p. 24.

45 Gordon, 1969, p. 182.

46 Milner, 1926, p. 15. See also Crabites, 1937, p. 226.

47 Sabry, 1933, p. 115, note 1.

48 Blunt, 1928, p. 13. Ninet, 1883, p. 155, estimated that the usurers were a catastrophe, a plague on the peasants whom they exploited along with Greek and Jewish money-lenders.

49 Adams, 1893, p. 69.

50 See Vallet, 1911, pp. 13–14.

51 See especially Salim, 1981, pp. 36–7, whose study was based on important primary and secondary sources.

52 *Idem.* On the mortgaging of property and the transfer of many peasant holdings to Greek usurers through the mixed courts, see Khanki, 1939. Raf'i, 1914, provides many statistical evaluations of these debts; he also writes about the failure of the banking

experiment in reforming the loan system (p. 172). Also see 'Ali, 1972; Mahmud, 1989, in which the role and impact of usury are discussed in detail.

53 Sarhank, 1964, pt 2, p. 34.

54 Nahhas, 1926, pp. 136, 140.

55 Barakat, 1977, p. 327.

56 *Ibid.*

57 Schölch, 1983, pp. 55–6.

58 Naqqash, 1886, pt 6, pp. 85–6.

59 Mahmud, 1989, pp. 79–80.

60 Fahmi, n.d., pt 1, pp. 103–4. In the second part of his memoirs (p. 153), he speaks of the Egyptians' debts in 1930 and mentions that real-estate banks played an active role in the confiscation of debtors' property, taking advantage of their straitened circumstances and their failure to pay their debts so that the *feddan* that had been worth 300 pounds was sold for 50 or 40 pounds.

61 Salim, 1981, p. 35.

62 Mahmud, 1989, p. 83.

63 Raf'i, 1948, pt 2, p. 29, note 1, pp. 263–4.

64 Cromer, 1958, p. 149.

65 Tal'at Harb, 1911, pp. 16, 32.

66 Dicey, 1902.

67 Rizq, 1997.

68 Kitchener, 1913, p. 7.

69 Nahhas, 1926, p. 95; 'Ayrut, 1943, p. 92.

70 'Irian, 1923, p. 145.

71 See Salim, 1981, especially pp. 301–2: some landowners from Shubra Balula in Sabk Munufiyya were imprisoned and their land confiscated by the *khawagas* Dimitri Badriko and Dimitri Kariazo, merchants from Cairo. See also p. 310 for details on how many of these usurers, notably Vastaria Busturi from Milig Munufiyya, forged stamps bearing the peasants' names and affixed them to documents presented to the mixed courts in order to appropriate their land.

72 From the introduction of Raf'i's book, *Niqabat al-ta'awun al-zira'iyya*, 1914, penned by Ahmad Bek Lutfi, councillor of al-Niqaba al-'amma li'l-ta'awun al-zira'i wa'l-manzili bi-Misr (The General Egyptian Union for Agricultural and Domestic Co-operation).

73 Kitchener, 1913, p. 15.

74 'Alluba, 1942, p. 51.

75 Amin, 1995, p. 36.

76 Mustafa, 1965, p. 74.

77 Blunt, 1928, p. 37.
78 Barakat, 1981, pp. 344–80.
79 Salim, 1981, especially pp. 321–3.
80 Naqqash, 1886, pt 5, p. 49.
81 Cited in Salim, 1981, p. 36.
82 Ludwig, 1997, p. 760.
83 Naqqash, 1886, pt 9, p. 767.
84 Schölch, 1983, p. 98.
85 Sharobim, 1900, pt 4, p. 238.
86 Blunt, 1928, p. 283.
87 Sharobim, 1900, p. 324.
88 See Mahmud, 1989, p. 286.
89 British archival material on the 1919 revolution in 'Abd al-Karim, 1945, p. 345.
90 Symons, 1925, p. 118.
91 Nubar Pasha, 1991, pp. 16-17.
92 The writings and speeches of Mustafa Kamil are of especial importance in this respect: see Kamil, 1898, written on the occasion of the Ottoman victory over Greece, and his rallying cry: 'Free in our country, generous to our guests'. He also published images of the victorious Ottoman soldiers: see Kamil, 1982, pp. 11–12. The renowned lyrical poet Ahmad Shawqi composed a poem of 250 verses inspired by similar sentiments when the Ottomans defeated the Greeks in 1897: see Husayn, 1954, p. 47. Shafiq Pasha, 1995, pt 2, pp. 231–43, mentions the news of the war and the Egyptian people's joy and support of the Ottoman sultan. In Sha'rawi's memoirs, 1981, p. 80, Egyptian support for the sultan is mentioned as being particularly strong at the time of Thessalia (1895).
93 See examples of his writing in Khanki, 1939, pp. 69–85.
94 Taha Badr, 1963, pp. 66–82.
95 22 Dhu al-Hijja 1297 (25 November 1880), al-Waqa'i' al-Misriyya.
96 Rida, 1906, pt 2, pp. 74–5.
97 Hamza, 1957, pt 2, p. 137.
98 7 August 1881, al-Waqa'i' al-Misriyya.
99 Cited in Hadidi, 1962, p. 179.
100 Saqr and Shahin, n.d., 233–4.
101 See Nadim, 1897, pt 2, p. 36 for the dialogue between the two peasants, Abu Da'mum and Abu 'l-Zalafi, and hajj Husayn and mu'allim Abu 'l-'Ila, both city-dwellers.
102 See Tunsi, 1994, pp. 65–9, 70–1.
103 Hifni, 1962, pp. 108–9.
104 Darwish, 1990, p. 254.

Index

The European Science Foundation

The European Science Foundation (ESF) acts as a catalyst for the development of science by bringing together leading scientists and funding agencies to debate, plan and implement pan-European scientific and science policy initiatives.

ESF is the European association of 70 major national funding agencies devoted to scientific research in 27 countries. It represents all scientific disciplines: physical and engineering sciences, life and environmental sciences, medical sciences, humanities and social sciences. The Foundation assists its Member Organisations in two main ways. It brings scientists together in its EUROCORES (ESF Collaborative Research Programmes), Scientific Forward Looks, Programmes, Networks, Exploratory Workshops and European Research Conferences to work on topics of common concern including Research Infrastructures. It also conducts the joint studies of issues of strategic importance in European science policy.

It maintains close relations with other scientific institutions within and outside Europe. By its activities, the ESF adds value by co-operation and co-ordination across national frontiers and endeavours, offers expert scientific advice on strategic issues, and provides the European forum for science.